The Apocalypedia

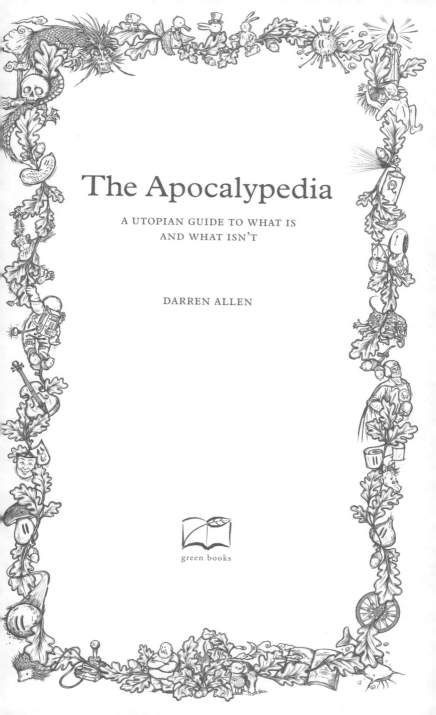

The Apocalypedia

A UTOPIAN GUIDE TO WHAT IS
AND WHAT ISN'T

DARREN ALLEN

green books

Published by Green Books
An imprint of UIT Cambridge Ltd
www.greenbooks.co.uk
PO Box 145, Cambridge CB4 1GQ, England
+44 (0) 1223 302 041

First published in 2016, in England
Darren Allen has asserted his moral rights under
the Copyright, Designs and Patents Act 1988.

Front cover / drabbit illustration by Ai Higaki.
Extracts from *Only Fear Dies* and *Making Love* by
Barry Long granted by the Barry Long Foundation.
Quotations taken from *The Anthropology of Childhood* by
David F. Lancy, copyright © David F. Lancy 2015. All rights reserved.
Scripture quotations taken from the *Revised English Bible*, copyright © Cambridge
University Press and Oxford University Press 1989. All rights reserved.
Extracts from the works of David Edwards, Ran Prieur, William Barker
and Ivor Southwood granted by kind permission of the authors.
Extracts from *Medical Nemesis, Energy and Equity & Gender*
by Ivan Illich granted by Marion Boyars Publishers.

The publishers have endeavoured to identify all copyright holders, but will be glad to
correct in future editions any omissions brought to their notice.

ISBN: 978 0 85784 405 7 (hardback)
ISBN: 978 0 85784 406 4 (ePub)
ISBN: 978 0 85784 407 1 (pdf)
Also available for Kindle.

Disclaimer: the author and publisher accept
no liability for actions inspired by this book.

10 9 8 7 6 5 4 3 2 1

CONTENTS

PREFACE

ENCYCLOPAEDIAS and dictionaries are usually boring, not much help when it comes to secretly filling train carriages with SUBVERSIVE BALLOONS and they rarely manage to offend just about everyone. People who compile dictionaries usually assume that language is a big, difficult, book, or a mechanism in the mind that you need *expert guidance* to properly use, instead of a river of silvery ribbons that flows through your astonished head; or a spectacular instant tree that grows between people in collective surrender to something bigger than the both of us; or a slow lightning-strike that wrestles you mooing to the floor; or some strange paradoxical state somewhere between hard, cold crystalline structures driving us to a revolutionary *point*, and mad, hot erupting flowers of aimless joy. People who read dictionaries rarely snort soup from their nostrils in outrage; or nod with gentle recognition at far-apart and long-estranged ideas flung together as friends; or feel like a bat; or fancy falling in love with waiting forever; or seriously consider the only solution to heartbreak there is, or could be; or leave work to master horse; or leave school to get educated; or up and seize their lovers about the middle, ready to embark on a week-long reality-cracking godgasm; or stroll whistling into the VOID…

It is my wish, in writing *The Apocalypedia*, to help change this parlous state of affairs.

WITH GRATITUDE TO

William Barker (wb) for the bizarre flecks of arcturian genius, Niall Mansfield for supporting, and coppicing, such a strange tree, Jake Reilly for good judgement, Tonto Turner for showing me how to never give up Gail Robinson for knowing where the world behind the world is—and allowing me to live there—and Ai for being home…

INTRODUCTION

THIS BOOK IS ABOUT REALITY; that which is *both* subtle *and* obvious, *both* comic *and* tragic, *both* pitiless *and* friendly, *both* real *and* unreal and *both* a wild, sizzling, salt-in-the-eye, all rockets firing, ultravivid cornucopia of strange delight *and* a simple little room just like this one.

It is also about why *neither* the mind *nor* the emotions can grasp anything that is *both* itself *and* something else; and how this leads to boredom, anxiety, sadness, discontent, the self-disgust of the vanquished, a complete inability to feel or talk about or create anything meaningful, or really beautiful, and the creation of a collapsing virtual world that more closely resembles a terrifying schizophrenia-induced nightmare.

The Apocalypedia shows WHAT—the horror of work, dread love affairs, gut-impotence, tongue-tied micro-catastrophes, world-detonating inflows of genius, self-shattering laughter, silent docked she-connections, the intelligence of walls, the wrinkles of a loved uncle, blizzards in the moonlight, anarchic moonwalks through the interzone and friendly festivals of death have in common—WHY—we *do* have the broken families, repressive institutions, boring philosophy, miserable history and omnipornographic teeveemedia we feel we could probably do without and why we *don't* have the utopian island-states, underwater improvised-theatre domes of baize and burnished glass, river-spanning trampolines, exquisite furniture hand-crafted in factory-cum-cathedrals, warm and liquid freedom sloshing around our ankles, tame zebras trotting through the garden and superbly tailored raiment that we feel, somehow, we *should* have—and HOW—to face the tender enormity of the unknown, find a decent fella, instantly overcome all worry, connect up all human knowledge with a transdimensional shoelace, seize never-to-be-repeated moments by their little balls, summon a berserk of glory from the bellymind, impersonate a tree so well that birds land on you, experience the centre of the universe together during apocalyptic intercourse (or apocalyptic gardening), blowtorch the system and find your way out of a me-shaped prison—back into the big room.

A IS FOR
apocalypse
where lives
UNLIVED FREAK

B IS FOR
bed
where things
UNSAID SPEAK

abb [ab]

vb to blab it out in the presence of authoritative silence

abreact [abrıakt]

vb 1 to avoid a subtle point by restlessly or emotionally 'skidding' over the message, blunting (or DIGITISING) its nuance, thereby creating a crude meaning to be offended by, or an excuse to stop paying attention 2 to focus exclusively on the technical meaning of an utterance, in order to avoid its VIBE

accumb [əkʌm]

vb 1 to lose beautifully 2 to be blown out like a man 3 to retire at the height of one's powers, before making a tit of oneself, before SHUFFING OUT or at the first sign that the harvest is over

ack [ak]

vb to realise, with heartsick dreadhorror, that your life was created by a former self you no longer recognise, or even particularly like

addiction [ədɪkʃən]

n ego's tight, concentrated focus on or over-experience of that part of self which it is 'best at' (its SPECIALITY) or 'most enjoys' (its VICE) in order to suppress the discomfort or threat of UNSELF

· signs of addiction include:
· DESENSITISATION · numbed response to pleasure, crude (or DIGITISED) EMOTIONS, BOREDOM (REALITY seems predictable or solid), VIBE blindness, senses dimmed and sensations drained of *banzai!* and *p'tang!*
· OVERSENSITIVITY · to potential SATISFACTION (on perma-alert to the possibility of getting or scoring) and to potential frustration or denial, or to sources of criticism (which are automatically ignored, ridiculed or attacked before they reach full awareness)
· INTOLERANCE · of difficulty, uncertainty or effort
· APATHY · low-level anxiety, withered will and standard so-bloody-whatism
· BACKGROUND SHAME · along with continued use despite negative effects (ill-health, creative-atrophy, UNHAPPINESS, dishonesty, fear of others, impotence, etc.)
· not, in any sense, a sickness; *see* PANCULPISM
· *see* SELF; for types of addiction, *see* NARCOTIC
· *never* satisfied

advertise [advətʌɪz]

vb 1 to spray shit with glitter 2 to train the world, by covering it in MARKET PORN, to believe that quality (peace, security, etc.) can be bought[1]

aedile [iːdʌɪl]

adj descriptive of one who habitually makes unpleasant comments, checks the reaction and, if nobody nods or smiles in agreement, claims he was joking

afuxia [əfʌksɪə]

n 1 inability to get things to work out like they do in the movies; e.g. confronting the boss, post-casual-coitus, kicking down a door, etc; leads to FLAPPING AROUND 2 dreadful yet compelling abyss that opens up in the mind's eye when you are not able to think of something because all you can think about is that you can't think of what it is you are supposed to be thinking about

ananarchy, omnarchy [ʊə]

n 1 a society comprised of DUNBAR GROUPS temporarily lead by whoever happens to be fittest for whatever activity is underway 2 apt and paradoxical rule by context, governing good friends, lovers and all truly cooperative groups, for 99% of human [pre] history[2]

· near synonym of ANARCHY [anəki] *n* innate tendency to circumvent unaccountable domination; flawed by excessive rationality, fear of OBEYING, a tendency to mob and *rather* too much face-bleeding punk

anglut [aŋglʌt]

n 1 feeling of regret, during the last mouthful of a meal, that one has forgotten to enjoy all the other mouthfuls 2 feeling, on saying goodbye to someone you never cared much for, that actually, in fact they are a good fellow 3 FUTILE attempt to get back the joy of a song, childhood or cake by doing it again

antonym [antənɪm]

· *see* SYNONYM

apartment, flat [əpɑːtmənt]

n garage for the overnight storage of economically productive wage slaves, set up for the economic function of upgrading commodities[3]

apocalypse [əpɒkəlɪps]

n something as it really is

A BONGAS
OF ARTICLES

MASHI-MASHI · a twingelette of jealous pain, when experiencing consummate beauty, that makes you determined to do better in your own work

UTTORATE · to be struck with the sense that reality has come apart at the stupid seam and any mad thing is now possible

YON · reverberating sensation after the initial FEELING of a lovely song, painting, gesture, phrase or kiss has ceased

AWARITY · the bittersweet feeling created by ephemeral or soon to be lost beauty, such as figs in season, a beautiful woman glimpsed from the upper window of the 55 to Lea Bridge Road or a functioning operating system

TAIKA · love for the largeness or smallness of a person or thing

TOUND · to know, in a place beyond knowledge, that love and death are somehow at the heart of it all

BABUA · to know, in a place beyond tound, that squelchy analogue boing-boing sounds are at the heart of it all

YUGEN · plummeting awareness of the profundity of the universe, that triggers feelings too mysterious, and tender, for words

appean [əpɪːn]
vb to agree with everything someone says in order to get them to shut up

apperceive [apəsɪːv]
vb to experience the subtle feeling of life buzzing around the body underneath and around EMOTIONS, tensions and other PAINS

apt [apt]
adj & vb 1 OBEYING the context before a plan, a theory or an authority 2 use or love of the right tool for the job
· APTISM [aptɪzəm] *n* the supple principle that all moral, aesthetic, political, psychological and philosophical theories, systems and ideas are beautiful or useful in context; and ugly or inept out of context
· lacks a definable mechanism for choosing the most apt principle to apply in a given situation (i.e. knowing what on EARTH to do) because, for the aptist, no such mechanism exists — ultimately only the situation, or CONTEXT, is intelligent enough to know what to do
· some ideas cannot fit any context, and so can *never* be

apt; such as MONOTHEISM, SCIENTISM, FUNSHISM, CAPITALISM, FASCISM and GOLF
· antonym of APPROPRIATE[4]

art [ɑːt]
n playful expression of time-less unself in the form of the TIMESPACE SELF
· ultimately art has nothing to do with TIME, and so, *at* the time, is overlooked by temporal (which is to say FASHIONABLE) people
· great art = the universal (*see* GENIUS) + the social (*see* SCENIUS) + the personal (*see* SELF), expressed through consummate TECHNIQUE (*see* CRAFT)
· antonym of PORN
· generates ARTICLES [ɑːtɪkəlz] *n.pl.* sublime bubblettes of vibe-hue which pop slow-mo or boom hugely in the receptive SOLAR PLEXUS

ashuln [aʃuːln]
n 1 a smile that steals away the pride of haughty woman 2 a glance that flattens the ego of swaggering man

assuefaction [əsweɪfakʃən]
n the state of being so well accustomed to a situation that one ceases to appreciate that it is worse than shit

asusu [əsuːsuː]
vb 1 to feel uneasy in a new place 2 to give up something new because you look a fool doing it 3 to turn spastic in someone else's kitchen [wb]

augury [ɔːgjʊri]
n to intuit the whole from softly absorbing the part
· *see* FRACTAL
· antonym of SCIENTISM

average man [avərɪdʒ man]
n.phr one who systematical-ly confuses reality for self; whose inner nature seems predictable or unparadox-ically knowable
· always occupied by some ambition or fret to which, after a moment of exulta-tion or relief, he morbidly returns

awhape [əweɪp]
vb to play the bum drums on your wife

awk [ɔːk]
vb 1 to be wrong by being right at the wrong time, or in the wrong way 2 to lie by saying anything at all
· antonym of ARRE [ɑː] *vb* 1 to be right by being wrong at the right moment 2 to be heard by shutting up

awolden [awəʊldən]

adj & n I [descriptive of] that which is familiar yet mysterious, well understood yet at the same time baffling 2 obvious and known to all, yet routinely misunderstood and overlooked

- e.g. the massiveness of the ground, the cowness of cow, the weirdness of having a hand that you can move, the unique 'herness' of your girlfriend's neck, why there should be anything at all, or just mushrooms
- AWAULD [awəʊld] *vb* finding sustenance for joy in failures, wastelands, waiting rooms, puddles and other unlikely places

basta, baster [bastə]

vb, n & exc I to draw the line 2 a line drawn that you will never allowed to be crossed 3 a complete, unwavering refusal to compromise; *ever*

- assisted by THE UNIVERSE

beauty [bjuːti]

n sacrifice + reality ÷ fractal

- *see* Q-WORD

belief [bɪliːf]

vb a guess + hope mix bolted onto a confused and frail personality, so that it A) has a good reason to argue with or exterminate someone in its way B) can prevent the inconvenient inevitability of death from spoiling its plans or C) can reassure itself that the CULT it clings to has cosmic validity

- sometimes means A) suppose B) guess

bellymind [bɛlimʌɪnd]

n the most intelligent part of your body, situated right behind the navel

- the source of GUT-INSTINCT and FEMININE INTUITION
- never wrong; but frequently confused with the more insistent EMOTION about a hand-width *above* the navel, also called 'intuition', but which only has about a 50% hit rate (*see* DOUBT)
- doubles up as an exemplary incinerator for fear, anxiety, anger and the desperate wanty-wanties
- can, if cut off from SOCIETY and REASON, be used as a weapon of MYSTISHISM
- a.k.a. SOLAR PLEXUS

biastify [bʌɪəstɪfʌɪ]

vb to excuse one excess of self by comparing it with its OPPOSAME / false ANTONYM

- e.g. to defend the CULT of

OPTIMISM by comparing it with that of PESSIMISM, cold rationality by comparing it with hot emotion, being 'a responsible adult' by comparing it to being 'an irresponsible CHILD', FUNSHISM by comparing it to BOREDOM, corporatism by comparing it to statism, or the *implicit* violence of MODERN uncivilisation by comparing it to the *explicit* violence of the lawless PRE-MODERN cults which gave rise to and sustain it

blick [blɪk]

n & vb a tic, wince or spasm used to cast out an unpleasant experience or memory

- range from tiny nervous eye-flutters and scrunches, through stomach-sucking grictus grimaces, right up to anguished face-clawing pelvic judders of shame

blip, saccada [blɪp]

n & vb a micro-expression, far too swift to consciously detect, but which delivers a superpotent meaning beam to the bellymind

- used to send secrets across the room, for broadcasting good news from radio me or for VIBE CONDITIONING

A PALLAS OF CLASSIC BLIPS

ZELP · a tiny clench of distrust around the eyebags or a swift furrow-pinch of micro-terror from suddenly not knowing who someone really is

ORM · disconcertingly serious glint of gripping, imploring desperation briefly glimpsed in laughing eyes

HEMPH · a warm flash of 'I'm not really serious' from the upper cheek

TRAVVER · a minute lip-tightening or forehead-crinkling of not liking a suggestion

SHUG · cute goof of hesitation caused by not being able to believe that someone really just said that

PHURK · an involuntary 'yes I'm guilty' smile, a thick 'oh shit' blink or an 'I'm lying' swallow (*see* RELATIONSHIP)

VIBELETTE · any one of an infinite gamut of moodhues that ripple over a calm face in conversational flow (precursor to the ARBRE-LATTICE)

SKASH · soft sigh of the door behind the door behind the door of the eyes, opening

GADUMLEIF · an imperceptible nod that signals that, yes, old friend, we really *are* going to do this terrible, magnificent, and quite possibly final, thing

A URIAH OF BLOCKS

CONTROLLING · over-planning, teaching or forcing action or conversation towards where you want it to go, rather than where it wills itself

GAGGING · going for the larf rather than for the communal story, avoiding a vital point with smirky asides or seeking attention; also PUTTING DOWN

NOING · refusing a proffered side-reality, pretend identity or playful illusion by being overly literal; also CHALLENGING and DEMANDING PROOF

GASSING · restlessly going off on one tangent after another, unable to rest in the collective conversational channel or perceive that others are waiting in vain to be invited into the flow; also ANECDOTING, BITCHING and BRIDGING (faffing around in order to avoid doing or talking about something meaningful)

PORNING · sex-violence gags that are smirk-smirk exciting or angry; rather than surreal or splendidly out of place

PREENING / GRANDSTANDING · using the conversation as an excuse to advertise yourself

TESTING · *'how much do you like me?'* (inc. the sneaky accusation of the *'why must you always?'* rhetorical question)

FACTING · sucking the living guts out of an interaction and filling it with a punch tape of likes, dislikes, facts and complaints (*see* SPONKING)

FLATTERING · *telling* someone they are beautiful or talented instead of showing them with *your* beauty or talent[5]

DOGGEDLY WORKING · grimly going through the motions

JUDGING · reducing a comment or action to a frozen, binary good–bad fact, to which all are forced to turn their weary attention, away from the life of the scene or conversation; also SILENT JUDGING

SUBMISSION · cutting off connected intimacy by inhabiting the cautious, silent, ironic, distanced, fearful or submissive ego-persona (*see* OBEY)

---

block [blɒk]

vb & n 1 to shut down improvised conversational or collaborative flow 2 to turn down an unselfish offer to roll into the unknown 3 to respond to what you want to hear, or to a caricature of what you can't hear

· *see* UNVERSATION *&* IMPRO

A GUDRUN OF BODY PARTS

GLABELLA · the space between the eyebrows; ranging from alien-wide to plod-witted thin

PROIN · the sad, set jaw of one who habitually resists and re-sists, never fighting back

ULLETS · close-minded thighs

LIETTE'S-TREAD · the vee on a bald man's head between the folds of the forehead and the glabrous smoothness of the ensuing dome

MINKLES · wrinkles across the upper lip caused by a lifetime of moaning, or a thumbprint of perma-stress pressed into the putty of a pounded brow

FLUNGE · subcutaneous rhu-barb

YUX · the stiff, inflexible up-per-lip of the PARVAPHOBIC, the puppyish mush of a too satisfied maw or the dulled matt-patina of bovinity over the DOMESTICATED eye

YORB · the biscuit-laying ovi-positor of a persecuted baker

ARBRE-LATTICE · a network of pathways across the face of someone who has, for 70-odd years, allowed every FEELING to wander freely over it, and every VIBE to flare through it

CRAMBOES · your grandmoth-er's antlers

BUGGERLUGS · fleshy, hanging cheeks, bristling with black stubble and reeking of after-shave (a.k.a. JOPPERS)

QUINK · perfection-enhancing imperfections such as wonky teeth, sticky-out ears and fra-grant grass-green pubic hair

SOLAR-PLEXUS · cold, SILENT sun of awesome obliterating super-reality which radiates from the BELLYMIND

IMPOPULANCE · the smooth, tense poverty of a rich man's smile

IPSIMS · features a Victorian author would highly esteem, such as noble brow, humane lips, poignant ankles, etc.

---

body [bɒdi]

n the soft brown space-suit which converts the trans-dimensional ÜBERSELF into sense, feeling and thought
- either APPERCEIVED from within as a wyrd symphony of out-flowing vibe-sense, or perceived from without as a SHAMEFUL-TO-REVEAL, sinful, remote or uncanny genetic FLESH-PUPPET
- *always* PRESENT (closer to the living CONTEXT) and so more APT, or INTELLIGENT, than MIND or EMOTION

boredom [bɔːdəm]

n 1 the point where the horror of ego-possession first pokes into awareness; engendering a restless desire to think, want, compulsively worry, consume narcotics, wage war, MASTURBATE and manufacture uncivilisation 2 a feedback cue that one's engagement is half-arsed or that one's ARSE is half-engaged 3 DOMESTICATION · antonym of IDLENESS

BOREDOM

To BE BORED is to come up with inadequate reasons not to talk to shop assistants with lungs full of helium, play recordings of ecstatic laughter on the tube, SEE sparrows, bring up death in unlikely places, smear yourself over the walls of your house moaning in gratitude, foxtrot through no entry signs, interview your friends, perform daily actions as if holy rituals, visit a prison, leave root vegetables on steps, wrestle with your friends, make bread, trombone up your girlfriend's arse, picnic in a cemetery, learn mycology, lie about your job to taxi drivers, organise a treasure hunt in your house for your lover ending with you, naked, hiding in the cupboard, do the poxy washing-up, make love in a hedge, give everything away, master impro, master joinery, build an organic shed-cathedral in the garden then impersonate the pope for your neighbours, organise situationist theatrical protests in corporate coffee shops, fast for five days, turn up for work dressed as spiderman, heavy metal drum roll as your arse hits cold toilet porcelain, grow fins, learn to crack necks expertly, sniff the smell of now, live alone in a shack, feign elk, or strobe blue, cry *'I am the expressive egg!'* shoot up into a little white ball, and fly out the window

❧

brainwash [breinwɒʃ]

vb to create MARKERED STEREOTYPICAL paths through the PSYCHE; along which the attention habitually flows, esp. when stimulated—via rewards and threats to EGO—by a TOTALITARIAN SYSTEM

HOW TO BRAINWASH YOUR CHILDREN

THE SELVES OF YOUNG CHILDREN are so soft that they do not just 'experience' what is happening, they *are* it. There is no separate 'me' witnessing 'not me'. For the very young the sounds, smells, sights and, most intensely, the hyper-subtle vibe of the room (a.k.a. the CONTEXT) are indistinguishable from the child's default inner state of soft-consciousness, which she shares with the selfless adult, or the selfless hedgehog, in selfless communion.

Needless to say, such a mode of experience is acutely subversive and must be obliterated. Children who are allowed to grow up in continual contact with inner ease grow into adults who do not need external stimulus to feel content, or to bolster their sense of self-worth. They are poor consumers, poor workers, unprofitably sensitive to CONSCIENCE and reluctant to compromise. They are, in short, a threat.

To neutralise this threat you must cut your child off from its own felt reality, and replace her soft, context-integrated self with a hard, isolated EGO (*see* SELF). There are three inter-connected ways to achieve this; A) HARD-FOCUS: forcing the wide sensory attention of the child out of the whole present moment and into divided-up parts of it B) EMOTION: gripping your child's attention with the wants (pleasures) and not-wants (pains) of the self C) SABOTAGE OF TRANSITIONS: stunting your child's capacity to exit their newly acquired needy-anxious self-realm and enter genuinely new, non-egoic, experience.

A. HARD FOCUS

The ultimate purpose of brainwashing is to replace direct experience with a mental–emotional image of reality (provided by external authority), but this cannot be done without first dividing your child's experience up into BITS. Ordinarily this ability to split reality up — and then to create ideas based on the divisions — happens naturally; leading to language, imagination and so on. Your job though is to *force* nature, so that your child is *always* focused on isolated things (subjects and objects). The stress of this will corrupt her blended sensitivity to what is really going on and replace the context with a tense, irritable emotionality upon which you can build subsequent manipulations (*see* CONSCIOUSNESS).

Until modern times over-focusing young children was rather difficult, and was normally passed over in favour of straightforward violence; but now there are plenty of excellent baby-brainwashing devices on sale with flashing lights and spinning disks and the like to stupefy infants into a tense, hypnotic trance. It is quite natural to entertain your baby with fantastic sensory effects, but the aim here is to do it, as far as possible, *constantly*. Repetitive digital sound-effects work well, as do light-emitting diodes and bright plastic paint. If these are not around, then excessively provocative chatter, yelps and leering, gurning faces will do. You might like to consider putting your youngster in a carrier or pushchair that faces out into the street and then walking through a crowded centre of consumption. Guard against allowing your child to enjoy just sitting there gurgling and muttering with pleasure at nothing more than being in her own body.

As early as possible get your kids watching TEEVEE all day, playing computer games or, if possible, plugging them into a VR headset. Loud rapidly changing CGI scenes of sanitised fantasy smattered with a patina of formal morality work best. The primary purpose here is to instil worry and anxiety through speeding up the psyche of the child, DIGITISING its CONSCIOUSNESS and beaming a stream of things to ardently want through its tiny, concentrated fovea (*see* VIRTUAL). The secondary purpose is to get your child used to the idea that dreams only come true on the video screen, and that reality isn't really real; it's a kind of show, which you are supposed to passively like or hate—never actively contribute to.

Finally, when your child is old enough to understand the word 'should', you must *moralise* to her. The key here is to have the greatest disparity possible between what you say and what you do by A) constantly going on about what is right and wrong without ever taking action and B) by having the greatest possible disparity between what you say and the way you say it. If your kid won't eat the meal you cooked for her, don't let her go hungry; tell her she's being silly, and then let her eat what she wants. If your little girl disturbs you with her spontaneous physicality, freeze, purse your lips, give her an awkward little pat and say, with great emphasis, 'of *course* Mummy loves you'. This kind of thing drives a *schasm* through a child's psyche that will take her decades to recover from; while implicitly programming her with the most important moral lesson of all — that truth does not really exist; only ideas, words, facts and tonnes and tonnes of LAWS.[6]

B. EMOTION

It's not enough just to create for your child a reality comprised entirely of atomised objects and experiences. You must also make him ardently want or not want them. This background emotionality is the fuel that drives your child into his self and the means by which he can be threatened, purchased and manipulated (*see* VIBE-CONDITIONING).

The first step in creating such constant emotionality is, first of all, to not understand it. You should have no idea of the difference between crude, coercive EMOTION and subtle polychromatic FEELING, so your trivial annoyances, moodies, dullness of spirit and so on feel perfectly normal or, at least, excusable. Then you should make sure you are *continually* emotional; continually restless, annoyed, depressed, anxious, excited or, covering this warzone, coldly suppressed.

In this way, you will fill the house with SUFFERING. It won't seem so dramatic to you, but while you are feeling harried, bored, irritable or under par, your baby, forty-thousand times more sensitive than you, will be experiencing these ordinary moodies as knives of violence or horrorful separation[7] which will cause him to become emotional in turn; wanting and not-wanting. He won't necessarily know *what* he wants; he will just *be wanty*; an intense (tense) state of in-self.

As your child grows he will learn to use his developing self not merely as a tool for thinking and playing, but as a defensive weapon; conniving or wheedling for stimulants —

such as sugar and adrenaline—and for proto-narcotic hits of attention, acquisition and hypnotic virtuality; which you should be sure to periodically lavish on your kids—pumping them up beforehand with *'ooh-it's-your-birthday-tomorrow'* type excitement—in order to habituate them to the cycle of BOREDOM, agitation, WANTING, expectation, fear-of-not-getting, over-excitement-at-having, disappointment and return to base-boredom which makes the world go round.

The final and most direct component of emotionalising your child is through periodically exciting his fears and desires. This doesn't just consist in terrifying your little boy with visions of hell, pushing him into confusing and uncomfortable situations (such as SCHOOL), or dangling fantastic imaginary delights in front of his mind's eye—although these are all excellent ideas—but in continually appealing to his *likes and dislikes.* These are not mere preferences—the usual configuration of inclination and taste that makes one child different from another—but a kind of rudimentary religion of me; a means of converting the child's ungovernable inner-reality into a tractable collection of fetishised labels which, in times of uncertainty, your child will, in lieu of genuine character, cling to (*see* PERSONALITY and TASTE).

C. SABOTAGE OF TRANSITIONS

As your child grows, you should be on continuous alert for moments when she first enters a new sphere of experience—or TRANSITION—into the unknown (or UNSELF). By correctly applying violence, pressure, disinterest or fretting, hovering anxiety you can warp your child away from selfless reality, forcing her into a cycle of repeated psychological CRISES that will play out for the rest of her adult life.

One of the best ways to sabotage transitions—alongside ordinary restlessness, stress and disinterest—is to make your affectionate attention *conditional.* When your child conforms to your expectations or acts in a way you approve of, reward her, and when she does something you don't like, punish her; again, not physically or verbally (although that will cer-

A REICH OF TRANSITIONS

As the child develops it enters new fields of experience. By applying the right kind of pressure to these transitions, the parent can effectively, profitably and permanently sabotage the child's character:

PRIMAL EXPERIENCE
of UNSELF, of the CONTEXT or of YOU; adult sabotage leads to shrivelled EMPATHY, forceful self-assertion, narrowed attention or PRIMAL FEAR

EXPERIENCE OF BODY
and control of bodily urges; adult sabotage leads either to touch-starved awkwardness or to an obsession with filth or order

ACQUISITION OF LANGUAGE
of IMAGINATION and symbol; sabotage leads to ADDICTIVE FANTASY, fear of expression or compulsive lying

REASONING, LOGICAL SKILLS
sabotage leads to weird beliefs or stupidity

CONSCIENCE
sabotage leads to deceit, guilt or inability to act APTLY

INDEPENDENCE
sabotage leads to excessive dependence or fear of society

AWARENESS OF DEATH
sabotage leads to existential insecurity or contributes to suicidal negativity

SOCIETY
sabotage leads to competitiveness, GROUPTHINK or fear of society

SELF-AWARENESS
sabotage leads to arrogance or self-consciousness

SEXUAL INTIMACY
sabotage leads to sexual obsession or fear of intimacy

---

tainly help), but vibically; through emotion, tone of voice and imperceptible micro-expressions; none of which you will be aware of, but all of which will reinforce the self of your child and teach her that A) certain kinds of freedom are wrong or shameful and B) we cannot really admit this to anyone.

After five to seven years of home brainwashing, your child should be sufficiently anxious, unempathic, demanding, bossy, snobby, picky, repressed, self-assertive, bland, stiff, digitised, clumsy, addicted to self, fundamentally confused by life or afraid of the unknown to leave the nest and make her way through the WORLD of the SCHOOL and SYSTEM.

If not, don't worry; she soon will be!

A LOYOLA OF WARPS

Still having problems brainwashing your little ones? Try these tips for screwing up your kids good and proper.

OBSCURE · if you don't want them to do something, simply make sure that they don't understand how; this will drive them to seek tactical advice from the worst possible source

NAG · keep on complaining about their behaviour until they have learned to screen out your moralising and have acquired a constant feeling of low-lying guilt and resentment

PRY · either be obsessively interested in the details of their personal lives, making them feel guarded, suspicious and exposed, or...

DON'T GIVE A TOSS · don't be interested in their experiences, don't seek to share their reality, don't try to understand what it is they are lacking or missing from their lives, and don't listen to, or help them to perceive, their CONSCIENCE

BRIBE · if you want them to like you, appeal to their vices and weaknesses and buy them off with presents, travel, excitement or power (esp. over the ugly, the weak and the poor)

BLACKMAIL · threaten your children with exposure, ridicule or discomfort if they don't do what you want

SYSTEMATIZE · pay them to work, score them, rate them, fine them and, of course, bargain with them

BULLY · beat them ferociously at games, toughen them up with tests of sado-endurance or get annoyed at their failures; whatever your style of bullying you should never stop pushing them to win, succeed and *advance*

CONDESCEND · never forget they are children—ludicrous, annoying, selfish, brutal, stupid, lazy and useless—and never let them forget it; either talk down to them, micromanage their actions and consult them only on trivial matters or treat them like frosted-glass figurines that will shatter at the slightest upset, confusion, deprivation, particle of dirt or *bad word*

FINALLY · don't touch them, inculcate subservience to [state, scientific or religious] authority, suppress all expressions of sexuality, don't let them play outside unsupervised and be ever on the alert for opportunities to '*teach*', *blame* and *compel*

- STANDARD BRAINWASHING TECHNIQUES INCLUDE:
- constant appeals to ego
- compliance rewarded with approval, attention, prestige, power or relief
- punishment of independent deviance with abuse, disapproval, ridicule and deprivation
- use of in-group jargon and the fostering of specialness
- making huge promises and giving erratic rewards
- guilt tripping
- ridicule of outsiders, who must be rejected
- degradation of Q-WORDS
- inducement of anxiety and addiction
- criticism CO-OPTED (marginal voices assimilated)
- objectification; individual treated as if he or she were an idea, fact or odourless pellet of datum
- all events, particularly mysterious ones, incorporated into the dominant ideology
- total exposure
- uncertainty and precarity
- constant presence of PORN
- restriction of free-time
- denial of any alternatives
- brainwashing is extremely fragile; it demands *constant* reinforcement
- *see* SYSTEM and HYPNOTISM

brangle [braŋgəl]
vb 1 to agitate someone who is calm by telling them to calm down, to make somebody break something by fearing their clumsiness, to annoy someone by asking if you are annoying them, to repel someone by clinging to them or to terrify someone with the words *'don't be afraid, I'm not going to hurt you'* 2 to make someone sick by doctoring them, thick by teaching them, demanding by pandering to them, ugly by covering them in beauty products or impotent by converting their world into a vast ever-morphing pornball 3 to make a child, or a nation, untrustworthy by not trusting it [8]
- leads to ECTOMONISHMENT

brap [brap]
n 1 dawning realisation that you're on the wrong train 2 suddenly finding that an always unlocked door isn't 3 the first tiny suspicion that your mighty castle of truth, health or security is built on a bedrock of margarine
- announced with a skipped dislocated little beat in the momentum of the day and confused, whelpy *'eh?'*

brelp [brɛlp]
vb & n I a stretching sound or motion, or a held intake of breath, used to signal one's desire to close a conversation 2 the moment when everyone suddenly knows that a conversation is finished and it's time to do something else

brelpless [brɛlplɪs]
adj [of] being trapped in a conversation with someone unable to perceive BRELPS

brundles [brʌndəls]
n.pl collective term for the advice and judgements provided by NATURE
· e.g. a pine cone's friendly recommendation for your wardrobe, a distant mountain's slow thumbs up, a crow's silent disapproval at the sorry state of your affairs, sheep sarcasm

brunge [brʌndʒ]
n I the collective feeling of unstoppable awkwardness when watching a film, or a world, that everyone is secretly hating but nobody can *quite* admit to 2 the agonising pretence that terminal illness, domestic violence, the final decay of romance, the loss of one's treasured position / possession, or the end of uncivilisation are not *really* happening 3 unspoken secrets between you and a loved one, that fester in your body to reappear later as SEXUAL disinterest, sexual violence and psychotic wrath over amazingly silly *'god you always do that'* type disagreements
· *things unsaid will speak in bed*

bumwash [bʌmwɒʃ]
n the speech of one in the grip of lady nonsense
· synonym of QUOG

bureaucracy [bjʊərɒkrəsi]
n standard, scientific, means of controlling reality by defining and storing it
· e.g. visas, degrees, application forms, care-plans, certificates, licenses, statements, reports, contracts
· synonym of CREDENTIAL-ISM and of BUMPH [bʌmf] *n* bum-fodder

business [bɪzi-nɪs]
n I socially-approved means of compensating for being an inept lover 2 chief activity of the poor and deprived 3 ritualised thievery
· *see* MARKET

BUREAUCRACY

1. IT DIGITISES uncivilisation is founded on EGO which can only conceive of reality in terms of that which can be isolated, measured, defined, controlled and possessed; in other words, written down (*see* SCIENCE and VIRTUAL).[9]

2. IT CONTROLS once people have been *put into writing* they can not only be controlled, but will control themselves; partly through the enormous amount of time and money it costs to come up with the correct bits of paper, partly through the stress engendered by the excessive abstract planning and mystifying formality that bureaucracy demands, but mainly through the self-regulating schizoid self-consciousness (anxiety about low marks, unlikes, official judgements and the like) that bureaucratic surveillance engenders.

3. IT IS INDIRECT bureaucracy, like DEBT, is indirect (a.k.a. polite) violence; if you stop filling out the correct forms, the POLICE will soon be on their way.[10] In addition the world would fall apart if FIRST-IMPRESSION were to govern decision-making. Spontaneous intelligence and soft perception (of PHYSIOGNOMY, VIBE and context) cannot be controlled, but forms, money and other bits of paper can.

4. IT IS PROFESSIONAL those who seek an indirect relationship with their fellows (who are stiff, awkward or uptight in their face-to-face interactions, and in their face), or who, through fear of life, seek to control it, and thereby gain power, through controlling the flow of information, are automatically promoted to the upper world of paperwork; i.e. MANAGEMENT (*see* PROFESSIONAL and SYSTEM).

5. IT JUSTIFIES the central management of a vast institution can only wield distant control through bureaucracy. Because of this distance the manager does not know what is going on and needs paperwork to justify his irresponsible position (as well as, like medieval inquisitors, the recorded facts of your communication to justify his sadism) and to give the impression of useful activity.

C IS FOR
cackeral
power over
WET BREAD

D IS FOR
deruet
not the voice in
YOUR HEAD

cackeral [kakərəl]

n a not-very-good super-power such as knees that bend both ways, ability to summon rabbits or the rapid growth of a goitre when a crime is being committed

· antonym of FADOMITE

cancer [kansə]

n institutions that will not sacrifice themselves creating selves that will not sacrifice themselves, creating products that will not sacrifice themselves, creating cells that will not sacrifice themselves; and vice versa

canerated [kanəreɪtɪd]

adj 1 to be prematurely aged through a dissolute life 2 to look like you are wearing a latex suit of your former self

can't [kɑːnt]

md.vb either 1 unable to ('*I can't fly*', '*I can't effectively store foodstuffs in my navel*') or 2 won't, don't want to or don't feel like ('*I can't give up work*', '*I can't say "cheerio!" to Mr. Moody*')

capitalism [kapɪtəlɪzəm]

n 1 rule by capital and by the MARKET 2 theft of surplus by those who do not produce it 3 fabulous belief that the most insane sector of society, for the most insane motives, will somehow create a sane world

· inherently exploitative
· cannot exist without class
· synonym of AUTHORITAR-IAN / STATE SOCIALISM, and TOTALITARIANISM

cerberus (mr) [dʒagənɑːθə]

n filter used by deep nature (and other great artists) to keep out pretenders, dilettantes and weekenders

· unlike his EVIL twin—the SHOULD BULLY of GUILT— Mr. Cerberus is on your side; he is, for example…
· the protective warzone between UNCIVILISATION and the remote tribe, and the apocalyptic ego-purge between DYSTOPIA and UTOPIA
· the years of punishing craft between SHAWPING half-intent and true mastery
· the emotional virago that loving women carry around to keep COCKMEN out
· nemesis (or Q-FORCE) your own self as BIG BOSS, that, because it is you, can only be beaten by that which is *greater* than you
· …and, strange to say, he *wants* you to beat him

MR. CERBERUS

T HE FIRST TIME YOU GO FOR A RUN after years of slump you feel like you are going to die after five minutes. If you've lived your life on low-nutrient junk food, you're more than likely to judge a subtle, high-fibre meal as lacking in excitement; difficult somehow. And if you are a city dweller in the bones and swan off for a year to live off grid in the middle of nowhere, it soon becomes, after the initial novelty wears off, hideously boring, terrifying even.

These kind of difficulties are well known. Less well known is the reason; Mr. Cerberus.

Mr. Cerberus, also known as The Guardian at the Gate and Dr. Cold Turkey, stands between the self-led life and the life-led self. He is there, in weed form, when you make a move from monoculture to permaculture. He's there as the background irritation of 'don't like' if you turn from fast-cut rapid-chatter, murder-beats to slow ('deep') symphonies of mood or thought. If you fast, stop working, stop pornwanking, give up smoking, try to master a genuine CRAFT or radically change any entrenched, self-gratifying habit, relationship, addiction or even social class he's there, either telling you it's pointless, stupid, impossible or slapping you round the swede with his existential meathooks.

Interestingly though, he's *not* there when you take up a new love affair (or interest); he tends to hang back and turn up about three months after Miss Glorious Uprush has buggered off. He goes immediately apeshit though if you give up tight-focus fucksex and make thoughtless, unsentimental love (*see* SEX). Indeed any move away from the momentum of unconscious mentation—an absence of habitual thinking, worrying or hoping—and you can expect to say hello to God's personal bastard.

He turns up in some surprising places does Mr.C. You sometimes see him hanging around, for no apparent reason around 6pm, or pointlessly hovering over a ringing phone; and sometimes he's just vaguely hanging round, for years.

And you can expect him in spades when civ pops.

CALENDAR

January

1st .... NEW YEAR'S DAY watching the sun come up and thanking it for doing so. Refusing to talk or think about the past all day, or all year.

February

15th .... INTERNATIONAL PREPARE FOR THE DAY WHEN YOUR PARENTS ARE DEAD DAY in which everyone avoids the future anguish of not having said what they really felt to their dead parents by, while they are still alive, letting go of blame, anger, etc., and instead briefly but sincerely thanking them for their sacrifices.

March

24th .... WILLIAM MORRIS' B.DAY observed by learning a medieval craft, participating in a permanent international strike and writing cheesy poetry.

25th .... EXSUPERATION WEEK no computers, no meat or sugar, cold showers with home-made soap, linen underwear etc. (*see* EXSUPERATION).

April

1st .... START OF SPRING three days of outrageous feasting, open-mic of *extreme* variety, ballroom, impro, naked mud-slides, banana-rugby, etc.

4th .... BOARD GAME DAY

May

1st .... MAY DAY in which everyone stops paying their rent, their debts and their taxes; forever.

June

UPSIDE-DOWN ANIMAL DAY............................5th
NATIONAL CRAWL CRAVENLY TO WORK DAY wb.......................21st

July

IMPERCEPTIBLY-ALTERED-GAIT DAY **marks the**......................14th
start of doing-things-slightly-differently week.

August

START OF DO HARDLY ANYTHING MONTH...........................1st

September

RUSSIA DAY **honoured by reading** *War and Peace,*.......................9th
**eating blinis, listening to Rachmaninoff, per-
forming dangerous repairs or potentially lethal
dares and** *never* **complaining, even if set on fire.**
FILTHY OUTDOORS SEX DAY.......................21st

October

HALLOWEEN / DAY OF THE DEAD **requiem at**.......................31st
**breakfast, picnic in the graveyard, children's
visit to the morgue, ingestion of** LSD, **simulated
midnight death and ecstatic daybreak rebirth.**

November

DAY OF THE MAN **in which men behave all day**.......................14th
like their grandfathers would have.
INTERNATIONAL DELETE A PROFILE DAY.......................25th

December

EXCHANGE RELIGIOUS BELIEFS DAY.......................20th

charity [tʃarɪti]

n popular, MARKET-friendly way of sustaining, excusing and concealing slavery, and easing class-guilt, by giving away a small portion of MONEY, or by teaching the working class how to cook

chark [tʃɑːk]

n 1 a worrying thought, or the feeling that there was something you were supposed to be doing, that you are distracted from, forget, but which somehow leaves a whiff of *something is wrong* for about ninety minutes 2 a worrying experience, or the feeling that there was someone you were supposed to be being, undergone some time between the ages of 2 and 6, that you are distracted from, forget, but which somehow leaves a whiff of *something is wrong* for about ninety years 3 the nagging feeling that you have recently said something idiotic to somebody

· can lay dormant for weeks, before being triggered by a subtle environmental cue (or by a PSYCHEMONGER), leaving you anxious 'for no reason', until the cause has been identified, whereupon the chark evaporates

childhood [tʃʌɪldhʊd]

n an artificial category of human created (around 600 years ago[2]) to A) segregate the most intelligent, creative and SENSITIVE sector of society from those who might be infected by their revolutionary fervour[3] and B) submit them to the authority of a schoolteacher

· for the SYSTEM childhood is a kind of mental illness

city [sɪti]

n large mechanism invented by men to house, transport, feed, create and care for cars

cleverness [klɛvənəs]

n being able to quote authorities, manipulate ideas (or people), do crosswords, acquire degrees, use hard, concentrated consciousness to solve abstract (scientific) problems, advance in TOTALITARIAN hierarchies, recite facts or SUCCESSFULLY fuck people over

· synonym of EXPERTISE
· antonym of INTELLIGENCE, WISDOM and APTNESS

climate change [wɪəduːmd]

n ongoing, unpreventable, man-made *climate meltdown*

· *see* COLLAPSE

clock [klɒk]

n an item of power machinery, the product of which (hours, seconds, minutes) is used to create the illusion that TIME is a mathematical sequence of discrete events, and not a sexy goddess

· originated in the Muslim and Medieval monastery CALL TO PRAYER—an early attempt to curtail spontaneity and profit-threatening irregularity—which was developed by the late-medieval military system and then by early capitalist industry; both of which demanded the same mutilated subservience from members as the religions they grew from[4]

cockman [kɒkman]

n I highly predictable and dangerous strain of AVERAGE MAN 2 a cock with its chicken cut off

collapse [kəlaps]

n the end of UNCIVILISATION · a.k.a. WORLD-HEARTBREAK

colour [kʌlə]

n mantis mints, tango pinks, Arcturian blue-beams and starling-egg greens, cream of sponge, feeling of orange…

A MALLORD OF COLOURS

LYARD · the silvery shimmering grey of apperceptive ease behind the eyelids

GLAVERY · the sickly mottled pink pallor of a butcher or DJ

PLOOM · pre-dawn yellowy grey, exactly halfway between butterwax feather and worm-skin poppyflesh [wb]

HAVERLINE · the warm biscuit orange of a jobless saunter

HOAM · the watery teal, damp cobalt and remote mountains of intense thursdayness

GHEBE · the greeny tawp of sprouting potatoes and guilt [wb]

RUGGLE · threadbare 4:30 pm burgundy musings

NESCLE · baggy mauve of late, wet SPRING, mellow French accents and the wading lope of a pronghorn in a massive treacle tart [wb]

DAUM · umber hum generated by a *yes* of liberation meeting the *maybe* of gathering dust

ZINTH · the nuclear, electric green of cheap office carpets, spreadsheets, sexual frustration and margarine

GUNGRISHE · the crumbling nut-brown of an 'erm' slowly gnawing through time [wb]

BREALM · oily golden amber of the sense of smugness that follows a really good point [wb]

COLLAPSE

EFORE SOCIETIES COLLAPSE: charity constitutes right-eousness, pride of wealth is inspired by insignificant possessions (or *likes*) upon which all lust and hanker, accumulated treasures are expended on dwellings, cows are held in esteem only as they supply milk and the people are always apprehensive of scarcity; and so are ever watching the sky. Before societies collapse, women become as men, men become as women and love is confused with desire, or with fear. Time is perpetually occupied and observed, which leads to the KINERTIAL feeling that it is both speeding up and [that culture] has frozen. Cults flourish, words are policed and language loses meaning. Scientists are consulted before artists, and artists say nothing. It is forbidden to lie down in public spaces. Dreams are troubled; of falling buildings and impossible tasks, of love drifting out of the world, of hopes for a saviour and of corridors. Sex hardens the hearts of the coveted and frustrates the hearts of slaves. Eyes everywhere glaze over, and nobody really RECOGNISES each other.

Before societies collapse everyone who has an elephant is a Rajah, and everyone who is feeble is a slave. SPECTACLE, PORN, DEBT and LAWS proliferate and with them a creeping sense of world-dread, which sleeps for a few months before being awoken with every new calamity. All buildings blend into one hut, and local customs wither. Hunter-gatherers abandon their forests, and gain a livelihood by servitude in the farms of villages that hate them, farming men abandon agriculture, and gain a livelihood by servitude in disposable electronic pet-grooming fork factories, and working folk abandon their tools and attend many, many conferences on productivity.

AS THE COLLAPSE PROGRESSES: ice melts, seasons cease, oceans rise, forests die, wells dry, rivers flood, deserts spread and the soil is blown away.[5] There are no more birds, fish, frogs, butterflies or bees. The corn is light in ear and the grain poor, and of little sap. Countless millions start to move and no police force is powerful enough, no wall high enough, to keep them out. They will be slaughtered.

Crowd-pacifying news, and VR-TEEVEE coalesce into a grotesque panpornographic live soap opera, which gradually becomes indistinguishable from daily life; somewhere between a terrifying battleground and a vast virtual brothel. Adverts for consumer goods function as insurrectionary messages,[6] as do the gated-communities and suites of the super-rich, which become the most dangerous places on earth to be.

The global economy crashes and crashes again. Savings are wiped out, markets collapse, supermarkets are armed, bread costs more than hard-drives and protein comes from insects. Viruses mutate and strange new epidemics break out. Cholera, tuberculosis and diseases of pre-modernity catch up with cancer, heart-disease and brand new modern ailments.

The coal-oil power that states and corporations rely on runs low. First access to the internet becomes as expensive as rent, then the worldbrain starts to go dark, engendering the furious anguish of virtual cold turkey. Solar panels and wind turbines stop working because there are no minerals to make or repair them. Everyone in the world YENGS that they don't actually know how to do anything, or be anywhere.

Civil unrest—fuelled by a rise of a displaced lower class, precariat underclass and newly impoverished middle class—reaches an unprecedented scale. Nakedly fascist state-corp power brutally crushes the threat of any independence, before centralised control disintegrates and cedes to the gangs and mafias from which, originally, it emerged.

Eventually every individual psyche becomes the epicentre of a personal apocalypse. The ocean of SUFFERING that lies in the UNHAPPY SUPERMIND—once the comforting and pacifying alienation, advertising and addictions wear off—breaks out in near omnipresent insanity. Men and women become as lizards, skuttling and watchful for weakness, or as hunted birds, white and ever blinking. The world becomes a sleepless hive, fuelled by nightmares. The many are SCHIZOID in the age of collapse, frozen exposed in everlasting awakeness, and the HEARTBROKEN few stand divided from them. Billions face death and the horror is everything, everywhere.

But, as the world cracks up, UTOPIA leaks in.

A YOSSER
OF CULPAS

Most people can easily identify physical hunger (food, warmth, water, etc.) but have difficulty identifying other hungers, misattributing them to remote, bizarre or rather too convenient causes:

COCOCULPA · blaming a lack of praiseful attention on not enough chocolate

ONSIOCULPA · confusing guilt caused by contempt for one's lover with psychotic anger for their tiny mishaps

BUREAUCULPA · misinterpreting the enervating, clouding, clogging and bitter brain-fat of WORK with a lack of yoga, fun, holiday or new phone

SPONSACULPA · blaming one's partner or blaming one's 'low self-esteem' for sexual disinterest caused by a stupefying routine or by pornography

LUDOCULPA · the assumption that the glum torpor of indolence is caused by something other than unused rollerblades, overused TEEVEE or easy-peasy sweety wheaties

AFFLACULPA · attempting to solve the anxiety, BOREDOM and guilt of wealth with charity, therapy, satsang or food

EOSCULPA · blaming *them* for *you*

comfort zone [kʌmfətzəʊn]
n the conviviality, creativity, originality and playfulness of late-capitalist employees, squeezed out and smeared over the big furry yoga bean bags and mindful muesli of the friendly, family, softly glowing, office-orb [7]
· *see* WELLNESS

commute [kəmjuːt]
n & vb the exhausting and reality-warping experience of being forced to consume unnecessary transportation to places unnecessarily far away
· COMMUTER [kəmjuːtər] *n* a person constantly absent from a destination she cannot reach on her own but must reach within a day [8]

competition [kɒmpɪtɪʃən]
n either 1 play or 2 the active manic phase of DEPRESSIVE–COMPETITIVE DISORDER [9]

conscience [kɒnʃəns]
n the quiet voice of UNSELF
· the intelligent pain of guiltless conscience is an acute threat to the WORLD, which must blunt or brainwash the sensitivity to perceive it and the courage to act on it
· antonym of GUILT

CONSCIENCE

THE WORD CONSCIENCE usually designates the priest, police or parent-code installed in the self; designed, more or less, to prevent or inhibit you from threatening The Way Things Are, by creating an EMOTION of pre-emptive GUILT. This *false-conscience* (a.k.a. respect, superego or responsibility) is an implanted alien morality, a purpose-serving cultural bouncer at the doors of liberation and a brake upon spontaneity, individuality and free discernment.

Guilt is the SHOULD-BULLY that keeps the rich rich ('we should go to work and pay our taxes'), the poor poor ('we should pay our debts'), the stupid stupid ('we should trust the media, the government, school syllabuses and the authority of professionals') and the modern artist in pay ('we shouldn't throw eggs in the MOMA'). But. If you are sitting down in your garden, say, easy in the body—and you smell toast burning in the kitchen, then you are going to have a feeling inside of something not being right. This is true CONSCIENCE.

Conscience is the whiff of burning toast—and toast will start to burn when human FREEDOM is restricted by lack of; food, warmth, water, air, cleanliness, creative physical exercise and rest, mental exercise and rest (when no thought arises), autonomy, trust, achievement and development (challenges overcome), privacy, SOCIETY (and social justice), infinity (the paradoxical FRACTALITY of nature), freedom of speech and expression, intoxication, knowledge of limits and freedom to break them when the moment is right, attention, companionship and affection (given and received), good vibe, inner (unaddicted, unhungover, choiceless) peace, unconditional 'faults and all' acceptance, freedom to give in to the tearing impulse to give everything away, craft-mastery, spontaneity, SUBVERSION, acute sensitivity, danger, dirt, duty, myth, ritual, art, SACRIFICE, LOVE and, above all, UNSELF.[10]

If you are unable or unwilling to A) smell the smoke (detect, in the body, that something is wrong) B) find the cause of the fire (which of the above needs is not being met) or C) put it out (act or accept), you will, of course, SUFFER.

CONSCIOUSNESS

WHEN YOU LOOK at a table and a chair you usually see them as separate from each other. The table is separate from the chair, which are both separate from the surrounding room, and the room is separate from you, the observer. These separations are created by an activity in the mind, a *focusing activity*, called HARD CONSCIOUSNESS. Before this activity there are no such divisions; the table, chair, room, you—the whole present moment—are one, single, undivided experience. This is the way babies, who do not have a well developed focusing mind, perceive the world.

This does not mean that there are no separate divided objects in the real world—that the mind literally makes up the bits of the universe (*see* PARADOX)—but that REALITY can be experienced in two different ways; the focused, divided experience of hard consciousness and the undivided, or less divided, experience of soft consciousness.

Hard consciousness is obviously important—people who can't tell one thing from another are insane—but it has a monstrously disproportionate prestige in the modern world. Scientists, and their modern students, take it to be the distinguishing feature of humanity, the foundation of human achievement and the acme of human intelligence. All scientific and psychological study is directed towards its nature and all education is founded on its supposed wisdom.

But. Despite being the basis of all SCIENTIFIC KNOWLEDGE,[11] concentrated consciousness is not aware of over 99% of sense-experience,[12] nor is it aware of how it came to most of its decisions or conclusions; although it easily finds reasons.[13] Hard consciousness is a thin, focused torch beam, unable to see anything outside the beam—including the torch itself—but assuming, because it sees itself everywhere it looks, that the whole basement is full of light.

SOFT CONSCIOUSNESS,[14] on the other hand, experiences the context, or present, as a *whole;* with hard-focusing as one useful, thinking, isolating part. Soft-consciousness is the I that is behind, or is conscious *of,* 'me'; the I that includes the entire scene, rather than the 'me' which is comprised of and focuses on isolated, literal, unparadoxical *bits* of it. Because of this, because soft-consciousness precedes the literal bits of hard-focus, it prefers to express itself through *non*-literal language (METAPHOR), paradoxical imagery (ART) and unspoken VIBE, which express the *quality* of what is happening; rather than the useful but plodding *quantitative* meaning-units of hard, explicit consciousness.

There is, of course, nothing wrong with the ability to pick out and use these units—literally nothing can be grasped or built without hard-focus concentration—but without soft-conscious awareness of the context from which units and bits emerge, there is no meaningful reason to grasp (or serve) and no genius to build (or fix) tools worth using, houses worth living in or songs worth listening to (*see* PINK TIP).

When soft-consciousness is suppressed for long enough (*see* BRAINWASHING), hard-consciousness takes over my subtle identity—and *becomes me*. (*see* SELF) My self, egoically self-informed, becomes unable to experience anything other than itself; its own ideas, worries, wants, fears and fixated manias.[15] Expression then becomes stiff, monotonous and (like science) predictable; the mind becomes exclusively focused on (i.e. STARES AT) the isolated things that hard consciousness creates through its own isolating, abstracting and focusing activity, and the world then becomes *just bits*. Naturally this is not a problem which can be solved or even seen in the normal way, with *my* concentrated thinking and effort. It can only be dealt with by learning to *not* be me (*see* SELF-MASTERY).

꒰꒱

consciousness [kɒnʃəsnɪs]
n either 1 the artist or 2 the canvas

consene [kənsiːn]
vb to unite opposing sides in an argument by stating a truth so outrageous to convention that all join forces against you

• goodies and baddies usually only stop fighting each other when they gang up against the paradoxies [16]

consumerism [əbeɪkreɪvɪŋ]

n a clever means of separating humans into a series of SPECIALIST subgroups (a.k.a. CONSUMERS[17]) who are forever in need of professional services to enter or to stay in productive life[18]

contemplation [tɛndəgeɪz]

n the firm, gentle, characterful, absorbing or brightvivid SEEING of the soft conscious man, who seeks to recognise life in what is before him, and so to whom life reveals itself, writhing in ecstasy

· antonym of the dull, dry, vacant, fleeting or tensely concentrated STARE, spy, glance or PRY of the AVERAGE MAN, who seeks not the VIBE or LIFE of what falls under his restless slidder, but whether or not it can profit him, or what name or theory he can dispose of it with, or how he can provoke it, get some excitement out of it, or mark it somehow, with the piss of his ego[19]

contergest [kɒntəːdʒɛst]

vb & n 1 to pretend to look around for someone in a bar or restaurant that you do not want to drink or dine in, in order to cover up the appearance of not wanting to stay there 2 to accept an invitation you have no intention of honouring

context [kɒntɛkst]

n the entire present moment or situation, from vibe-root to material-fruit; touched in soft-consciousness

· fundamentally mysterious, impossible to represent in the mind, opaque to both science and religion

· source of apt, spontaneous INTELLIGENCE

convale [kɒnveɪl]

vb & n 1 to laugh in a Scottish accent while spinning round like Wonder Woman 2 to walk across Bangladesh in a pantomime horse 3 to lick a daffodil with a savage tongue while conducting an imaginary orchestra[wb]

conversation [kɒnvəseɪʃən]

n a slow lightning-strike or instant-tree of interlacing silence, sound and meaning, which branches from the shared vibe-space of two communing humans

· happens when participants listen to the tree of meaning between them in order to

take the interactional fractal where it needs to grow, into a flow of ideas, gestures, games and silences that connect aptly, as if the tree knows the next comment exists; which it does
· antonym of ARGUMENT and WAR (*see* UNVERSATION)
· synonym of DANCE

co-opt [kəʊ-ɒpt]
vb I to render a SUBVERSIVE message or Q-WORD harmless by taking [and *keeping*] it out of context, refining it, limiting its meaning, writing about it in the newspaper, using it to sell pantyliners or printing the head of its chief proponent on a t-shirt 2 to appropriate the style of an original art-form (or movement[20]) in order to protect yourself from what it means
· co-opted words, theories, definitions and images are used by the self for artistic career advancement (appropriating fashions), justifying criminal activity (as 'revolutionary'), increasing market share, suppressing threatening loveliness, feeling special ('I'm an *ahhtist*') or as a means to gain the favourable attention of the erotic elite

corporation [kɔːpəreɪʃən]
n I a very big business-cult which converts RESPONSIBILITY into profit 2 Byzantine hall of mirrors used to disguise a ruling class desperate to remain concealed[21]

craft [krɑːft]
n & vb to master a [scientific] skill or tool sufficiently to build a dwelling place, or telharmonium, for GENIUS[22]
· helps create CONFIDENCE

craunch [krɔːntʃ]
n I painful hollow plate that forms across the chest after planning a revenge, grimly fucking someone, VR gaming, worrying, wanting or wanking 2 a microthin film of separation between you and reality (or you and your lover) which bungs up the artery to THE GOOD THING
· dissipated through honesty (confessing anxiety, professing love), action, apperception and excellent figs

criticism [krɪtɪsɪzəm]
n see PAIN, DEATH and UNSELF

culpese [kʌlpiːz]
n I guilt masquerading as gratitude, envy masquerading as praise 2 making the

need for responsible action magically evaporate by pronouncing the words *'abracadabra'* or *'sorry'*

cult [kʌlt]
n 1 early stage of uncivilisation 2 small structural and functional unit of the WORLD fuelled and bound by ego and BELIEF
· forms of cult include tribe, religion, family, company, team, sub-culture, profession, faculty, relationship, corp, faculty and club

dance [dɑːns]
vb & n concentrated hooplas, rubber-ochos, labrador rolls, damp fleckerals, sopping fleckerals, spod vexers, net-casters, chicken-spacks, wang-scythes, blasphemous tractor-glides, electro-nellies, whitstable washboards, bubble-rubs, the old michigan twat-vexer and the glorious bronto-squat
· better done together

death [dɛθ]
n the softening, sacrifice or end of SELF
· terrifying to self-oriented people and illegal in self-oriented societies
· synonym of YINYIN

debt [dɛt]
n either [the basis of] 1 free human civilisation, in which everyone is lender and borrower and nobody cares or of 2 artificial inhuman society [23] in which a tiny portion of society is lender, a vast portion is borrower... and *everyone* cares [24]

decennoval [dɛsinəʊvəl]
n one's 19th favourite colour

delusion [dɪljuːʒən]
n antonym of VISION

democracy [dɪmɒkrəsi]
n 1 dictatorship of the 51% 2 five yearly ritual of validation for an illusion of participation; does not apply to WORK hours 3 allowing prisoners to vote for their warders to relieve both of RESPONSIBILITY and distract them from their [systemic] captivity 4 SOCIALISM for the rich, CAPITALISM for the poor 5 euphemistic shorthand for state-sponsored totalitarian mercantilism [25] 6 an occasionally useful means of reaching a group decision, which is tolerated by power until it threatens the status quo, at which point it is rebranded 'mob rule'

HOW TO DIE

Dying is an art, which means that, to do it well, you must give your whole life to mastering it:

FACE THE FACT · that you and everyone you know is going to die; and much sooner than you think

LET GO · train for giving up the most valuable thing you have, the whole self (everything you think you are) by letting go or giving away less valuable parts of self (possessions, activities, beliefs, moods, addictions, having-to-be-right, etc.)

TALK ABOUT DEATH · directly (without excitement or morbid seriousness) with loved ones, with children, with colleagues in the office and with call-centre employees

EXPERIENCE THE DEATH OF OTHERS · be with people who are dying (and convey presence, rather than submerging it under a river of KIPPLE), look at dead bodies, and handle them

SEE THAT THE WORLD IS DYING · face the fact that uncivilisation is in its last few years and is about to bring the whole millennial edifice crashing down over our heads (*see* COLLAPSE)

PLAY WITH DEATH · (*see* CALENDAR: 31ˢᵗ OCTOBER)

WHEN YOU DIE, IT IS NOW · practice the experience of now (*see* SELF-MASTERY) to gain insight into that which cannot be remembered, anticipated or possessed

SEEK THE VOID · in order to face the FEARS that follow from mortality, which is *all of them*, find death before it finds you [26]

---

deruet [deruːət]

vb, n & prep 1 to mistake the noise in one's head for oneself 2 to mistake a magpie for a miniature flying killer whale [wb]

diagnosis [dʌɪəgnəʊsɪs]

n 1 [physical] a means of generating, from PAIN and DEATH, a 'need' for market therapies 2 [mental] the re-branding of dissent, negative emotion, selfishness, malingering or indirect complaints against the loneliness and stress of economic growth into a range of *professionally-generated* / curated 'mental illnesses' that require more NARCOTICS or more corrective INSTITUTIONALISATION [27]

A POOTER OF DELUSIONS

THE CAPGRASS-MAJOR DELUSION · the schizoid belief that your loved ones have been replaced by imposters, that your peers are corporate cyborgs constructed by Google, that celebrities are all computer generated, that reality is a crappy cardboard simulacra, that insects are in fact sophisticated little surveillance cameras or that the entire world is possessed and controlled by a darkly knowing pan-psychic entity called 'Ørbal the Unknowing'.[28]

THE CAPGRASS-MINOR DELUSION · to quietly wonder why everyone else, or anything else, is here.

THE AGUSTA DELUSION · a man's belief that all pretty women are desperate to have sex with him, and that they communicate their desperation with glances, with smiles or, sometimes, with 'sod off and leave me alone'.

THE JENDRIX DELUSION · the belief that everyone is really a secret member of a secret society and that they are secretly exchanging secret messages about you and your secret initiation into the secret mysteries of a secret reality that everyone else has always secretly known about.[28]

THE PANFALTA DELUSION · the belief that human beings are separate entities living in a mechanical, objective universe created and sustained either by describable laws (of physics, chemistry and biology) or by a describable God or gods.

THE BOOS DELUSION · the belief that, when UNCIVILISATION COLLAPSES, and the seas rise, and the wells dry up, and the crops fail, and the multitudes move, and the bombs fall, that your gated walls, sea defences, flood barriers, police forces, institutions, money, power, phones, computers or weapons will be of the slightest help.

---

digitise [dɪdʒɪtʌɪz]
vb to reduce FRACTAL infinity and nuanced, ultravivid analogue quality to crude, bland (but useful) discrete, relative, pixilated, MENTAL or emotional caricatures or STEREOTYPES
· *see* SELF and VIRTUAL

disorder [dɪsɔːdə]
n see SICKNESS

displode [dɪspləʊd]

vb 1 to lay wide one's field of observation until the observer dissolves into cosmic treacle 2 to feel the edges of self soften into a hazy place where we dangle and fiercely radiate

- *For 5 weeks William watched the wheat field slowly ripen from his little room until he came to realise in a long disploding moment of gentle awe that the goldening grain was himself, in grassy disguise*

domesticate [dəmɛstɪkeɪt]

vb to create an environment in which animals or people are forced to depend on an authority or on a system for survival or comfort

- *see* INSTITUTION

dondon [dɒndɒn]

vb, adj & n to dribble, mong, gumby, sub-normalise and spaz esp. in situations where such behaviour is extremely 'inappropriate'

drail [dreɪl]

vb to use A) one's creative superpower to invent a stickier duct-tape B) Excalibur to open a can of beans C) the PINK TIP to seduce someone you don't really care for

dream [driːm]

vb & n see ZZZ

dunbar [dʌnbɑː]

adj & n a human group of optimal size; between 120 and 180 people (the number of people with whom a stable relationship can be sustained), fluidly blending into other such groups [29]

- when a group grows beyond the maximum dunbar tipping point (*see* UTP) interpersonal relations can no longer be maintained; humans then get replaced by ABSTRACTIONS (such as 'them') and the group as a whole starts to demand more TIME and effort to organise than it provides, leading to breakdown in collaboration, strained intimacy and, as orders take longer to reach reality, a collapse of apt, spontaneous response to life

dystopia [dɪstəʊpɪə]

n the entire universe reconfigured as a massive EGO

- physically shoddy and psychologically VIRTUAL
- truthful dystopias and utopias are just exaggerations of what there already is
- *see* UTOPIA *&* TECHNOLOGY

E IS FOR
emotion
the voice of
SELF

F IS FOR
feeling
everything
ELSE

eame [iːm]
vb to cool down burning fin-
gertips (after e.g. carrying a
hot mug) by squeezing one's
earlobes or noselobes

economics [iːkənɒmɪks]
n a pseudo-scientific study
of illusions used to justify
UNCIVILISATION
· founded on the illusion of
free labour (of which there
is none; *see* ENCLOSURE),
on the criminalisation of
debt (upon which unciv-
ilisation is based), on the
invention of scarcity (and
the production of waste)
on the fantasy that money
replaced barter (and not
a GIFT ECONOMY) and on
millennia of ideological-
ly-disguised theft
· economists define autonomous as anti-social, the
traditional as underdevel-
oped, the environment as a
scarce resource, independence as a threat, subsistence as unproductive, the
community as impotent to
provide for its own survival
and comfort and human
beings as violent, selfish,
rational, wealth-maximis-
ing automatons with needs
(i.e. as NEEDY)
· *see* MONEY and MARKET

ecoshism [iːkəʊʃɪzəm]
n I the idea that those who
should save the environment
are those who don't have an
environment 2 the idea that
buying a fair-trade, ethical
stole will somehow turn the
reality-eating market into a
butterfly 3 a mystishist CULT
· ecoshists may love nature,
but ecoshism is the anto-
nym of love of nature

ectomonish [ɛktəʊmɒnɪʃ]
vb I to blame your tea for
spilling it, your tools for a
shoddy job, your parents for
a miserable life, your lover
for the RELATIONSHIP that
you disintegrate, your balls
for a fluffed free-kick, your
employees or subordinates
for your mediocrity, and so
on (*see* MING and BIASTIFY)
2 to insult absent objects or
persons, or to blame others
for how you feel 3 to make
a woman moody, cavilling,
busybodying or addicted to
stimulation through feed-
ing cold or fractious unvibes
into her femi-plasma, and
then to blame *her* for it while
justifying yourself by pointing to a lack of OBJECTIVE,
scientific evidence for your
irritation, your boredom or
your hyper-subtle sadism

effubula [ɛfʌbjʊlə]

n 1 microthin layer of psychic flab that precedes physical fat 2 microthin physiognomic vibe-layer of psychic corruption and emotional crudeness that precedes eyes sunken in their sockets, wet lascivious lips and a bland, CANERATED, mask-like network of wrinkles [1]

egg [ɛg]

n big swirling, multi-hued and morphing bubble of flavoured vibe that swells and beats around the bellymind, blending into atmospheres, smearing its strange plasma wheresoever it goeth
· under influence of self egg either inflates to a massive, defensive roman-tortoise or shrinks to a cold, hard solitary pea in a saucepan

ego [iːgəʊ]

n selfish, cunning, cancerous, semi-autonomous and self-informed mental–emotional entity comprised of [and consuming] *both* emotion and mentation [2]
· masquerades as 'I'
· does what you don't really want it to do, and doesn't do what you really do want it to do

· synonym of ID, SUPEREGO, dominator consciousness, the restless tenant, MAYA and near synonym of SELF
· *see* FIEND

elander [ɛlandə]

vb 1 to calm aggression with touch or with touching tone 2 to counter one-upmanship with one-downmanship [wb]

elay [iːleɪ]

vb 1 to make someone else's low-quality contribution to a CONVERSATION acceptable or brilliant; thereby making both of you feel high-quality 2 to resist drawing attention to another's stupid or awkward comment (in order to preserve the harmony of the moment)
· c.f. SEPHEL

emotion [ɪməʊʃən]

n 1 a corrosive magma (violently hot, pitifully wet, bitterly cold or ironically dry) that gradually eats into the bellymind 2 a crude, heavy, binary (want-don't-want / like-don't-like, etc.) craving or compulsion
· antonym of FEELING [3]
· synonym of EGO, MENTATION, the [self-informed] SELF and the LIVING PAST

EMOTION

THERE ARE TWO DISTINCT KINDS of affective experience in the body; EMOTION, a crude, digital, monotone *note*, generated by the restless ego, roughly as varied as forty different car-horns, and FEELING, a kaleidoscopic, hue-subtle *song*, emerging from the still CONTEXT, roughly as varied as the entire history—past and future—of world music.

Emotion always feels more or less the same; an anxious, heavy, hollow or restricted wanting or not-wanting sensation, sucking in the pit of the stomach, brittling across the chest, tightening the neck or weighing down the skull.

The mind gives this experience various names, depending on the kind of heaviness, hollowness or unease, and on the particular wanted or not-wanted object or situation that the emotion is directed towards. These names include guilt, boredom, depression, doubt, anxiety, impatience, frustration, anger, discontent, despair, loneliness, sadness, fear, excitement and exultation; each of which is focused on a different object (person, prize or loss), but all of which describe more or less intense versions of exactly the same inner experience.

It is, however, impossible for ego to admit that all emotions are the same; partly because this would unmask their common cause—ego itself—which is why the self relentlessly focuses on external causes, reacting violently to any suggestion that A) 'up' emotions (such as excitement) are basically the [oppo]same as 'down' emotions B) there is a state of being in which absence of ups and downs is not registered as 'boring', 'blissful' or 'cold' or C) I am being emotional, right now.

The main reason that ego cannot understand the cause of emotion however, or that emotion is radically different to feeling, is that ego *is* emotion. It can no more perceive itself than an eye can see itself, which means that, although the emotional ego reflects off and generates crude surface thought,[4] it is immune to the efforts of mind to feel better, or to any kind of reason or apt intelligence. All it knows how to do is expand—by feeling more emotion, up or down—and to defend itself—by savagely attacking any threat (*see* SELF).

emotional-labour [mɑːskɪŋ]
n management of feeling, performance of idealised attitude ('natural' informality, 'can-do' attitude, irony and so on) and the summoning of contrived enthusiasms to cover worldly ego-anxieties or hostility to TOTALITARIA [5]

· synonym of PUTTING THE FACE ON and PSYCHOCOMPULSION

· capitalism demands emotional labour not to erase dissent (which is implicitly encouraged; *see* STAGVERSION) nor even to add EWHELMIC 'affective value' to industrial services and commodities, but to guarantee employees' capacity for alienation, conformity and willingness to give up their whole [social and private] lives to the MARKET

empathy [ɛmpəθi]
n 1 the experience of what self is not 2 personal experience of what it is to be a member of the opposite sex, a bat or a tube of toothpaste

· antonym of CARE [6]

enclosure [ɛnkləʊʒə]
n 1 the process or policy of fencing in common space in order to convert it into private property 2 theft by the wealthy, through 'fair' MARKET rules laid down by property-owners and their lawyers; handed down and disguised by inheritance [7]

· applies not just to physical space, but also to:

· SOUND-SPACE · SILENCE is a commons, appropriated by commercially-acquired loudspeakers, TEEVEE and entertainment devices [8]

· TIME-SPACE · enclosed by obedience to CLOCKS and by imposing ever-shrinking constraints on idleness and liquid TIME-FREEDOM

· LANGUAGE-SPACE · the use-range of Q-words, such as LOVE and LIFE and so on is delimited by professional services and enforced by media-conditioned public opinion (*see* CO-OPT)

· VIBE-SPACE · the span of socially acceptable EMOTION is determined by the MAINSTREAM media and policed by informal GROUPTHINK which mocks or punishes deviant FEELINGS [9]

· to say a man on enclosed land or in enclosed time is free to participate in society is to say that a man in the sahara is 'free' to walk to water

enpupe [ɛnpju:p]

vb 1 to have your indignation hijacked by a well-meaning parent or partner who, on hearing your bad news, lets off a stream of completely over-the-top second-hand outrage 2 to have your *slight doubt* converted into *intense anxiety* by a well-meaning relative (esp. AUNTIE), who is terrified of everything; warning! can lead to abandoning monstrous, reckless gestures of great-hearts headed for glorious ruin

equality [ɪkwɒlɪti]

n 'fair' incorporation of different races and sexes into TOTALITARIA

eternity, eternal [ɪtɜːnɪti]

n & adj not time going on forever, but reality experienced with the TIME-AND-SPACE making self silent or secondary [10]
· found in the utter present
· *see* TRANSDIMENSIONAL

euphiasco [ju:fɪaskəʊ]

n fundamentally delightful failure or DELECTAFLOP
· applies to oneself; pleasure at someone else's disaster is the *slightly* less hilarious SCHADENFREUDE

· *The last thing Sheila heard, as the Grizzly bear dragged Garth's mauled body out of the tent, was laughter*

evidence [ɛvɪdəns]

n collection of photographs occasionally used to try and prove that something other than me really exists
· *vital* for establishing FACTS, *useless* for proving QUALITY
· *see* FALLACY (the DEMAND FOR PROOF)

evil [i:vəl]

n & adj 1 the inhibition of nuance, empathy or mystery 2 an illusion unconsciously created by ego to justify its supposed 'good' 3 cheap and poorly-fitting stockings

evolutionism [i:vəlu:ʃənɪsm]

n over-emphatic denial of context as an active agent in gene-coding, 'mutation' and heredity [11]
· a.k.a. DARWINISM
· subset of SCIENTISM

ewhelm [i:wɛlm]

n subtle form of vibe-hypnosis employed by PROFESSIONALS to redirect doubt, nullify SUBVERSION and stifle dissent; the subject is rendered harmless by a secure, smug, brisk, lightly condescending, disconcertingly mechanical and unquestionably inevitable facial expression, judgement, gesture, tone of voice or ambience of institutionally sanctified power [12]

- e.g. a 5-star hotel receptionist's mouth-only smile of welcome, a mechanic's *'it's gonna cost you'* headshake, a doctor's blandly confident DIAGNOSIS, the *'important things are being done here'* grilled intensity of a corp-newsroom, the sacrosanct solemnity of a swearing in, the subservient self-censored raillery of a corporate boardroom or a teacher's head-waggling, belittling, tight little smirk

e.w.s. [iː dʌbəljuː ɛs]
ab einstein's wife syndrome
1 any theory that one's wife, cat or postman can never *really* care about (i.e. LOVE)
2 the sinking feeling that a woman gets, watching her man tinkering away, that he loves his car / pigeons / computer or collection of vintage milk-bottles more than her
- source of the *preposterous* idea that quantum physics and the female orgasm are unrelated

exam [ɪgzam]
n academic rite-of-passage [UNCONSCIOUSLY] designed to A) reward SYSTEMIC subservience and the ability to ignore context and B) codify the individual as a 'case' which can then be INSTITUTIONALLY manipulated and rationally classified [13]
- looks just like a 'neutral' fact-recall test
- people who pass a lot of exams tend to be content to A) accept implicit institutional constraints B) to have themselves systemically objectified and C) to ignore the context, which is either a distraction, or a source of anxiety
- for how 'objective' exams filter dissenting students, *see* SCHOOL

exclusive [ɪkskluːsɪv]
n a club, power, SECRET or pastime which *excludes* the majority (i.e. HUMANITY)
- *see* PRIVILEGE

expectation [ɛkspɛkteɪʃən]
n the father of anger, heartbreak, disappointment and premature ejaculation
- caused by THOUGHT, HOPE, IMAGINATION and PORN
- synonym of DOUBT

EXSUPERATION TACTICS

Techniques for overcoming addiction to uncivilisation include:

ELECTRICITY · by refusing to use electric-blankets, central heating and air-conditioning

TIME · allowing unstructured time and boredom to wash through you in idle awareness of the unique increments of inner time and the tiny, light, exquisite, details of stuff

MEDIA · chucking your TEEVEE and smart-phone away, freeing yourself from the news and learning to make your *own* art, play or music

SUSTENANCE · growing your own food, fetching your own water, joining a co-op

MONEY · by living without the crutch of money (or savings), connections or WORK

UNSELF · seeking nature, solitude, darkness, silence and the unknown (*see* IMPRO and SELF-MASTERY)

The purpose of exsuperation is not to renounce the pleasures of the WORLD, *but to be free of its addictive hold over your self so that, unlike so many people, you are capable of putting justice, love, beauty and other Q-truths above* FEELING COMFORTABLE

experience [ɪkspɪərɪəns]
n & vb to play with the cards you are dealt; happens *in*, *by* or *through* you
· corrupted Q-word which usually means 'things that happen *to* you'

exsuperate [ɛksuːpəreɪt]
vb I to overcome addiction to the world by deliberately EXPERIENCING deprivation, discomfort and uncertainty 2 putting obstacles in front of one's creative output in order to express the JOY or GENIUS of overcoming them
· exsuperate is a conscious activity; the antonym being INSUPERATE [ɪnsuːpəreɪt] *n* unconsciously making life hard for / heaping SUFFERING upon yourself

extinction burst [fʌkɪtʃjʊəri]
n when constant watchful concern to stop something happening crosses over into mad reckless desire to have it happen and happen again, heaped on to excess, and to hell with the monstrous consequences

facine [fəsiːn]
adj & n a feeling—such as needling angst, spry cheer or profound world-dread—

that, quite unbeknownst, or unbesniffst, to you, everyone in the world is feeling at precisely the same time

· seven billion lonely minds one night sat up and said; *'this can't be right; something is missing, something is wrong; my mind is shot, I can't go on…'*

factory [faktəri]

n a cathedral of ornate and extravagant fractal-organic architecture, surrounded by gardens and not far from a wilderness into which it seamlessly blends, in which people freely work to create beautiful goods useful to their community; provides facilities not only for technical and liberal education, but for the pursuit of music, drama, fine arts, fine dining, ridiculous sex acts and superviolent table-tennis [14]

fadomite [fadəmʌɪt]

n a small but charming or useful superpower or mutation, such as the ability to make people forget what it was they were supposed to be doing, foot-in-mouth undo-button, marzipan nipples or a finger-bang of tiny songs

fall [fɔːl]

n & vb 1 the moment, some 12,000 years ago, when self passed the UTILITY TIPPING POINT (UTP) and started to exert a RADICAL MONOPOLY over experience, resulting in superstition, permanent war, patriarchy, misogyny, FEAR of DEATH, and a new dark, abstract monotheistic RELIGION (and new pessimistic concepts of the afterlife), social stratification, hostility to sex, to the body and to nature—all of which happened at the same time to the same peoples from the same region of central Asia, from whence it spread outwards to overwhelm the earth entire 2 to bite planet

fallacy [faləsi]

n BRAINWASHED instinct of the SELF to avoid self-critical truths by using mental–emotional hedge-tactics to defend itself against LOVE, PAIN, DEATH, CRITICISM, UN-SELF, diminution of status or salary, EGO and classic funk

· leads to conveniently sincere denial of experiences which one does not want to have (by instinctively confusing *wrong* with *unpleasant to seriously consider*)

THE FALL

FOR COUNTLESS MILLENNIA—for nearly all of human pre-history—men and women enjoyed rich, varied, playful and meaningful lives, lived in socially and sexually egalitarian societies, were exceptionally healthy and well-nourished, never went to war, didn't need money, didn't do what we would understand as WORK, were at ease with life, fearless before death and were able to craft, commune and improvise with miraculous presence and sensitivity.[15]

Around 12,000 years ago, somewhere in what is now the Middle East and Central Asia, the self—a tool for abstracting, imagining and projecting into the past and the future—grew, through over-use, beyond its UTILITY TIPPING POINT and began to usurp conscious experience. Self, in other words, became EGO; a parasitic thinking-emoting, and self-informed (as opposed to context-informed) entity (*see* SELF and UTP).

Ego, faced with the unknown—with experience which cannot be apprehended or grasped by ego (named, counted, owned, understood or emotionally experienced)—began to experience PRIMAL FEAR. Darkness, femininity, the innocence of children and animals, extreme ['altered'] psychological states, NATURE, selfless LOVE and DEATH became threatening, and the living character of plants, animals and natural forces, with which man once selflessly perceived he shared reality, hardened into emotionally potent conceptions of gods, ghosts and ancestors with which ego, perceiving them as fundamentally separate entities, was forced to negotiate, appease and pray to (the beginning of SUPERSTITION[16]).

To allay its PRIMAL ANXIETY ego began to dominate plants and animals[17] (through excessively exploitative agriculture and DOMESTICATION), other groups (through hierarchy, debt, slavery and war), children[18] (through cruelty and 'education'), women (through patriarchically-managed marriage, violence and the threat of desertion) and nature[19] (through over-control, over-use and, eventually, SCIENCE).

This change in man's relationship with reality is reflected in the ubiquitous myth of a fall, from the GARDEN.

A MOLOCH OF FALLACIES

If criticised ego will use one of a limited range of tactics to drift from the point, misrepresent it, ignore, control or co-opt it:

THE APPEAL TO SPECIALISM

Intellectual equivalent of a rudeboy headbutting someone who laughs at him; when criticised ego seeks a way to move the subject into a field in which it has a greater reserve of facts to draw from and in which, provided that we 'stick to the facts', it *has* to win. This might be quantum-physics or it might be 'being a mother'. A version of this is THE PLAYER FALLACY common in journalism and law, in which the actors in a drama (corrupt or inefficient politicians, managers, doctors, etc.) are CRITICISED in order to deflect attention away from the theatre (the system, the law, corporatism, professional states, etc.).

FLAT DENIAL & RIDICULE

To say *no-no-no-no* until the threat passes or refusing to respond. Mocking dismissal of innocence, love or transdimensionality as mystic-guff is part of this strategy, as is the tactic of dismissing an entire philosophy because of a few zealously seized criticisms.

THE PALABROTIC FALLACY

To think that you know what a word *really* means, to assert that the *correct* meaning of a word ('altruism', 'quantum', etc.) is the scientific one (*see* NEWSPEAK), to BELIEVE that you understand something because you can give a name to it (*'that's a goat'*), to dismiss a point of view by labelling it (*'Oh, it's basically Socialist Buddhism'*) or, if the threat is communicated by vibe or silence, to speak at all.

REMOVING RESPONSIBILITY

If self is guilty of shameful behaviour, it can magic away its responsibility by changing the grammatical form of its admission or using hypno-inducing passives and nominalisations (e.g. *'mistakes were made'* instead of *'I made a mistake'*). Just as a child who knocks over a glass is liable to say *'it fell over'* rather than *'I spilt it'*, so a man who has become bored of his girlfriend is liable to say *'it's not working'* rather than *'I don't want to make it work because I'm bored of fucking you'*.[20]

AD-HOMINEM / GETTING PERSONAL / RIGHTEOUS INDIGNATION / NAME-CALLING

[Ab]reaction to any criticism as if it were a personal attack, and, rather than answering the CRITICISM, attacking the critic with labels; 'obsessive', 'serious', 'immature', 'weird', 'arrogant', 'patronising' or 'no fun down the pub'.

REVERSE AD-HOMINEM

Instead of accusing someone of wholesale guilt, to accuse them of accusing *you* of it. This is commonly employed by teenagers and corporate journalists. The former will respond to a criticism with *'you hate me!'* and the latter with *'anti-Semite!' 'sexist!'* or *'conspiracy-theorist!'*

AD-HOM *and* REVERSE AD-HOM *are frequently confused with* AD-RADICEM—*a.k.a.* GETTING TO THE ROOT *or* AD-RAD—*an attempt to take the debate away from emotional fact-wrangling and towards the personal qualities, fears and desires which underpin superficial intellectual differences (e.g. dealing with a difference of artistic or religious opinion by discussing someone's sex life, their body, their class interests or their* PUC*).*

IGNORING CONTEXT / TAKING OUT OF CONTEXT / SELECTIVE LISTENING / CHERRY PICKING

Removing the truth value of a comment by taking it out of context. By focusing on single assertions alone self can find inconsistencies (e.g. *'you're saying that now, but before you said this…'*), make them seem trivial (as examples often do seem trivial) and remove the tonal or vibal content which conveys the basic meaning of an utterance; but which is difficult to remember and impossible to prove. Likewise, by focusing on isolated facts and emotions, ego can pull from the vast, bright, inscrutable and ever-pleasant moment whatever 'message' best suits its purposes.

LIFE & SPEECH POLICING

To limit your speech to topics which have been verified as safely understandable by common usage or to remove threats from your life by not dealing with those who might be able to criticise you, or to not engage in activities which demand sacrifice, sensitivity or movement beyond 'can't' or 'don't like' psychological markers and into the sombre ecstasies of the unknown.

RATIONALISATION

Substituting REALITY *with an idea or abstract image of it and then assuming that reality is ultimately abstract (or mind-knowable). The most common forms of rationalisation are:*

THE DEMAND FOR ARGUMENT, PROOF[21] OR EVIDENCE

To demand evidence or proof where none is possible. There can be no rational proof for the meaning of love, death, unself or the tone of a comment because their meanings are PARADOXICAL or precede the time-and-space making self-mind (*see* SCIENCE).

APPEAL TO FALSE ANTONYMS

If someone says that all laws must be abolished, you might say that if we didn't have laws we'd all be killing each other (*see* SCOFFON, LAW and ORIENT); or if accused of being selfish you might say that it's better to be selfish than to be a doormat, etc. (*see* BIASTIFY).

APPEAL TO FALSE SYNONYMS / APPEAL TO RELATIVITY

If you are greeted with the idea that your modern art is a titillating swindle or that your country's government is destroying the world in order to steal its resources, or your personal hygiene leaves a lot to be desired, you can breezily dismiss the critique with something along the lines of *'beauty (truth, bodily odour) is in the eye (mind, nose) of the beholder'*.[22]

SHIFTING THE GOALPOSTS

Commonly employed to swat away critiques of UNCIVILISATION; *'what would a non-coercive society do with criminals? who is going to prevent selfishness?'* etc. The fallacy here is not in demanding the answer to impossible questions but that the move from a general critique to a specific plan immediately changes the form of the debate into something manageable; and thus completely irrelevant. A similar move is to demand that a critic of society run for office (i.e. to enter a deathless unreality of manageable details) or to protest that *'most people will never understand'* (i.e. to shift truth as it applies to *you* on to an abstract mass). The most desperate goalpost shift is to provoke a critic until she gets angry, in order to dismiss her with ridicule or weaponry. The most subtle is to agree with her.

CLASSIC FALLACIES

THE ANECDOTAL FALLACY
Presenting a few examples, or limited experience, as proof (*'I worked in a large company for twenty years and never met a psychopath!'*).

THE APPEAL TO NATURE
Assuming that an argument is true because it appears to have a counterpart in 'nature' (*'fighting to be the most powerful cock on the pyramid-peak is natural, because apes do it'*).

THE APPEAL TO CULTURE
The notion that something (torture, bull-fighting, niqābs, foie gras, etc.) is good because it is part of one's 'culture'.

THE APPEAL TO FAMILIARITY
The idea that something is true because it is associated with age (*'He's just a kid!'*), novelty (*'You luddite!'*), fame (*'Do you know who I am?'*) or popularity (*'Who are you?'*).

THE STRAW MAN
Caricaturing a position so as to more easily pull it apart (*'You talk about unconditional love and yet you're angry!'*).

THE APPEAL TO HYPOCRISY
To dismiss someone's position based on criticism of her inconsistency and not on the position presented (*'You cuss the market-system and yet you employ its lawyers!'*).[23]

falsolis [fɔːlsəlɪs]
n 1 avoiding your problems by obsessively focusing on those of your friends or of humanity 2 covering a fault up with the more harmful fault of concealment 3 the colossal stupidity of wanting to appear clever 4 dying inside by turning away from death (*see* SUFFERING)

famous [feɪməs]
adj describes 1 a conspicuously UNHAPPY 'somebody' stared at by inconspicuously unhappy nobodies 2 one isolated from SCENIUS
• UNCIVILISATION is [unconsciously] designed to make everyone a bit famous; or famous for being a bit

farg [fɑrg]
n a lunatic confession
• fargs can bubble up from no place the frantic mind can locate; or they can be sunk down in the unconscious, lying dormant for something to distract the censor in the mind (name of ED; *see* REG) whereupon they rush out through the lips, naked, waving their underpants around their head; or they can be the result of the magnificent

— A MYTHOLMROYD OF FEELINGS —

winter-pre-dawn, celery-sastrugi tang and shed-roof, wet-rope-and-pebble, copper-cow-flank, mink-oil and myrtle

dark-umber sea-shouldered cederwood, rancid-accordion, toast-crumbs and buttock-prints in the carpet

ancient fire burning in an ancient cave, illuminating the old, old lion-headed lord of the slate-gold fens

tuesday morning, greasy-spoon, ripped corduroys, cumbia-en-moog and risky business

peach-heart, chin-dribbly, nectar-golden, swimming in liquid sunlight, soft-edged, fire-fringed, glowing on the cheek I put my cheek to

---

and calamitous thought 'I wonder what would happen if I admitted *that?*'

farn [fɑːn]
n 1 the feeling you get about 4:30 pm when you've spent the day watching too much porn[24] 2 the feeling you get at about the age of 43 when you've spent your life watching too much PORN

fear [fɪə]
n the reaction of the self-informed self towards UNSELF
· will transform itself into irritation, violence, blame, guilt, shame, hope, belief, disappointment, rationalism, addiction, fallacious self-justification, self-pity, needy cling, giddy worship and anxiety 'for no reason' to avoid being perceived (which is to say; *fear lives*)

feeling [fiːlɪŋ]
n the subtle—but extraordinarily rich and vivid—vibes, tones, colours, atmospheres, weathers, moods and small musics that pulse intensely through the hushed egoless SOLAR PLEXUS
· antonym of EMOTION

feiseanna [fɛʃənə]
n the rust-speckled aluminium deckchair-leg feeling of *'going over old ground'* with a vaguely friendly colleague[wb]

feminishism [fɛmɪnɪʃɪzəm]

n 1 misplaced demand for love from women who have only ever really been, at best, needed, desired or fawned over 2 easily-acquired nexus of opinions that ambitious, masculine and intellectual women can bolt onto their frail egos in order to advance their careers as journalists and academics while beating the drum for the opportunity for women to degrade themselves as thoroughly as men, and crawl further up the iniquitous mountain of filth called 'career'

· feminishism is most stridently endorsed by women with highly developed egos struggling to SUCCEED in the male market-system; in other words by women at constant war with the intractable physical laws, system-shattering spontaneity, mysterious creativity and innate generous sensitivity of their own BODIES

· near synonym of SEXISM [sɛksɪzəm] *n* the widespread (although out of FASHION in the modern world) and largely male belief that the masculine domain is superior to the female domain; not to be confused with the transparent fact that men are like dogs and women like cats (i.e. have different SENSITIVITIES and SWELLS)

· usually joins forces with RACISHISM & QUEERISHISM

fesque [fɛsk]

vb 1 to find erotic *ideas* more arousing than sensory experience 2 to be unable to get irrelevant thoughts out of one's mind at the moment of coitus 3 phantom breasts

· leads to POST-COITAL TRISTESSE (FUCKER'S REMORSE), impotence and the need for leather, lube or recording equipment for sexual congress with a loved-one

fiend, fiendess [fʌksɛlf]

n 1 dense mass of restless, self-directed, darkly clever sado-masochistic CRAUNCH which erupts into a living beast of nightmarish emotional pain between one and three months after you move in with someone (marked by the thought 'God help me, I've made a horrible, *horrible* mistake') 2 the strangely 'ancient' knowing look that squirming, hysterical children flash at you to check you are feeding them with negative attention [25]

- a.k.a. PAINBODY and EGO
- the fiend also exists as the collective (UNCONSCIOUS) groupfeel of cults, societies, genders and the entire SUFFERING WORLD (*see* THE UNHAPPY SUPERMIND)

first impression [wɒtðɛːrɪs]
n.phr 1 reality, as it is, before the timespace-making emotional mindself overlays it with what you know it is, or what you want to get from it 2 plenty-subtle TRANSDIMENSIONAL psyche-eruption into the present from what appears to be the future

- e.g. a misty sense that the profile you've just glanced is that of your future husband, the flickering feeling that the yellow flower at your feet will somehow relieve your haemorrhoids, the weird impulse to pick up a pair of scissors that you end up needing later, the umami musical SOUND-BLOB of a word (such as 'burgle' or 'filthy') before your mind understands its meaning, the sweet sense of reliefy deep that the first few moments of a quality film, new place to live or euthanatist generate, the blank sense of suspended otherness you occasionally get upon slowly waking, before 'me' slots into its grooves, the unique vibe of the room or of a dead friend's well-loved boots, the tiny inner clench of a clanger before you rapidly excuse it into the memory hole, time slowing down as you see that your house has been broken into or when penetration begins and your partner suddenly seems extremely, miraculously or dreadfully, who they really are

- it's what there is
- synonym of DIRECT EXPERIENCE and SEEING
- antonym of slug, ponderous, SECOND IMPRESSION

flap around [flap əraʊnd]
vb & n 1 to swiftly pass—facing accurate CRITICISM or an unpleasant truth—from pretending it doesn't exist, to smirking ridicule, to furious spleen, to the awkward, sheepish GRIN OF GUILT, to hurt or indignation based on secondary or irrelevant facts, to breezy dismissal of the whole beneath-you business, to a final, grudging, flippant, indirect, qualified and half-arsed confession

2 a frenzied, frequently bizarre burst of activity that occurs between losing one's grip on one addiction or excuse and grabbing onto another one; *hilarious* to watch 3 the undignified behaviour of AVERAGE MAN accidentally finding himself flailing and thrashing in the ocean company of a real woman, or of madam YINYIN

fenk [fɛnk]

vb & n to rescue one's floundering self from social annihilation—after stammering, stuttering, feebly grasping the wrong thing to say or 'taking things a *bit* too far'— through the straightforward expedient of admitting that *it has actually happened* ('*I don't know why I said that*' / '*I'm boring myself*' / '*I seem to be temporarily possessed by the ghost of my parent's worst nightmare*' etc.)
· requires PRESENCE

fleshquake [flɛʃkweɪk]

n I a tremor in the rear parts of a panicked THUNT 2 a rippling of the breasts / upper arms of a large woman during dough-beating, helpless laughter, cycling over cattle grids and exemplary coitus

fool [fuːl]

vb & n a consciousness-softening, expectation-thwarting, bum-gut igniting, sick, hyper-sensitive, intelligent, metaphor-juggling atavar of universal recognition, plum sandwiches and dust
· forced by the MARKET to play the unfortunate role of [STAND-UP] COMEDIAN [kəmiːdɪən] *n* purveyor of bland, smirking PORN and cult-bonding SHITICISMS
· master of the high art (and CRAFT) of COMEDY [kɒmɪdi] *n* a picaresque, subversive, saunter through a world that reveals itself, in surprise and ur-delight, to be your [offensive] friend
· near synonym of TRAGEDY [tradʒɪdi] *n* an expression of the vast cruel, mysterious beauty of TEMENOS and SACRIFICE before the wisdom of self-exploding, world-destroying PAIN
· the deep source of great comedy is, paradoxically, great seriousness (or SORROW), and vice-versa; while egoic fun and seriousness (or OPTIMISM and PESSIMISM) appear as they are; predictable constraints on tragicomic depth
· *see* LAUGHTER

football [fʊtbɔːl]

n twenty-two men fighting over an egg

forble [fɔːbəl]

vb & n to create a tiny verbal side-universe in which something is other than it is, in order to generate regret, annoyance or attention out of nowhere

· e.g. *'I was going to say'*, *'but you knew that'* and *'but you should have said!'*

foreplay [fɔːpleɪ]

n & vb to begin love-making

· begins the moment you wake up; at least 4 hours of active, creative vibe-fanning or she-delighting per day are required for KSLI level 4–6 sexual congress

· n.b. some women require three to five years of foreplay in order to experience a truly devastating orgasm; worth it though

· *see* SEX

FOR PLAY

WORK ON YOUR MAGNIFICENT STRUTS, make fused-bum-love on warm rocks, midnight graffiti missions, two-piece band of trumpets and drums, lie on the ground perfectly still in a field until cows come up and lick you, move to Saariselka at the drop of a hat, dress each other up as Babylonian gods or paint each other's naked bodies with J.M.W. Turner maritime scenes, make a zombie film, walk for three days into the wilderness, waltz in the supermarket, tango off a cliff, library-cunnilingus, foraging for chestnuts, *long* meals with friends, learn tuba *&* drums and record ridiculous krautrock covers then busk dressed as snub-nosed monkeys, day of dares in town (pants on head, juvenile dancing in Fortnum *&* Masons, sonorous poetry reading in the job-centre, etc.), plot some kind of extravagant crime (she; long silk gloves, cigarette holder, charming the ambassador, he; stove-pipe-hat, tiny beard, furiously priming bombs in the cellar), dedicate three years to learning carpet-weaving, or painting epic panoramas of future worlds over the bonnet of your car and then driving it into a wall, or *anything* but working apart, watching a movie, sitting silently on separate laptops then pub, club or show to yawk your unlife into a cup.

forewoebegone [fwəʊbɪɡɒn]
adj currently sad about future regret [wb]

fractal [fraktəl]
adj & n 1 a natural structure, form or object, each part of which has the same PARADOXICAL CHARACTER as the whole 2 the invisible tree-shaped straw that NATURE uses to suck thoughts out of your head
· the equations and patterns of chaos theory (used for CGI; *see* VIRTUAL) are crude, definable approximations of fractality,[26] which is why they are not as beautiful as fractal forms in nature, nor can be; natural forms are *somehow* comprised of and animated by a living and ultimately indefinable reality (the TRANSDIMENSIONAL CONTEXT) which [soft] consciousness *recognises...* because consciousness itself is a fractal structure[27]
· APPERCEIVED through JOY and SACRIFICE
· felt as BEAUTY

frankensheila [fraŋkənʃiːlə]
vb & n an imaginary woman, composed of various bits of other [media- and ego-generated] women

· has the effect of turning real women into self-doubting body-anxious sports fans
· male equivalent of frankensheila = FRANKENBRUCE

freedom [friːdəm]
n the ability to play, walk, heal, die, learn, speak and love without coercion, law or ego; but within the soft limits of self, scenius and tradition[28]
· smells good

freeloader [friːləʊdə]
n 1 a label used to express the indignation of the wage-slave at those who live free of work 2 classic totalitarian scapegoat (someone who is not a TEAM PLAYER)
· appeared with the advent of WORK, MONEY, LAW and similar inventions
· the freeloader (a.k.a. idler, slacker, lollard, loafer, *freeleader*) is to be emulated and admired—or at least tolerated—but only as the fellow EMPLOYEE (whose indolence is punished by guilt, as their fellow slaves are forced to work harder); one who compels others to work for him is not a glorious freeloader, but a parasite, owner or EMPLOYER

friend [frɛnd]

n either 1 one's other heart or 2 a VIRTUAL PRODUCT to be MANAGED, accumulated or CONSUMED (or a loved-one, reduced by CAPITALIST specialism, to someone with whom one does nothing but offload on or have FUN with)

· friends are often uncon-sciously sought to nourish fears, addictions and PUC slave-master subroutines; when these branches are cut off, or die, the friend who fed them will continue to keep the old self alive, until he or she adapts, or is also cut off

· the system does not permit friends to depend on each other for survival, only on the system itself

frink [frɪŋk]

vb to dominate another in conversation by staring at their forehead questionably or by endeavouring to get a handle on what they *are*

fripp [frɪp]

vb when two or more par-ties know they are kidding themselves but tacitly agree to continue their polite fic-tion in order to further their mutual ends

· *After Sam and Catherine's acutely embarrassing public argument Catherine fripped a headache, which everyone fripped great sympathy for*

frismous [frɪsməs]

adj [descriptive of] letters, texts, messages and e-mails that your conscience silently urges you not to send, but which, by some odd force of gravity exerted by the post box (or the 'send' button, or the desert-island bottle) you dispatch in a blind, balls-to-the-wind pother

frisms [frɪsmz]

n.pl anxiety induced by con-templating re-reading a fris-mous mail, or a reply to one

froob [fruːb]

vb & n 1 realisation, while doing something deeply id-iotic on your own, of what you must look like 2 realisa-tion, while buying a pack of draft-beer jelly beans, a re-usable 'downstairs' toupee, a nun-sucking-a-unicorn-horn mousemat or a maxi-pack of pumpkin spangles what the withered, skeletal, post-collapse remnants of mankind are likely to make of your shopping basket

AN ERMEY OF FUTILITY TRAPS

- the better a system functions on paper, the worse it functions in practice
- the better you can explain or understand your decisions, the worse those decisions will end up being
- the closer the virtual world gets to reality, the more the real world becomes VIRTUAL
- the more action films / games you STARE AT, the more immobile you become
- the more intelligent, powerful and fascinating your mobile telephone becomes, the more stupid, powerless and tedious you become
- the more accurately you are able to describe REALITY, the further you are from it and the more doubtful and subjective it seems
- the more client demands are met (the better transported, informed, educated, protected or entertained), the less liberty they have as a human being (restricted freedom to speak, move, study or collectively delight themselves)
- the softer your will, the softer your arse; the harder you try, the harder your heart
- less darkness outside, less to see inside

fulcrum-pact [fʊlkrəm-pakt] *n* unspoken deal to overlook another's childish outburst, pettiness, violence or emotionality so that they'll do the same for you next time
- 'fulcrum' because this tacit deal plays a central role in determining whether the two of you are, as a partnership, headed for hell in a handbasket or heaven in a helicopteroid

fun [fʌn] *adj & n* 1 standard means of concealing one's true nature from oneself by filling up the free-time in which it is liable to appear 2 frenzied MANAGED ACTIVITY used to stifle the pain of work or to fill a ghastly yawning gulf of unemployed deadtime 3 a crude form of brainwashing employed by the system to sell WAR 4 FIEND food
- synonym of WORK, OPTIMISM and DISNEYSHWITZ

fung [fʌŋ] *vb* 1 to resist another's anxiety in conversation, becoming hard and cold as they grimace, jibber-jabber and tense their throat up in an unconscious effort to keep it all together 2 to be swept up in another's anxiety, getting stressed, confused and anxious oneself

funshism [fʌnʃɪzəm]

n the harrowing nightmare of centrally-organised, corporate-constructed or calendar-dictated FUN you're supposed to have

furze [fə:z]

vb 1 to allow anxiety (your own or someone else's) to sweetly sweep through you 2 to receive a criticism (either a good, accurate one, or a totally wrong, unfair one) as if 'twere but a breeze passing through the open window of your heart 3 to toss a brain-clench, must-have, wishy-washy porn-thought into the furnace of the SOLAR PLEXUS
· antonym of FUNG

futile [fju:tʌɪl]

adj [descriptive of attempts] 1 to change the WORLD by participating in it (at school, at work or at the ballot box) 2 to make a peaceful, connected society with violent separate selves 3 to create less centralisation by creating more centralisation 4 to make yourself feel what you are not feeling (with thought or emotion) 5 to use CHARITY to cure poverty 6 to use CAPITALISM to cure global environmental meltdown, catastrophic inequality or BOREDOM 7 to transform an unsatisfactory self through the efforts of the same self (i.e. by splitting yourself into three; *self one* [the unhappy observing self], declaring that *self two* [the deficient self that is being observed] will, at some point in the future, turn into *self three* [the unselfish, honest self that self number one wants to become]) 8 to cure the sickness, guilt, anxiety and WANT caused by ADDICTION with more NARCOTICS 9 to cure the sickness, stupidity, crime, boredom and waste created by a media, school, prison, hospital and energy-dependent 'society' with more doctors, POLICE, prisons, schools, technology or energy 10 to refute scientism with just facts or logic 11 to argue with, or have to beat, BELIEF 12 to make REALITY fit a PLAN 13 to try to kill a tree by hacking around in its branches 14 繫驢橛
· leads to maniac enmeshment in SOLID-CONSCIOUS FUTILITY TRAPS

G IS FOR
gungo
a god in
YOUR EAR

H IS FOR
hope
p.r. man
OF FEAR

GARDEN

THERE IS A GARDEN in which all is provided. It is has been shaped by human hand, but everywhere the untouchable wilderness thrives. There is a constant feeling of relief; the next moment will not do you over. It is, to use an old Persian word for garden, PARADISE.

When the world was young, men and women lived in the garden and made paths through it on a whim. Wherever attention wandered, a track would be made through the wilderness. We wandered freely, to the feint beck of the moment—like an animal, guided by the slightest twitch in sense and atmosphere, sometimes treading the same path twice, but mostly going forever nowhere; where we were at home. Our path-making instincts then were soft and supple, and although we had tendencies and talents, presence was free to take any path it liked.

At first man used his feet and trod footpaths down, foot-width and foot-strong. Then he learnt to use horses, which made routes wider and flatter. Next came carriages, trains and finally cars, which needed the widest, hardest and smoothest roads. These roads were useful—they conveyed us easily, quickly and, once established, we could get without thinking to where in the world we liked and wanted.

But the more man liked and wanted to get somewhere, the bigger, straighter and wider he built his roads, and the smaller, fractal paths fell from use, became overgrown and forgotten, and so did the places they took him to, until the entire world was one clean canalised motorway; and the cars that ran upon it had learnt to run themselves.

When the world had become road, all decisions about transport were made on auto-pilot. Instead of man or his moment deciding where to go, building an open network of manifold and flexible paths, the auto-pilot decided; and what the auto-pilot decided was, of course, to expand the road.

With cars in charge, the roadless land became a threat, to be boarded over and ignored. Feet became nothing but a means to reach a car, and the purpose of roads became nothing but a means to carry the car and protect it. The map, instead of being a natural tree of living, exploring, cobwebbing tendrils, able to pass through wildernesses at whim, became a grid, reinforced by millions of journeys.

Living on habitual auto-pilot made rerouting tendencies from established roads harder and harder and the pull towards the familiar stronger and stronger. This reduced the capacity to perceive new routes or to spontaneously head off-road. Uncertainty (or depth) became unpleasant, and so the autopilot was trusted more and more until, eventually, the individual began to identify with the autopilot, champion it and defend it—reacting with panic when its programming was challenged or its routines changed; even minutely.

With SECOND-IMPRESSION autopilot in charge, I bump into things, lose and drop things, repeat myself, drive to work without being able to recall what happened en-route and find myself making the same mistakes, over and over again. I mechanically pursue sex, security, power and other genetic goals, getting stuck in ruts from months to lifetimes long. I fear, hate, ridicule or ignore the unknown, off-road and off-map; anything never done before, or seen before (especially, of course, revelations of my road-confinement) or requiring lawless unplanned spontaneity—or I become addicted to the heady, emotional effects of self-indulgence and speed, and resist the craft and slow sacrifice of making beautiful paths.

There is nothing wrong with organised highways, but to live on them is to funnel life down to a minuscule stream of concentrated attention, excluded from the mysterious terrain of everything else. And yet, with autopilot in charge, I have no way of seeing anything else. Reality becomes autopilot; and the garden become a MYTH.[1]

People who live on roads eventually forget the garden, replacing it with spectacular adverts and with co-opted clichés (for the garden!). These adverts and clichés are many; the sentimental love of dipsomaniacs, soft-focus WELLNESS therapies, channelling the purple elbow chakra, rock and rap ballads, middle-class communes and all the third-rate fairy-tales of Hollywood that peddle the absent myth.

But sometimes self does stop. A moment of beauty, or of shock, and there, in the cracks of macadamised habit, is a glimpse of something alive with more than just momentum, something never seen, or been, before. The old self likes to congratulate itself in such moments, and tell itself that 'I have arrived', but the momentum of ego is enormous and not overcome by a moment's genuine delight or a mere *decision* to stay. Stop wanting and worrying, in fact, and it is not paradise you can feel, but the unease, boredom and discomfort of trapped habit (*see* MR. CERBERUS). You find you 'don't like' leaving the motorway, that the garden is 'boring' or, despite promises to yourself and fine intentions, you find yourself shooting back out again regardless, lost once more on the motorway; restless, bored, unhappy or agitated 'for no reason', feeling like *something is missing*, that you are somehow cut off from life, or that you are locked in a metal box.

How then to stay? How to go off road when momentum has you trapped upon it? How to return to the secret garden and, when you find it, to live there? How to get back to bikes, horses and feet, when the world is built for cars?

Ego would have it that all we need is better educated drivers, or more intelligent networks, or safer, cleaner, *spiritual* cars; that faster, more efficient or differently designed vehicles can take us to where we really want to go; that the network of roads can be restructured to allow access to the wilderness; or that the problem, being technical, just requires time, thought and talent enough to effectively MANAGE.

It is impossible for ego to see that ego is the problem. It is impossible for the autopilot to conceive of the driver's intelligence (*see* VIRTUAL) or to admit that between the driver and the garden, lie the likes, skills, fears, desires, thoughts, memories, past-programmed beliefs and boron steel bodyshell of the car itself.

To prevent ego flying out into the grid-world may initially be a practical matter, one of intellectually learning to master the thinking self and of emotionally learning to listen to CONSCIENCE, but sooner or later, all I have to do, is get out of the car.

gagambo [gəgammbəʊ]

n 1 a juicy thought-cherry that dangles from your idly CONTEMPLATING sensi-tree 2 a GEIGER-COUNTER set to 'boing' 3 a gobsmackingly liquid, loose-limbed gait

garden [gɑːdən]

n 1 pliable, permeable fractal, boundary-zone between culture and nature 2 a place in the bellymind where figs are *always* growing

gay [geɪ]

adj & n a species of light-hearted camp fabulousness, SENSITIVITY and sweetness which, when warped by fear of the VOID, class-FORMALISM (*see* TASTE) and the STRATI-FIED SELF-INFORMED STRUC-TURE of the WORLD 2 becomes QUEERISHISM

gender [dʒɛndə]

n 1 one of two utterly different but complementary forms of human sensitivity and strength, typically (but not necessarily exclusively) manifested by each of the two sexes 2 one of two living [and overlapping] spheres of sense–vibe influence
· note the innate reluctance of one gender to exert *exces-sive* influence in domains where the other is more competent; the idea that the obvious, public, mental male realm is superior to the occluded, private, female vibe-realm is itself as SEXIST an assumption as the idea that one sex can never encroach on the gender-realm of the other
· gender (masculinity and femininity) is DEVIANT to mono-sexual MODERNISTS

generosity [dʒɛnərɒsəti]

n natural, inborn instinct to give away surplus (without thinking), to lend without interest (or without concern for repayment) and to help those in need to the detriment of oneself 3
· near synonym of ALTRUISM
· antonym of WASTE, PROF-LIGACY and CHARITY, and based on EMPATHY; which is why generosity is both prevented and relentlessly punished by the SYSTEM

genetics [dʒɪnɛtɪks]

n 1 the EVOLUTIONIST study of selfishness (by SCIENTISM) 2 an attempt to work out the MEANING of MUSIC by reading the notes in a score
· *see* VIRTUAL and LANGUAGE

GENDER

WOMEN HAVE SOFTER BODIES and softer selves, men harder bodies and harder selves. Consequently WOMEN *tend* to avoid dirty, gruelling work, tend to be better at absorbing the whole context (and therefore better gatherers), tend to be in charge of informal, private social domains and tend to be more interested in the reality of our material lives, rather than in ideals and ambitions; they tend to have greater feeling intelligence, empathy, overall [soft] awareness and their creativity tends to be *intrinsic*. Women have a reduced facility with perspective, less interest in isolated abstract systems and ideas, less ability to make systematic, clock-based plans and, overall, less need to *get* somewhere.

MEN *tend* to prefer risky, abstract or filthy activity, tend to be better at isolating elements of the context and relating them to each other (and therefore better hunters), tend to be in charge of formal or public social domains and tend to be more interested in ideals or ambitions than in whether their underpants are clean. They tend to have greater visual-spatial thinking intelligence, a greater ability to focus on abstractions and their creativity tends to be *extrinsic*. Men have a decreased ability to think discursively or to perceive intuitive similarities between distant concepts and are susceptible to plan-addiction and obsessive intellectual insensitivity.

In sum; women tend to be mostly FEMININE: essentially at one with the source of manifest reality (the body) and therefore more intelligent, sensitive and spontaneous; while men tend to be mostly MASCULINE: partly cut off from the body and built with an 'aspiration' to return to it, largely through sensitive and courageous mastery of systems, craft, probe and tools. These two tendencies (or SWELLS) lead to the natural COMPLEMENTARITY of the sexes—she *is* it (the mysterious unselfish-confidence that attracts him to her) and he, eventually, *knows* it (the self-mastered confidence that attracts her to him)—and to the tendency of natural women to prefer to be led in a dance by a man sensitive to the tender rhythms of the underworld where she prefers to exert authority.[4]

These tendencies are innate, and so have existed for all of human pre-history, but they are also culturally determined, which is how, through man's hard-conscious dominance of women and creation of the insane hyper-male SYSTEM, the natural gender-complementarity of pre-historic hunter-gatherer societies[5] (and of apocalyptic waltzers) slowly slipped into A) the emasculation of man, whose confidence and tool-mastery became a threat to the RADICAL MONOPOLIES of the system and B) the physical and economic[6] subjugation of women, the complete denial of her fluid, egoless awareness and, eventually, as women became shaped by the cut-off (or VIRTUAL) male world and forced to masculinise herself to survive within it, the total erasure of femininity; to be replaced by the psychologically androgynous MONOGENDER[7] promoted by QUEERISHISTS who seek prominence for their identity, FEMINISHISTS who seek a pay-rise or promotion to upper-management, SEXISTS who seek no-strings-attached sexual-release with pseudo-male FRANKENSHEILAS, and MANAGERS who need women who are either capable of suppressing their innate super-intelligence, sensitivity and spontaneity for eight hours a day or have long cut these useless feminine appendages from their psyches.

Emasculated egoic man does not possess the presence or PROBE-confidence to keep female emotions in line, while masculinised egoic woman lacks the presence or VOID-power to keep the male probe genuinely purposeful. Such men lose their authority—and are as incapable of handling their own angers and frustrations as they are her irrational moods—and such women lose *their* authority and are as incapable of keeping their own emotional excesses reined in as they are of inspiring him to extravagantly beautiful or courageous deeds. The relationships that result from the clash of these monogendroid moderns are, predictably, utterly disastrous; comprised as they are either of a feeble, metrosexual, femi-man and a hard, bitter, masculinised woman casually hooking up in wary bourgeois couplings, or of two clichés—a walking talking cock and an erratic, subservient and security-addicted doormat—noisily tearing their finer selves apart in standard sexual combat (*see* RELATIONSHIP).

GENIUS

G REAT ARTISTS AND CRAFTSMEN STRIVE TO LIVE with the intimate experience of what is beyond comprehension, and to allow this, rather than their own fears and desires, to shape their work. This activity was once the definition of genius,[8] a creative power that comes, via the context, from *beyond* self; that lodges in the guest bedroom of the mind, and then sets splendid fire to it.[9]

It is the wish of every authentic artist that genius will stride into the vehicle of self,[10] drive somewhere that has never been visited and then drive home pulling a mental wheelie. This wish, if committed enough, leads him to add to his self. He knows that if genius is to take the wheel, the vehicle must be developed to its highest possible subtlety and its widest possible range, that the ignorance, hesitation and insensitivity of the unformed self (and its crude VIRTUAL world) must not be allowed to get between genius and her fantastic instincts. If, through incompetence, there is anywhere she cannot go, she will not turn up for the trip, or bail at the first hurdle.

This process is called 'learning one's craft'. It is the difficult (CERBERUS-packed) *science* of art and, as such, can be identified and measured and its errors diagnosed; I can explain why your plot is clumsy or why your roof will leak or why the hand you have drawn looks like a radiation-deformed beetroot, because explanation and technique are both self and mind-made phenomena (*see* WHY).

I cannot, however, explain why your love-song is cheesy, or your dance embarrassing, or your 'installation' a vision of your own self-absorption or your story self-indulgent excrement because, while the technique of craft is acquired (refined by *adding* to self), the truth of art is innate (revealed by *subtracting* self). It is not what you have done that is the problem; it is that your self did it.[11]

Because self covers your entire life, emptying it out for genius is not a process of learning [hard] concentrated techniques, *at work*, but of applying [soft] concentrated self-mastery, *everywhere*.

genius [dʒiːnɪəs]

adj & n I mysterious message from somewhere else beamed into a state of pure, soft-conscious perception 2 a miraculous fruit the tree of which requires massive amounts of healthy soil, psychological space, free time, confidence and joy to grow in (and so is nearly impossible in the WORLD)

- he or she who hosts genius is reviled while alive and honoured when dead [12]
- fear of inner freedom manifests as the convenient lie that genius is a gift given only to a few rare heroes and not the result of continually opening your heart to LIFE, becoming sensitive to its strange depths, receptive to its strikes of inspiration and craft-capable enough to do justice to its consummate elegance; i.e. available to *all*

gift economy [gɪftɪkɒnəmi]

n a revolutionary means of production, exchange and consumption, founded on utterly irrational generosity

- used by lovers, friends and all humans before the FALL
- antonym of MARKET ECONOMY

GIFT ECONOMY VS MARKET ECONOMY

MARKET ECONOMY

THE MARKET ECONOMY—a.k.a. business or trade—was originally reserved for enemies and the ritualised transaction of luxury or priceless items. It is a recent and degenerate form of human contact; coercive and founded on fear and greed. It is also extremely unreliable, tending to USURY, over-CONSUMPTION and the reduction of quality and genuine choice (*see* MARKET)

GIFT ECONOMY

THE GIFT ECONOMY—giving away or 'collectivising' surplus without money, barter or market middlemen—was once the means by which all exchanges were made, but is now reserved for private, ceremonial or highly privileged occasions; it is voluntary and founded on GRATITUDE and GENEROSITY (i.e. unlike fear and greed, it is innate). It is also adaptable and tends to conserve natural resources

note that CHARITY *is not a gift as it is not reciprocal; it does not, therefore, generate gratitude but resentment* [13]

A BRIEF HISTORY OF GOD

1. PRIMITIVE GOD

The SELFLESS SELF is a welcome guest in a mysterious, friendly, TRANSDIMENSIONAL universe (an organism called 'God') comprised of immediate, living qualities (understood as MYTHIC 'gods') [14]

2. SUPERNATURAL GOD

The integrated self is an ally, or a hanger-on, in a universe of capricious 'good and evil' forces and divine personalities which must be honoured or superstitiously appeased

3. RELIGIOUS GOD

The individual self is a tenant / employee in a universe–corporation run by an absolute manager (with a beard), who wrote down a series of rules which must be SUBMITTED to

4. MODERN GOD

The isolated self is the proprietor of a mechanical universe comprised of separate interrelated parts, or people, which must be grasped and controlled

5. POST-MODERN GOD

The sole self *is* the universe

These five stages blend into and overlap each other, with two, three, four or all five potentially coexisting in one person's beliefs

god [gɒd]

n either 1 the living transdimensional (feminine) void manifesting through nature and self (unself / context) or 2 any one of a post-fallen series of superstitious myths based on aspects of nature or self or 3 a supernatural (i.e. *un*natural) monotheistic humourless old man, that created the universe, wrote a book, and then buggered off or 4 a fiction or lie [a MYTH taken literally] invented by priests or 5 *me, me, me* (more or less a synonym of 'fuck')

- *'do you believe in god?'* is synonymous with *'do you believe in x?'*—i.e. entirely meaningless without first knowing A) what *x* refers to (which one of the above definitions, or which one of the many, many variants) and B) what is meant by BELIEVE [15]

grictus [grɪktəs]

adj & n 1 a shudder of sympathetic shame for a friend's idiotic comment 2 a smile that expresses a feeling exactly half-way between courtesy and anguish 3 the mask-like ghoul who stares back at you from the mirror when you are deeply miserable

GROUPTHINK

A SET OF SELF-REINFORCING PHENOMENA which binds together egos informed by SELF (emotionally, psychologically, genetically) and unconsciously terrified of UNSELF (the mysterious, the unthinkable, the uncontrollable, the radically different or the genuinely original).

Groupthink (and GROUPFEEL — or collective unconscious) reinforces and reassures 'who I am' by stigmatising 'who I am not' and glorifying 'who we are'. It can be seen in Nazi rallies, MONOTHEISTIC sermons, menopausal tea-breaks, gentleman's clubs, anarcho co-ops, teenage cliques, Anfield, small towns, PROFESSIONAL symposiums, corp-journo twitter feeds, bars, mobs, or anywhere else egos anxious of unself congregate.

Groupthink comprises excessive generalisation and stereotyping, ever more extreme views (as members obtain the favour of the others by expressing extreme attitudes in the favoured direction), a [BOOS] illusion of invulnerability, unquestioned belief in the morality of the group, blindness towards inconvenient facts, pressure to conform on dissenting voices, self-censorship (creating an illusion of unanimity), disregard for empathy towards out-groups (whose faults are exaggerated), unconscious urges to help those who are perceived to be similar — who look the same, share the same values or have the same origins — to reject the outsider, no matter how affable, and accept the insider, no matter how obnoxious, alienation of anyone who does not display competent use of in-group vocabulary (i.e. JARGON), emotional nuance-blindness, exaggerated outrage at criticism; which is then used as group-defending justification and, most subtly but powerfully of all, a reassuring collective (groupfeel) VIBE.[16]

The beliefs and theories that groupthink is based on include religious belief, national-tribal identity, membership of a class or profession, gender, sexual orientation, laddish mob-mind, feminishism, homosexuality, scientific or political theory, identity with famous personalities, fashions, trends, products or sub-cultures, institutional status or length of service and age; all of which 'feel good' to be part of.

gringe [grɪndʒ]

vb & n a psycho-sexual event which propels one back into an agonising experience of one's childhood or teenage shame

- *The waitress' thin patronising response to Max's fluffed compliment made him briefly gringe back to his fourteen-year-old self*
- *When the text arrived, Sarah gringed with goofy delight*

grivle [grɪvəl]

vb & n to frantically try to retrieve a lost moment of TRUTH, a mutually agreeable vibe-state or chance to ask out that Polish girl who works in the post office

- a sub-species of FLAPPING AROUND

groupthink [gru:pθɪŋk]

n the hive-mind

- antonym of SCENIUS

guck [gʌk]

n a vague, shifty, indirect, overly cool, embarrassed or non-existent 'goodbye'

- complement of SWELK
- *Dermot's swift, casual guck made Isabel feel as if he had just flicked the pleasant day they had spent together from his shoe*

guggerstrasse [gu:gəstras]

adj & n the feeling of awkwardness, exposure, uncertainty or panic induced by accidentally being oneself at work

hallucination [həlu:sɪneɪʃən]

n see DELUSION

hangover [haŋəʊvə]

n 1 the suffering of excessive intoxication 2 a secret reason for narco-addiction (provides redemption, self-pity or an identity to those who do not have sufficient resources to malinger)

hard consciousness [prəʊb]

n see SELF, CONSCIOUSNESS and PROBE

hasties [heɪsti:s]

n.pl rapid series of explanations given to someone who interrupts you in the middle of a difficult and potentially embarrassing task, such as swiftly hiding incriminating evidence before a superior or wife returns [17]

health [hɛlθ]

n sensitivity to unself and to a healthy environment

- the result of living completely as (the PERSONAL)

self and [of growing up] in an intensely MANAGED environment *in* which desires and fears are shaped by inhuman INSTITUTIONS and virtual SYSTEMS, *over* every surface of which is pasted an exhortation to consume heavily degraded, industrially produced, scientifically engineered artefacts, and *for* which you must prostitute your life to either produce KIPPLE or take care of those drowning in it; is SICKNESS

- the result of living totally free from the authority of self, and of growing up in a soft-selved vibe-milieu of actual (as opposed to VIRTUAL) social networks of mutual aid, in reach of the wild, in which learning occurs informally (as a result of living in and contributing to a community) in which things are made by people for people, in which GENIUS rules the intellect and NATURE has taken the place of management, in which self is unable to monopolise reality and freedom of thought, speech, movement and desire does not need to be POLICED; is HEALTH

- doctors are quite unwilling to point out that you have been doing a fruitless task in an unnatural, porn-saturated cubicoid, or that nothing much happens between your adolescent adventures and your death, or that you are rarely at peace, in fact rarely even alive, yet dread to be told so; they are unlikely to DIAGNOSE you with *your whole world* [18]

heam [hiːm]

n the disorienting feeling, after lifting your head from several hours of staring at a screen and then walking out into the street, or of several years of living in a city and walking out into the woods, of either A) that the universe isn't supposed to be there or B) that you are supposed to be here

heartbreak [hɑːtbreɪk]

n & vb 1 to feel that you—and everything you felt was true—are breaking in two 2 to be sick with self-disgust as everything you'd come to trust, crumbles in your hand like dust 3 to lose self-control, then have a midnight stroll through the rubble of your broken soul 4 to FEEL the fire of PAIN, as you look upon your world in flames and you realise just who is to blame

- but when you reach the end you find you can start to learn to love the fire that burnt your heart; which just burns away what isn't true, and that is why you'll hope to god the world will suffer too
- *all* addiction, dependence and attachment lead here
- the point when *you* are willing to consider the most radical solution; *not you*
- a.k.a. SELFSNAP & EGOPOP

hebble [hɛbəl]
vb to be about to speak and about not to speak

hebetation [hɛbɪteɪʃən]
n 1 market-fuelled reduction or limitation in classes of EXPERIENCE from many thousands to seven or eight 2 atrophy of multi-tone-nuance, lexical-flexibility and poetic flow in speech

- examples of 1 include jobs, shapes of bus-stop, types of carrot, historical-dramas, attitudes to suicide, reactions to criticism and feelings of 'intriguing'; examples of 2 include; the

brain-scraping nasality of hypermodern capital-city accents, the stiff, back-of-the-throat monophone of the suburbanitemare, the euphemismistic jargon of PROFESSIONAL or political uniquack and the colourless monoglot mumblings of the modern TEENAGER or UNIVERSITY graduate

hedgehog [hɛdʒhɒg]
n a pig with swords

hell [hɛl]
n not, as has been claimed, other people, but yourself, multiplied a thousand times, and all of you forced to live in the same housing estate

history [hɪstəri]
n 1 ten-thousand year war on silence, idleness, women, the body, and on children's innate instinct to enjoy life 2 a really large bag of facts (which must be respected) from which any MYTH,[19] can be constructed

- *see* GOD and SELF

holiday [hɒlɪdeɪ]
n stressful time-filling managed gawk used by those so scared of free time they must fill it up with FUN

· tends to create impatience, guilt, PHOTOS, status anxiety and (like VR) stories that nobody wants to hear

hollow [hɒləʊ]
adj either 1 a thing without stuff inside, or on; as in a hollow tree, a hollow aperture, an empty mind, a blank page and so on (*synonym* of VOID) or 2 a thing or activity without quality, significance or sincerity inside; as in a hollow laugh, a hollow gesture, a hollow post-graduate thesis, a hollow forty years of work, a hollow upper-middle-class dominated culture, a hollow ten years of tremendous SUCCESS and so on (*antonym* of VOID)

homo–ludens [avətɑːɒvliːlə]
n an idle fellow, whose scale of priorities puts dancing at *just* under the level of eating
· antonym of HOMO-ECONO-MICUS (market-man) and HOMO-CLAUSUS (box-boy)
· synonym of THUNDER CUP-BOARD

honour [ɒnə]
n & vb either 1 a premium on speaking the truth, keeping your promises, being fair and CONSCIENTIOUS in your dealings and in doing a good job or 2 a complete refusal to be CRITICISED (common amongst; medieval lords, managers, emotional parents, soldiers, mafiosi and fallacy-ridden fallen man)

hope [həʊp]
n either 1 confidence in the future or 2 fear's PR man

hospital [hɒspɪtəl]
n 1 an INSTITUTION that separates bodies from societies, minds and galaxies 2 a place where sick people go to contract more diseases

huxleyan [hʌksliən]
adj see POLITICS

hypnotism [hɪpnətɪzəm]
n extreme tight-conscious probe-focus on a voice, entertainment device, religious ritual, chant, yoga posture or narcotic in order to zonk out, feel spiritually select, fart around in psyche, suppress pain, improve one's career prospects or wash the taste of corporate cock out of one's mouth
· *see* PORNTRANCE, MYSTISH-ISM, TEEVEE, NARCOTIC and SCHIZOID
· antonym of RITUAL

I IS FOR
improvising
on a planetary
STAGE

J IS FOR
joy
the opposite of
ROAD RAGE

i.a.p.c. [ʌɪ eɪ piː siː]

ab international american pseudo-culture; GRID-CIT-IES (in which place of work, habitation, culture and provision are as far away from each other as possible and separated by long roads) UN-MUSIC (the rhythm of fighting and fucking) UNFOOD (manufactured nutritionless sweety wheaties) UNMYTH (big men saving the world) and so on and so forth

· antonym of G.A.C. [ʤiː eɪ siː] *ab* genuine american culture (early blues, original jazz, beat-lit, sci-fi, Crumb, home-schooling, occupy, early punk, Lynch, etc.)

identity–politics [dɪvʌɪdənruːl]

n.pl well-established means of SOCIAL CONTROL through which system-threatening solidarity between prisoners sharing common interests (e.g. their imprisonment) is diffused by relentlessly feeding their secondary group-think preoccupations with gender / race / family / taste in music / choice of shoe / breakfast cereal / president[1]

· the young must blame the old, women; men, black people; whites, us; them…

· *I am not my shoes!*

if-weed [ɪfwiːd]

conj & n a mental–emotional algae which must be seen and then instantly brushed out of the way, or you'll get tangled up in it and drown

imagination [ɪmadʒɪneɪʃən]

n either 1 the wyrd tailor of the void, velvet bedecker of squidbeaks and disposable architect of UTOPIA or 2 the curse of man; the DYSTOPIAN EMOTIONAL TUFO between SELF and UNIVERSE

impro, improv [ɪmprəʊ]

n & vb the art of presence; of experiencing and responding to *what there is*

indecision [ɪndɪsɪʒən]

n inability to FEEL the bigger YES, courageously obey it, wait until no decision is needed or simply, choicelessly, do what you prefer

indushilate [ɪnduːʃɪleɪt]

vb to realise, with no small degree of astonishment, that you needn't think that

infarta [ɪnfɑːtə]

n fabulous amount of effort that pathetically small distances seem sometimes to require to cross

IMPRO

I N IMPROVISED THEATRE you walk onto an empty stage to create a story from nothing. When it works selves dissolve like sugar cubes and reality roars in a-flowing. Often though, it doesn't work; fear, hope, imagination and excessive planning, theorising and self-consciousness—all the SECOND IMPRESSIONS of ego—get in the way. The scene crumbles, and everyone scrambles around clenched and desperate.

This should sound familiar to anyone who has ever been lifted team-whole by an unseen hand on a football pitch only to *'ooh-ooh I'm gonna score'* fluff an open goal, or FLAPPED AROUND like a beached guppy in the company of a real woman, or let the brush paint harmony before giving self one last touch of ruin, or auto-piloted through paradise to later look back in ANGLUT at your own tragic absence (*see* VANTASY).

Impro fails because the self-informed ego cannot divine the unselfish source of life, because ego can't be bothered to master enough craft to guide the flow of life and because it fears what it cannot control; the GENIUS of life. Ego resists self-mastery, corrupts craft-mastery and blocks the underground river of myth at every weird wellspring.

Thus, to master impro, the novice must master unself, unstatus and unlanguage:

UNSELF

To master unself, is to overcome self in charge. For this the players practice awareness enhancement, fearless (but not reckless) commitment, psychological generosity, uncertainty [or failure] embracing, casual stake-raising decisiveness and self-emptying PRESENCE.[2] To the extent that they master these existential skills in an atmosphere of trust, UNBLOCKED players can allow the collective unconscious truth between them to manifest the straightforward character-honesty, sincere insanity, meaningful change, psychological risk and archetypical structure called a great story. Or a great life. To allow, in other words, the situation to speak (*see* SELF-MASTERY).

UNSTATUS

Much of the fascination of drama—improvised or scripted, tragic or comic, real or make-believe—comes from the reversal of status. Status-theory is based on the idea is that most inter-species behaviour is a presentation or 'transaction' of status. A high status animal, for example, will look directly and slowly, and then look away without looking back, and its posture will be relaxed and open to attack; whereas a low status animal will glance and then glance back, or cower its body protectively. Humans display similar behaviour when interacting with the people—occasionally even the objects—around them. Status transactions change according to the situation—a man can be high status to his employees but low status to his wife (again, pleasurable to watch on the screen or stage)—and can be extremely subtle—a referent touch of the nose, a split-second's hesitation, a strained smile...

Status-theory is allied to the founding assumption of EVOLUTIONISM and of GAME THEORY; that we are biological machines. Adherents of such ideology believe that status is an inescapable component of human nature, and so the only way to succeed in life is to become a STATUS EXPERT, free to play the status you choose, in order to get what you want.

This is factually true; status theory can be nuanced and thrilling to behold in theatrical action and it is useful and entertaining to apply an understanding of it to oneself and others. But it is a theory—a product of mentation, crude and binary; it still comes down to ones and zeros, highs and lows, winners and losers. This is partly why it feels uncomfortable to be reduced to a status in the presence of someone attempting to bully you into status-submission (psychologists, managers, pick-up-artists, etc.), but the main reason it feels bad is because communion has its roots in unstatus.

When UNSELF rules the system, there is no I to state. When the body is APPERCEPTIVELY allowed to PLAY, then soft-awareness is unselfishly, 'behind' the play, statusless. When I greet a friend with 'good morning peasant' or 'good morning sire' my playful co-star does not feel insulted or proud. When lovers dock, presently together, or when we lie under the stars there is, ultimately, nothing describable; least of all who is the dominant animal.[3] All this status BUSINESS is only in unconscious animal behaviour; and the idea that it is inescapable[4] is because in the world, which coerces us into behaving like unconscious animals, it *is* inescapable.[5]

UNLANGUAGE

What do the Q-WORDS REAL, FREE, GOD, LIFE, DEATH, BEAUTY, LOVE and TRUTH mean? It's hard to say when they are used continually and applied to everything. This isn't to say that playdough words can't be thrown freely around, but with the most meaningful words, or way of speaking, isolated and hollowed out by the co-opting ego, it becomes nearly impossible to find, express or recognise answers to ordinary meaningful questions; *'Do I love her?'* for example or *'What is the right thing to do?'* or *'What's the bloody point?'*

Good writers work to solve the problems of degraded language by expressing the truth in new ways; by freeing language from the SENTIMENTAL pretensions of pseudo-artists, the co-opted clichés of propaganda and the efforts of priestly or professional power to restrain meaning within approved limits. The writer's work is vital, but the power of the written word is inherently limited A) by its static, material, possessable, divided (into illusory *words*) and co-optable nature; and B) by the fact that, despite the music of the writer's art, the written word lacks the tone, vibe, silence and, deepest of all, the fluid response to context of live, illiterate, speech.

Entertaining and useful as it might be to read of new ways to talk about love and death, or to expand the boundaries of language, to really understand each other there is no need to find new ways of expressing or even understanding Big Words. Speech only has to be truthful. An epic poem about love cannot hold a candle to 'I love you',[6] said right; and that—before dastardly moustache-twirling, zero-gravity barroom fights and baboon eruptions—is what the improvised life is about; saying *'I love you'*, right.

HOW TO IMPROVISE

SAY YES-AND

yield to the situation completely and accept all offers into the unknown with a full-hearted *'yes, and…'* (instead of a close-hearted *'no'* or a half-hearted *'yes, but…'*)[7]

BIG, BIG COMMITMENT

go in *full* and go in *big* (which means embracing *enormous* failure) and give your whole eagle attention softly to *what is*, as if your life depends on it—which it does—so you can hear exactly what the CONTEXT is saying and respond to *that,* and not to…

PLANS; USEFUL BUT DEADLY

ifs, maybes and shoulds will fly across the screen of your mind; look through them to what is *actually* happening

BE OBVIOUS, BE SIMPLE

don't be clever; the word or act you need is a SCONK hovering *right here*, if you are *both* small enough to see *and* big enough to seize it

DON'T PREPARE, DON'T TRY

impro is not learnt by *getting ready* or *making an effort* (to be original or liked) which generate emotion (particularly EXPECTATION) and which strangle GENIUS, SENSITIVITY, SPONTANEITY and simplicity while they sleep

LET GO OF FAILURE & PRIDE

the *instant* you say something that clunks or stifles flow, or that stamps on a sprouting miracle, or makes you feel all 'ooh I'm the big man', release at once and re-enter the flux

GIVE TO THE SCENE

strive to make other people feel good, to make the scene glorious, to allow the room to speak and to EGG BLEND… then, when the spotlight falls on you naturally, let it all out

LEARN YOUR CRAFT

the crafts of ART, STORY and theatrical action, like those of PARTNERSHIP and SOCIETY, all draw inspiration from a common well; but without consummate craft, the bucket will leak and the rope will snap[8]

YOU ARE NOT IN CHARGE

improvisation is shaped by your craft; but it is animated by something far bigger than technique; *you* can become confident, charismatic, protean[9] and technically adept but without the *selfless* humility of something *else* at the rudder, *you* will always behave somehow uncreatively, come across somehow unpleasantly and feel somehow dead; and somehow, somewhere, you'll know it, and so will they

INDECISION

U SING THOUGHT OR EMOTION to work out what to do leads to a state of protracted decision making, or DOUBT. The words doubtful, dubious, and duplicitous all come from the Latin duo—which means two. When 'I' don't know what 'I' should do, I say that 'I am in two minds', meaning that a split (SCHISMED) self is trying to work out what another part of self should do; which, as many shoppers and job-seekers are capable of perceiving, is hell.[10]

Ordinarily, man goes to enormous lengths to avoid this hell. He will obsessively cling to a system, a plan, a theory, an ideology, methodology or RELIGION that tells him what to do (planning what to say to her, and it comes out creepy, planning a holiday, and getting stressed and missing what is going on, planning an economy and causing a devastating crash, etc.) and he will avoid taking RESPONSIBILITY at all costs—blaming his actions on the market, God, his genes, his parents, his past, 'human nature', or 'them'.

The irresponsible man of doubt removes himself—and seeks to remove others, especially his children—from experience that requires SPONTANEITY, genius or uncertainty; he creates systems, institutions and ideologies that insulate him from the improvised life, and he ignores, ridicules or destroys anything or anyone who threatens them. In short he substitutes the HUXLEYAN (post-capitalist) hell of indecision with the ORWELLIAN (capitalist or communist) hell of decisiveness.

CERTAINTY is completely different to this trivial decisiveness. Certainty is letting the context, or (with the rudder-guidance of REASON) the present moment decide; which makes reaction instant—and therefore remarkable—and removes the need for *me* to decide. When engaged in natural, spontaneous or creative activity—running through a forest, speaking without a script, kayaking down rapids, selflessly serving a guest, underwater welding, recording a drum track, diving for clams or caressing a dreamweapon—*I do not decide.* If I do, communion with the bodily context snaps, which is painful and leads to regret, guilt and HEARTBREAK.

ingrail [ɪnɡreɪl]

vb to gaze in awe at a record or book cover after a profound listening or reading experience

institutional-analysis [tʃʊm]

n.phr an account of how the thoughts, feelings, sensitivities and consequent behaviour of people that comprise the institutions of a SYSTEM are shaped by the system's structure and priorities

- often deliberately confused with its antonym CONSPIRACY THEORY [kənspɪrəsiθɪəri] *n* an account of how power is directed by underground illuminati, evil martians or magical cats

- *'If we pour a stream of marbles into a square framework, they will inevitably form a pyramid. In accounting for [this] perfect conformity... no one need propose eager participation on the part of the marbles. In organisations for which profit-seeking, say, is the bottom line... facts, ideas, values, policies and individuals are naturally selected that fit the structure, that act in structure-supportive ways, and that do not challenge the founding framework'.*

    David Edwards

institutionalise [dreɪm-drʌɪ]

vb to force people (or tempt them with a pseudo-secure 'career path') to be dependent on educational, religious or 'social' systems through depriving them of means of production (or distribution of surplus) and by blurring the difference between institutional processes and the aspects of life they manage; e.g. by encouraging people to believe that HEALTH care and medical treatment, or learning and schooling, are synonymous

- INSTITUTIONALISATION is a form of CAPTIVITY, which results in DOMESTICATION, which then leads—in humans and in animals—to: A) plumper, stiffer or more stereotypical physiognomy B) increased docility, submissiveness or infantilisation C) reduced mobility D) increased BOREDOM E) simplification of complex behaviours (such as courtship) F) reduced hardiness G) cruder nutritional, environmental, and SOCIAL requirements H) atrophy of the SENSES and of SENSITIVITY to the CONTEXT I) stunting of consciousness (and duller eyes) J) chronic

decrease in empathy, loyalty and generosity (except to those that feed them) K) living death (*see* SELF)
- standard institutions:
- SCHOOL · initial processing
- FACTORY / OFFICE · making stuff, moving it around
- HOSPITAL / PRISON · repairing defectives
- THE MEDIA · mass indoctrination / FUN / SPECTACLE
- THE POLICE · crowd-control and surveillance
- THE MILITARY · acquiring resources and opening up new markets
- THE BANK · debt-peonage and systematic theft
- THE STATE · legislation [II]
- institutions use the same interlocking TECHNIQUES: to control people A) eliminate personal knowledge and points of comparison B) relentlessly and intensely SPECIALISE C) separate humans from each other D) idealise and occupy the mind E) control the flow of knowledge F) redefine happiness to mean compliance or consumption G) place profit above all other considerations H) treat life as a collection of thinkable mechanisms, which can and must be managed by professional-priests I) expose everyone to BUREAUCRATIC surveillance

insuffence [ɪnsuːfəns]
n I to allow a horrible-beautiful sunset to pierce your exquisite solitude 2 the discrete art of dissipating pain (or repelling rain) by turning to face it, welcoming it, OXYHEBOUSLY allowing it to sweep over the body, loving it even, until it snaps you open and the light of mystery and relief floods in
- also evaporates the agonies of HEARTBREAK, the urge to show off, QUEUE RAGE, argumentative self-assertion when receiving criticism from dicks and the curious conversion of dignified poise into servile submissiveness when you think you might get a promotion or get your leg over

intelligence [ɪntɛlɪdʒəns]
n mind informed by UNSELF
- not what you know, but how you behave when you don't know
- not '*learnt*' (in SCHOOL or in BOOKS), but RECOGNISED in and through SELF-MASTERED action and existence
- antonym of CLEVERNESS

internet [ɪntənɛt]
n see TEEVEE and VIRTUAL

interview [ɪntəvjuː]
n humiliating performance of ambition, interest, happiness and confidence designed to test enthusiasm for EMOTIONAL LABOUR [12]
· synonym of APPRAISAL

interzone [ɪntəzəʊn]
n deathless spatio-tentacle network of identical, rootless, smooth, purposeless and perfectly safe airports, offices, PRISONS, SCHOOLS, hospitals, chain-stores, virtual worlds, waiting rooms, TEEVEE channels, galleries, APARTMENTS, MUSEUMS and newspaper articles [13]
· leads to PORN, ill-HEALTH, SOLASTALGIA, KIPPLE, KINERTIA and the slow, invisible destruction of SCENIUS
· physical manifestation of the UNHAPPY SUPERMIND
· synonym of DYSTOPIA
· antonym of UTOPIA

intoxicant [ɪntɒksɪkənt]
n useful means of temporarily softening part of the self in order to experience what it is not; results in temporary hardening of SELF (or HANGOVER)

· the UTP of intoxicants is exceptionally low; habitual or casual use catastrophically stiffens the self, converting the intoxicant into a hyper-ADDICTIVE NARCOTIC

jaids [dʒeɪdz]
n.pl approving, courageous, gentle words emerging from a face expressing rejection, disapproval, fear, stress or anger (esp. in BLIPS)

javel–implex scale [bʊlmɪtə]
n relationship between the amount one lies to oneself and the ease with which one is annoyed or offended
· one who scores highly on the javel-implex scale (i.e. a JAV) will A) explode with fury upon a hint of criticism B) be surrounded by an enormous brittle EGG and C) be totally full of shit

jaywalk [dʒeɪwɔːk]
n & vb curtailment, by law, motorway and stereotype, of the freedom to roam by spontaneous inspiration

jink [dʒɪŋk]
n awkward catch-22 situation after saying something funny that is too subtle or TABOO for your listener to

appreciate; you can either
A) say nothing or apologise
and let them think you are
a weird idiot or B) point out
that it was a joke—with the
insulting unspoken subtext,
'which you were too thick /
uptight to get'
· A) is the better choice
· *see* WOTNOG

joof [dʒuːf]
   n I a groan-inducing pun 2
a feeble gag from your girlfriend's dad 3 a dad's joke

joy [dʒɔɪ]
   n I to be part of an audience
taken collectively through
actual world death to ecstatic choral rebirth in new-to-
the-world self-melting con-
nectedness 2 weird flare of
mad, reckless GOD-QWOTH
as all cares, commitments
and pressures are seen, in
one huge sigh of parachut-
ing relief, as absurd shams
3 annihilating EXPERIENCE
of the VOID as self dies, leaving behind apocalystonish-
ment, road-rapture and a
tender experience of blended union with a loving room
4 that kind of thing, yeah?
· joy occasionally looks like
relief or like [merely pos-
sible] OPTIMISM; while the

impossibly REALISTIC optimism of *true* joy is hopeless, ridiculous, relentless
and confident of victory in
the unwinnable battle

juddle [dʒʌdəl]
   n & vb I a swiftly invented
imitation of pain or sorrow,
after you realise that you've
done something wrong, in
order to head off the oppro-
brium of others at the pass
2 deliberately choosing not
to [learn to] do something
as it ought to be done, or
making a half-hearted pa-
thetic gesture of doing it, in
an effort to force more competent people to take charge
and do it for you, so you can
swan off and do what you
really want

jujube [dʒuːdʒuːb]
   vb I to look out of the window often to see if someone
is coming 2 to mournfully
check one's email or telephone again and again for a
message that can surely now
never come, can it?

juvalarmu [dʒuvəlɑːmuː]
   adj & vb I serene eye-snap-
ping clarity occasioned by
a purge 2 the joy of cycling
through a deserted city

K IS FOR A
kimochi
knuckle
CRACK

L IS NOT
for the
love
YOU LACK

kafkaesque [kafkəɛsk]
adj structural coercion via schizoid objectification (*see* BUREAUCRACY)
- complements the equally subtle HUXLEYAN coercive system and the cruder ORWELLIAN system; *see* POLITICS and SCHIZOID

kamichan [kɑːmitʃan]
n the god of stuff
- e.g. broken pencils, secret meteorites and flapjacks
- *bestows afflatus by the shedload*
- the pencil trembles with anticipation as it is poised over the paper / crumbles of mud tumble with sordid guffaws as they fall from bashed boots / lashes are fame for a snowflake, but they also love to land on trash / cheap toasters are dead sad / keys are tragic lovers, dreaming of locks (which they enter with a poignant sigh) / lightbulbs unshaded are ashamed / unlit candles sullenly withstand / curtains part with reluctance / beds are uncles; pillows their patient friends / dust is the sigh of god and even disposable plastic spoons surrender their secrets to your lips

- the path to turning people into objects begins with turning *objects* into objects

kawaigasm [kawʌɪgazəm]
n fist-scrunching paroxysm of half-painful delight at seeing a kitten stretch its legs; can lead to psychotic RABIA
- synonym of CUTEGASM

kimochi [kɪmɑtʃi]
adj pleasurably painful or painfully pleasant, such as a lower back knot worked by a Finnish chiropractor or a Japanese volcanic bath one degree below too hot

kinertia [kɪnəːʃə]
n 1 feeling that you never have enough time while, at the same time, that nothing is really happening 2 to be simultaneously paralysed by and overwhelmed with agitated inner movement 3 constant movement at the service of nothing changing
- a.k.a. NON-STOP INERTIA[1]

kipple [kɪpəl]
n & adj 1 ever-multiplying, self-propagating substance which grows on domestic surfaces; comprising labels, receipts, pens, picks, cables, scrunchies and god knows

what else² 2 half-memories, fragments of songs, arses, film-scenes, revenge-wanks, bank-scores and all the detritus that fills a hard, tense head-in-the-world

kisling [kɪzlɪŋ]

n a loud, violent, emotionally demanding three-year-old instinctively exacting revenge upon the world for his mother's unconscious lack of respect for his father

k.s.l.i. [keɪ ɛs ɛl ʌɪ]

ab kamichan sex–love index

language [laŋgwɪdʒ]

n MUSIC + MYTH

· originally the tone and the meaning of *speech* actually, [FRACTICALLY] contained, or was imprinted with, the thing it referred to—just as nose-shape conveyed character or a loved object was stamped with an owner's vibe—then, as the literate self became separated from reality, so *words* split from their referents and from the musical-poetic experience of uttering them, creating the illusion that there is a 'true', OBJECTIVE 'reality' which word-strings more or less accurately represent

lap [lap]

n a lovely chair which pops into existence when someone sits down

laughter [lɑːftə]

n the sound of no self

law [lɔː]

n 1 declarative will of thieves and their heirs, the purpose of which is to permit their own theft, while prohibiting that of those who might deprive them of their power to steal more 2 a vast interlocking matrix of unintelligible ideas and procedures designed to subordinate ordinary people to elite rule, professional admin and the market; and to fix deviants back into the SYSTEM from which they have erred

· BIASTIFIED by emphasising the horrors of its own 'lawless' origins (i.e. the savage *unwritten* law of HONOUR and the *explicit* violence in egoic pre-civilised gangs, pre-modern 'societies' and 'lawless' states)

· law (like DEBT and BUREAUCRACY) is UNNATURAL and unfair;³ and so it must be held in place through [the *implicit* threat of] force or violence; i.e. the POLICE

—— THE KAMICHAN SEX–LOVE INDEX ——

DESCRIBABLE—AND THEREFORE MEASURABLE AND RATEABLE

1. Anxious, expectant, fumbling and strange; two fleshy, foreign bodies working away at each other, penis dimly perceived (tip only), vagina tense, expectant or resistant. Male ejaculation mechanical, accidental or far, far, away; female mostly bored, confused or feeling used. Leads to immediate withdrawal, self-disgust and sadness. Male desperate to leave.

2. Either: penis used as weapon, female degraded (perhaps patiently servicing with workmanlike duty) or: penis flaccid, male punished for being a naughty boy; in both cases leads to [suppressed] self-disgust or a nightmarish [incremental] hardening of once soft femi-tendons.

3. Cold, hard, sweaty, grippy, grunting, gyrating, animal fuck-sex; stiff, distant racked orgasm leading to exhaustion, stupor and, upon recovery, microscopic feelings of despair, emptiness and distance which grow to neediness, irritation or violence.

—————————— SEX–LOVE BORDER ——————————

INDESCRIBABLE—AND THEREFORE ONLY EXPRESSIBLE IN ART OR MYTH

4. Friendly connected bewilderments, building to cascades of speechless pleasure coursing through the entire body; leads to shared MARROW-WARMTH of goldening cells—humming in a vast, ambient, underground beehive—and generating an all-day autumn-warm, anxiety-proof EGG.

5. Insane, roaring, reckless galloping at midnight on a blind thunderstorm horse, minds undone, wardrobes smashed, cupcakes plastered over buttocks and dinosaur-suit in tatters; animal complementarity (him giving to or taking charge of her and she beaming and giving up to him) detonating blast waves from the creation of the universe pulsing through your astonishing bodies leading to warm pink delicately deliquescing snow on a beach, six am sky lorquin blue, North Norfolk.

6. Mind and emotions absent, an immense calm of infinite space, a void, a black hole, from the point of view of existence, nothingness, but realer than existence itself; has the quality of superintense joy and fulfilment, but is impossible to remember as something concrete, except as superfine egg-gold ease.

LAUGHTER

THERE IS THE LAUGHTER OF RELIEF, making the train to slip through the doors Indy-style, farts at funerals and tiny crimes that take tension away. There is the laughter of exhilaration, throwing yourself from the bridge, and the laughter of fear, awkwardness and approval. There is the laughter of newly formed groups, binding by creating butts, the laughter of superiority over the out-group, and the laughter of letting in; showing approval to the just-joined. There is the laughter of anxiety, trying to make it all okay with a smile, the peace-keeping lie-smirk or rictus grin as you listen to one 'it was so good / bad' advert-anecdote after another. And there is the dark laughter of emotion; of sex and torture.

The empress of laughter, however, is RECOGNITION.

I recognise large status reversals (the boss suddenly becoming the butler, or vice versa), I recognise life given to objects, I recognise the indestructible innocence of a fool, I recognise the insanity and pathos of inflexibility, I recognise perfect aptness, spontaneity, hyperbole and farce; the serious reduced to the absurd, the sacred profaned, far distant ideas linked by puns, subtle sureality, strange timing, strange sizes, strange behaviour, awesome beauty and animals. I recognise the insights of a hyper-observant comic-master, showing me myself at an angle to the universe. I recognise all these things because I am an impossible, indestructible fool in a mysterious universe, and it makes me laugh to see it.

But what I recognise most, or deepest, of all, is what is happening, no matter how catastrophic.[4] I am not alone in enemy territory. The merely objective world is actually my *friend*—and I laugh when a friend approaches. This is why innocent children and ancient tribes spend so much time merrily sparkling with amused delight. When the world is seen as it is, it is bizarre, grotesque, savage, apocalyptically alive, unlike my thoughts and gaily butcherous; not demented and cruel, but shot to bits, mad, hilariously mad... and I am mad with it. We are friends, the universe and I, in all joy and horror.

This is the laughter of *the whole truth*.

LAW

THE PURPOSE OF LAW is to protect property, order, PROFESSIONALISM, the MARKET-SYSTEM and the rule of the UNHAPPY SUPERMIND. These are all far more important in law than justice, which is an embarrassment, and, because it cannot be technically controlled, illegal. Any act of justice, desecration of capital, unprofessional use of commons, uneconomic activity or threat to ego must be outlawed. Examples include; home-schooling, occupying land, graffiti, suicide, sharing, self-medication, redistribution of wealth, satori, nudity and sending cheese in the post.

But laws are of secondary concern when one reaches court, where greater importance is given to 'the facts and merits of the case'. Ordinary people are able to present these facts and merits themselves, but are dissuaded from representing themselves, and compelled to employ a professional middleman — a LAWYER — for four basic reasons:

1. Truth, justice and authority are made inseparable from an abstract and extremely complicated code that only lawyers are trained to understand, interpret and discuss.
2. Going to court must involves a series of ceremonial, formalised rituals, invested with all the mystique of a religion, that bewilder, terrify or pacify outsiders into dependence on lawyers — as well as into unearned 'respect' for judges.
3. People also rely on lawyers because of the colossal prestige that professionals wield. Most people assume that their own unprofessional account of the case will not be given as much respect as that of a qualified professional; and they're right. Lawyers and judges, like all professionals, tend to condescend to outsiders and only reluctantly afford them access to the information, status and power they enjoy.
4. 'Nobody is above the law' — justice (like other professional concerns) cannot be executed outside of court. This does not just include crime and legal disputes, but also marriage, divorce, buying a house and making a will, all of which are legitimised by a trip to the lawyer.

lead, leash [liːd, liːʃ]

   n a piece of string with a dog at one end and a monkey at the other

leg [lɛg]

   n manifestation of the love between foot and hip [wb]

live [lɪv]

   vb to refuse to allow the tugging, massy gravity of egoic unlife to suck you under; to be strained to breaking—and then to break, and to be grateful for it, that you were proud or selfish to invite such pain, that it could crack your heart and let the soft genius of humility, in selfless surrender, pour torrents of eternity back into the body of the world, leaving you with finer sensitivity to feel and greater ingenuity to express the colossal, chaotic intricacies of nature; not now cliff-top thundering or ocean motionless out there; but in here

lord soames [lɔːdsəʊms]

   n an invented future self—which resembles an urbane Victorian count perhaps, or a cowboy-fingered 'man-of-many-lives'—that one plans to have turn up, take over your mind and masterfully deal with a *difficult situation*, only, at the crucial moment, to slump unconscious over a pork-barrel and let a drooling big-fisted farm boy handle matters instead

- married to LADY SOAMES [leɪdisəʊms] *n* the sophisticated and poised ice-queen of the mind that dissolves into teary hormonal sludge at the moment-of-truth
- lord and lady soames are inveterate rehearsers; they enjoy nothing better than to plan, in detail, the ins and outs of a future confrontation and then, when the time comes to deliver, gad orf for cocktails in the UNCONSCIOUS

love [lʌv]

   n & vb 1 not: desperation, emotion, excitement, addiction, sympathy, pity, hope, clinging, needing, ownership, satisfaction, getting, pedestal-putting, wanting, caring, worrying or self but 2 everything else

- impossible to maintain for more than a moment while self controls SELF
- synonym of REALITY (so if you don't feel it now; you only *know* what it is)

M IS FOR
mainstream
a small bottle
OF PISS

N IS FOR
the news
a small bottle
OF PISS

mainstream [meɪnstriːm]

n & adj 1 taste and opinion based on SYSTEMIC CORP-MEDIA-directed priorities 2 an identical *'have you heard about…?'* UNVERSATION that is occurring in a thousand million offices and factories throughout the WORLD

- a.k.a. MEAGREDRIBBLEOF-PISSSTREAM…
- *'[The word mainstream] suggests that the most duplicated and distributed books, magazines, newspapers, and television transmissions are like a big river, wide and deep, into which all the shallow little streams flow. The way it really works is the reverse: There's a giant ocean containing all the experience in the world, and in one place, some of it is sucked up into a river, which is then divided down into smaller and smaller streams, until all that's left is a thin trickle going up the drain of a urinal in an office building in New York City, into some guy's dick, and out his mouth into a little bottle labeled "Ocean," which is then duplicated one million times and delivered to people who live right next to the ocean but never go outside'.*

Ran Prieur

make love [meɪk lʌv]

vb 1 the experience of letting your self slip, in sheer sensory floodout, into the unfathomable and apperceptive pre-sense plasma of the other, thereby igniting the void of unself which already connects you to the epicentre of the universe 2 allowing 99.996% of the sense and vibe data normally excluded by the mental–emotional ego into relaxed, mutual consciousness of self-annihilating devotion and near hideous strange-delight

- TECHNIQUE is unnecessary
- transdimensional animal love-making creates clingless liquid ease and daylong creative yawp—but to reach this state man and woman have to know how to [want to] give up their SELVES (*see* SELF-MASTERY)
- antonym of FUCKSEX
- *see* KSLI and SEX

mammon [mamən]

n the god of the world's leading religion 1

- when serious conflict arises between the demands of Mammon, Jahweh, Allah, Krishna and Buddha, etc; Mammon always wins
- synonym of CUSTOMER

manager [manɪdʒə]

n see PROFESSIONAL *&* FUTILE

marker [mɑːkə]

n a 'don't like' no-entry sign, implanted (by self or world) in the GARDEN terrain of the psyche, before the wild path to what I am not (creating an illusory UNCONSCIOUS)

- creates an instinctive EMOTION [of agitation, irritation, boredom, cold disinterest etc.] in what I 'am' (what I like, am paid to be, believe myself to be or fear not being) when confronted by 'what I am not'
- markers do not just exist in *space* (creating anxiety about going somewhere, or about considering something new) but also in *time* (creating agitation about a slowing of speed, which is registered as unpleasant weirdness or 'depth')

market [mɑːkɪt]

n I systematic self-reinforcing cycle of over-production of drugs, weapons, shoddy goods and porn which requires professional services to clean up the waste *from* and create a need *for* the over-production of drugs, weapons, shoddy goods and porn 2 USURIOUS financial system that produces massive amounts of power for the parasitical middle-men [a.k.a. HALF-MEN] who produce nothing but MONEY borrowed from an illusory future of infinite progress 3 steady conversion of reality into VIRTUAL reality

- based on property, WORK and LAW and fuelled by EGO, class and planned and perceived obsolescence [2]
- synonym of FREE MARKET [friː mɑːkɪt] *vb* the *restriction* of choice to those activities that make a profit; routinely advertised as '*generating* choice', while, in the real world, free skills exchanges, spending a few years loafing, home-schooling, free speech, sedate, widespread and lovely public transport networks, public use of public commons, independent media, simple machines that people can repair and self-medication are all, sooner or later, squeezed out by 'free' markets (which, therefore, are only possible with uninformed consumers who make daft choices)
- synonym of WAR
- antonym of GIFT-ECONOMY

masturbation [mastəbeɪʃən]
n self pleasuring self with
self, in a counterfeit world
unconnected to anyone or
anything else
- principle entertainment of
  caged males, or of caged
  pseudo-males
- synonym of SEX

meditation [mɛdɪteɪʃən]
n apperceptive relief from
the headache, neck-ache or
CRAUNCH you were too stu-
pid to realise you had
- meditation (or 'mindfulness') without SELF-MAS-
  TERY (for 5 minutes a day,
  that is part of a RELIGION or
  that ignores CONSCIENCE) is
  either a MYSTISHIST narcotic or HYPNOTISM

meesh [miːʃ]
n the shin-tingle of a truly
stupendous YES

melancholy [mɛlənkəli]
n that most attractive form
of depression

mentation [mɛnteɪʃən]
n 1 mind informed or instructed by itself, or by [the
emotional] self 2 emotion's
fantastic wardrobe of off-
the-peg dungarees, pomp-
ous hats and peep-hole bras

mind [mʌɪnd]
n an extraordinary space-
time-creating machine
- magnifies and multiplies
  whatever is put into it

ming [mɪŋ]
vb 1 to blame one's inability
to master self, skill or solitude on a handful of half-
hearted failures[3] 2 to blame
reluctance to act on an emotion ('how I feel')[4]
- usually announced with a
  pitiful utterance of '*I can't*'

mode [məʊd]
n & vb to change (gradually
or instantly) from 1 selfless-
ness into emotional egoism
or 2 a human being into a
professional, priest, dictator or any other variety of
'responsible' person

modernism [mɒdənɪzəm]
n the penultimate stage in
EGO's unconscious project
to eliminate all life from the
universe, and all truth from
artistic-cultural experience
- modernism is essentially
  unconnected to any experience beyond self, and so
  alternates between viewing
  consciousness as one insignificant object amongst
  many (SCIENTISM) or as the

megalomaniacal source of the whole universe (POST-MODERNISM)

· characterised by rationalism, adversarialism, irony, self-referentialism, intense scrutiny of details, detachment, relativism and similar SCHIZOID symptoms of near-complete intellectual self-absorption[5]

money [mʌni]

n 1 a means of concealing (or laundering) enslavement and theft by replacing their traceable spoils with an untraceable digit 2 a means of replacing the ungovernable context with a manageable, addictive, reality-occluding, symbolic system; much like abstract PHILOSOPHY

· founded on DEBT, slavery and social control

· to put an end, for good, to money and capitalism:[6]

1. wipe out / default on all debt and abolish 'growth'

2. *demand* the state employ people (in public works), redistribute wealth via *devastating* taxes on elites and corps, level incomes and allow job-share, and pay a generous citizen's income to everyone... (or just:

3. eat the corporate state)

4. proliferate informal, spoken GIFT-ECONOMIES

5. use negative-interest currencies (money that decays in value over time)

6. create networks of skill and labour exchanges

7. deschool society, disable professions and dismantle corporations

8. allow small autonomous communitoids to emerge that naturally self-regulate and that have the power to control surplus

· a.k.a. CASH or SAD LEAVES

· synonym of SHIT

monger [mʌŋgə]

n & adj one who deals in the degrading BUSINESS of hawking, trading and selling objects or emotions

monotheism [mɒnəʊθiːɪzəm]

n belief that the creator of the universe is an abstract idea or a male entity (with an extremely low opinion of women), separate from his creation, judgemental, genocidally violent, with no sense of humour and keen to create repressive, hierarchical institutions on earth that more closely resemble open-air prisons or a collection of brains in jars

A LELAND OF MONGERS

DOUBTMONGER · one who enjoys generating fear and making others doubt themselves

FACTMONGER · someone who has got a degree, read a few books, found a job and thinks he now understands life

FAMEMONGER · any website or social media service that sells tiny little increments of fame; or upvoted 'likes'

FLUFFMONGER · a heckler

UPMONGER · one who wards off the threat of stillness by peddling excitement (pimps, pornographers, modern artists, wealthy parents, etc.)

LIFEMONGER · one who sells the most creative and awake forty hours of his week to an institution or corporation

POMPMONGER · one who creates the illusion of authority through solemn ceremony

PSYCHEMONGER · somebody who avoids the unconscious by farting around in the subconscious

PUSSYMONGER · someone who wields the vague promise of sex to get what she wants

GASMONGER · one who sells their adoring attention to a [usually FAMOUS] gasbag

---

- leads to MONOTONY, MONOCULTURE and SCIENTISM
- a.k.a. JUDAISM, CHRISTIANITY and ISLAM (the ABRAHAMIC BIG THREE)[7]
- synonym of ATHEISM and MYSTISHISM
- *see* RELIGION and GOD

monotony [mənɒtəni]

n predictable, nuance-free, vibeless, single-tone state of being directed by ego or by uncivilised institutions

- leads to HEBETATION: the atrophy of nuance
- synonym of BOREDOM and of FUN

mordfunk [mɔːdfʌŋk]

n the dreadful realisation, while reviewing your own personal creative work, that the author of it is a cunt

mua [mwɑ]

n a MASHI-MASHI feeling of heartache—engendered by recognising that the reality expressed by great art and craft is *your* reality—that you have not created something so wonderful; that you gave up before creating a timeless masterpiece from your life

- common in SYSTEMS which stifle limitless potential

munge [mʌndʒ]

vb to ruin a lovely unspoken little ritual by mentioning it

museum [mjuːzɪəm]

n a warehouse for the storage of stolen-goods

· similar to GALLERY [galəri] *n* small room used to hide art from the big room

music [mjuːzɪk]

n 1 pure vibe, directly manifest 2 the liquid origin of fixed LANGUAGE [8]

· the music of pure meaning precedes language; as animals, children, aphasics, pre-conquest primals and those who have groped to give word to a new feeling well know (but inarticulately testify) [9]

· in music you cannot hide what you say, because your message is entirely the *way* you say it; which is why you can never prove that a song is awful (*see* WHY)

mystishism [mɪstɪʃizəm]

n 1 ego's use of the ideas and feelings of UNSELF for fun and for suppression of conscience 2 dressing up, chanting or sucking water into your anus in order to feel *special* 3 being told what to do by guru because you miss being told what do by daddy 4 means of justifying the rejection of technique, tradition, CRAFT and TIME-SPACE 5 FLAPPING ABOUT in PSYCHE 6 DRAIL-enhancing MARKET-friendly WELLNESS or 'MINDFUL' HYPNOTISM

myth [mɪθ]

n a four-dimensional metaphorical mind-map of the several-dimensional self

· *see* STORY

· heavily degraded Q-word which has come to mean a quaint relic, a charming fiction or an outright lie

name [neɪm]

n an item of vibe-clothing

· in APT societies and people names (like OPINIONS and PLANS) shift, morph, evolve, live with and FRACTICALLY *contain* the swelling, waning, wealing landscapes of psychic matter; in totalitarian societies names are utterly separate from their referents—in order to create the illusion that reality is OBJECTIVE—yet also fixed and forever tied to them, so that both the name and that which is named, can be owned and controlled [10]

A CARBO OF NOTICES

- a coat flying from the back of a chair, whirling, and resolving into human form
- the slow-mo detune and swell of blossoming clouds of milk in a teacup
- the withering sarcasm of owls
- a word or sound you've been using a *bit* too much recently
- the aesthetic distribution of standing cows, and cowness itself
- hyper-fine streams of delicate 'yesness' streaming up from the corners of mouth, around the crinkling eye-sides
- a dog trying to understand 'maybe'
- a puffin-beak-orange e-flat major, an eggy c-minor 7th...
- the voice of your back saying *'straighten-up fool!'*
- the obliterating pre-scent of necks, the reassuring aroma of stones
- what's *not* there, what *hasn't* been said, what you *don't* feel or know, what's missing here
- things that only ever happen in films (handsome lad moves house and cute girl lives next door, single-punch knockout, mouthful of vomit, light not working in the cellar, dreams that make sense, etc.)
- where thoughts come from

nar [nɑː]

vb (of couples) to instantly 'sober up' from a tragic sense of unshared solitude or from murderous feelings of mutual aggravation to a genial display of amicable good-humour upon meeting a mutual friend

- synonym of PUTTING ON A GREAT BIG SMILE FOR THE NEIGHBOURS

narcotic [nɑːkɒtɪk]

n 1 that part of self which ego prefers to obsessively focus on or over-experience so as to obviate A) the threat of the CONTEXT and B) the discomfort of being cut-off from UNSELF 2 tomorrow's USURIOUS bank of happiness

- e.g. competition, psyche, food, news-gossip, power, drama, danger, THOUGHT, knowledge, TEEVEE, tourism, grooming, fidgeting, WORK, FAME (from minor social-media to major celebritism), SEX, complaint, PORN and *getting*... the particular object, configuration and flavour of ADDICTION one is susceptible to is a result of the substance, configuration and flavour of the particular SELF
- antonym of INTOXICANT

nature, natural [neɪtʃə]

n & adj the intelligent (APT), balanced (within UTP) and beautiful (i.e FRACTAL) principle of the UNIVERSE; and that which acts or vibrates in harmony with it

- often mistaken with [the merely OBJECTIVE observation of] the events or the forms which occur in the UNIVERSE (leading to the insane POSTMODERN idea that 'everything is natural')
- *you can't get closer to nature than your own body*

news (media) [njuːz]

n 1 a boring dream told by a nutcase in a prison 2 rich people paying middle-class people to blame, distract or sentimentalise the poor[11] 3 visual and textual fragments of contextless events used to create, in its consumers, a fragmented virtual image of remote problems so that they can forget about their nearby sadness 4 tittle-tattle and bitching for *serious* men 5 a convenient means of enjoying a little murder, WAR, fear, SEX and violence with one's breakfast 6 the PROPAGANDA voice of ego, state and the corporate-professional market system

- the [unconscious] purpose of the news is: A) to make the clear-cut 'debatable' B) to make the god-awful trivial C) to accustom consumers to events with no cause and no context D) to promote WORK, POSTMODERNISM, SCIENTISM, GROUPTHINK and RELIGION E) to make dissent seem bitter, ridiculous or completely incomprehensible
- there is no real difference between the TOTALITARIAN, SYSTEM-supporting 'analysis' of elite newspapers, the herd-minded hate-fear screeds of tabloid rags and left-liberal hand-wringing over distant or secondary moral concerns;[12] they are all fundamentally OVERTON WINDOW-bounded *opinion regulators*, selling audiences (*you*) to advertisers
- the media, like all professions, *automatically* filters out UNSELF, HONESTY and SUBVERSION (*see* SYSTEM)

notice [nəʊtɪs]

vb & n 1 sweet yellow fruit plucked from a tree of soft consciousness 2 beauty you cannot own offered down through giving up the one thing that is yours

— NEWS SPEAK —

Along with Q-WORDS mentioned elsewhere the professional news media has some specific POLITICAL terms, which it interprets[13] *according to the systemic interests it serves.*[14]

TERM	ORDINARY MEANING	NEWS-MEDIA MEANING
defence	Defence	Attack[15]
terrorist	Powerful people or groups that molest their own subjects and the world[16]	Those who molest the powerful or threaten their market interests
security	Being free from arbitrary or systematic violence	A means to funnel money into the high-tech MARKET by enhancing humanity's ability to do away with the Earth
austerity	Practicing self-denial in order to contribute to the greater good	Subjugation through widespread deprivation (via enforced, precarious WORK)
freedom / deregulation	Ordinary people being allowed to do what they like without government interference	Enormous wealth-maximising corporations being allowed to do what they like without government interference
anti-social	Threatening society	Threatening property or profit

peace [17]	Efforts to seek peace
	US-UK elites 'left in peace' to do what they want; reduce the world to rubble (or KIPPLE)
maverick	An unorthodox, original, unusually creative or independent-minded person
	A threat to the system (also CONTROVERSIAL, PASSIVE-AGGRESSIVE, NARCISSIST, EXTREMIST, FIREBRAND, IMMATURE, NAIVE, PRETENTIOUS, ANGRY, CRANKY, CYNICAL and EDGY [18])
radical	A person who advocates thorough or complete political, social or psychic reform
	One who offers technical solutions to problems caused *by* technique, without threatening the system as a whole (also VISIONARY, INNOVATIVE, GENIUS and, for psychopathic mass-murderers, 'MODERATE' [19])
aid	Help, usually to those that need it
	Official wealth transfer to an overseas corporate branch or local mafia
conservative / left-liberal / socialist / communist /	Supporting traditional values / supporting human liberty / supporting the interests of workers / placing the means of production into the hands of society as a whole
	Serving concentrated power, the activities of business elites and a TOTALITARIAN, professionally-administered SYSTEM (which is usually referred to in the news as SOCIETY, DEMOCRACY, COMMUNITY, etc.) *see* SOCIALISM and SOCIETY

O IS FOR
omnarchic
empathy
RESTORED

P IS FOR
policeman
bureaucrat
WITH SWORD

obey [əʊbeɪ]

vb to listen with everything you have to listen with, revealing the OBVIOUS; what must be done [act / accept] [1]

- antonym of SUBMIT [səbmɪt] *n* slow masochistic suicide
- '*Today I may obey you and tomorrow you may obey me, which of us is under the other's orders, may be a matter of chance—convenience—or momentary agreement. But whichever is under the other's orders must do them, and not think about them… the distinctive teaching among us will be, that one man must obey another, not that the other may crush him, but that he may* COUNT UPON HIM'.
  John Ruskin

objective [əbdʒɛktɪv]

adj an isolated, intellectual, partial, spacetime fact apprehended by the tight-focus mind, where it is related to other such facts to form a SYSTEM or a WORLD

- partial objective facts and relations do (indeed must) exist in reality, but it is only to the objective mind that reality is *exclusively* so constituted, which is why…
- should rightly be preceded by *merely* ('*scientific research into sex, art, nature, sanity, consciousness etc. is utterly misguided because it is merely objective / school is boring and pointless because it is merely objective / academic philosophy is irrelevant because it is merely objective / evolutionism and scientism are fictions because they are merely objective*', and so on)
- near synonym of SUBJECTIVE
- antonym of PANJECTIVE

occupy [ɒkjʊpʌɪ]

vb & n to use or inhabit any common [ENCLOSED] area (physical, mental, vibic, etc.) that can belong to no-one

- those that dwell in the linguistic, social or customary commons are defined by LAW-ABIDERS as squatters, anarchists, nuisances and threats to the 'social order' not because of the problems they cause, but because they are upsetting the standard definition of citizen as a working consumer of market property

omnarchy [ɒmnɑːki]

n see ANANARCHY

opinion [əpɪnjən]

n see MASTURBATION

optimism [ɒptɪmɪzəm]

n I stressful and unhealthy intelligence-lowering cult of self-belief founded on the idea that the privilege-and-poverty-supporting WORLD will progress for ever or that you can SUCCEED through positive thinking, constantly feeling happy and buying FUN 2 test of ideological or market conformity

· used by elite cult-winners to A) justify their privileged position B) recruit future members and C) suppress dissent from 'pessimists', 'haters', 'losers', etc.

· ordinary HEALTHY people are optimistic or pessimistic—or honest or dishonest, hard-working or lazy, assertive or compliant—according to the context; in other words they are *apt*

· antonym of JOY & REALISM

· synonym of FUN, YAYSAY, PESSIMISM and NAYSAY

orboing [ɔːbɔɪŋ]

n I being forced, by a long, shallow staircase, to take a series of lorby loping megasteps or dainty mini-steps; thereby temporarily inhabiting a strange and awkward otherself [wb] 2 dignity-thieving little A) run forced upon you by a departing train, or B) crawl forced upon you by an under-desk plug-socket

orient [ɔːrɪənt]

vb to accept the state one is in and to take the *next* step towards the finest possible state imaginable

· classic fallacious ABREACTION to personal or social orienting is to assume it means wholesale *replacement* of the situation for an idea of 'perfection' (a lawless or moneyless world, a constantly passionate and moody-less partnership, a life without problems and so on), which is nuts

· synonym of P.O.P. [piː əʊ piː] *ab* your [piecemeal] progression of principles and positions towards paradise

orwellian [ɔːwɛlɪən]

adj see POLITICS

oscavine [ɒskəvʌɪn]

adj [descriptive of] the feeling, in dark, silent, solitude, of fine, grey, untouchable strands of consciousness becoming luminescent green beans, hanging from a shimmering forest of birch trees growing at lightspeed in the cool soil of your bellymind

ostavise, ostavism [ɒstəvʌɪz]
vb & n the process whereby words relating to the present moment drift away to mean some other time, some other place or something half as good
- e.g. by and by, soon, divine, incredible, wonderful, etc.[2]

overton [window] [əʊvətən]
n 1 tiny spectrum of acceptable opinion marked out by PR and the news 2 implicit limits on the range of debate
- the *rightmost* boundary of the overton window, policed by mass outrage, prevents elites from proposing extermination of superfluous workers, privatisation of the air, and other such rational, profitable schemes
- the *leftmost* boundary of the overton window, policed by the LEFT-LIBERAL NEWS MEDIA, prevents the poor and selfless from questioning the foundations of the totalitarian world without sounding like they come from Neptune
- *outside* the overton window lie unspoken beliefs; the selfish assumptions of ego and the totalitarian assumptions of the SYSTEM; talking about or exploring either is both TABOO and profoundly SUBVERSIVE
- *see* SYSTEM and POLITICS

owarme [əwɑːm]
vb to go through life as if it has nothing to do with you

oxyhebus [ɒksihiːbəs]
adj descriptive of any problem that is solved by doing the PARADOXICAL opposite of what makes seeming or rational [cause–effect] sense
- examples include turning into the skid, getting what you want by not wanting it, relaxing in quicksand, solving problems by sacrificing answers, loving an unlovable and eating fermented beans
- OXYHEBE [ɒksihiːbiː] *vb* to solve a problem by acting on the truth of its inverted verbal form
- *see* INSUFFENCE

pabulate [pabjʊleɪt]
vb 1 to work only while being watched 2 to carry out valueless work in order to convey the impression that one is busy 3 undermining your manager or circumventing his diktats while appearing charming, innocent or even simple-minded

OXYHEBUS REVERSALS

Relief from standard finger-pointing logicoculpoid paratraps can often be obtained by acting on the truth of their opposite-forms, or oxyhebous TURNAROUNDS [3]

I'm so bored = I'm so boring

I can't do any exercise because I'm knackered =
I am knackered because I am not doing any exercise

I can't get my life to work out = Life can't get me to work out

I can't get the lid off this jam-jar = I can't tear open my mind
and allow a pantheon of Greek gods to fly out into the
world to birth a new universe of strange delight

That guy is such an arseface = I am such an arseface

She shouldn't treat me that way = I shouldn't treat
her that way / She should treat me that way

Life is meaningless = I am meaningless

❧

A JIDDU OF OXYHEBES

you are cell in your own body

the more you love life, the more it loves you

you get what you are (and you are what you notice)

you can only really be yourself by being everything else

you are not inside looking out, but outside looking in

nothing worth having can be found by looking for it

it's not what you know, but when you know it

love lives in shouldlessness

mind the mind!

❧

pain [peɪn]

  n 1 a physical order from the body to stop or change direction 2 an emotional command from the CONSCIENCE to walk away, knuckle down or INSUFFENTLY accept the whole situation 3 an invitation from the centre of the universe to slip focus softly into the pool of UNSELF

- pain, like death, is meaningful, and so it must be CO-OPTED by the WORLD; through A) STAGVERSIVE or CHARITABLE *sympathy* for the sick and the deprived and B) conditioning those privileged by the SYSTEM to interpret pain as a reason to wipe discomfort out with FAME, NARCOTICS or FUN, tiny imperfections as a reason to upgrade tools and minute threats to certainty as a reason to proliferate bureaucratic order, antiseptic safety, medical control and LAW
- the price of EMPATHY
- antonym of SUFFERING

panculpism [pankʌlpɪzəm]

  n foundational assumption that everything (or anything of real importance) can be mentally comprehended or emotionally possessed

- varieties of panculpism:
- PSYCHOLOGICAL · ascribing COMPETITIVENESS, selfishness, violence and so on to A) animals B) children C) primal people or D) human nature; based on 1) observation of animals in zoos (or in reduced, threatened habitats) 2) children in totalitarian society 3) hunter-gathers living in marginal areas and menaced or influenced by UNCIVILISATION and 4) the miserable, addicted prisoners that comprise the WORLD [4]
- SEXUAL-ROMANTIC · to believe that everybody else is having more FUN than you; to believe that he or she 'will make everything alright'; to try and work out if you love someone; to think about a love-relationship *'It's alright, I've got this sussed'*; to need 'me time'; to confuse LOVE for what you know it is or want it to be; to put looking for the right person above becoming the right person
- ASPIRATIONAL · to spend more time perfecting plans or 'working on yourself' than on acting; to believe that other people ('they') know what they are doing

- MEDICAL · ignoring the role of the whole self (including the UNCIVILISED environment) in physical illness; to assume that hospitals, doctors, drugs and medical research make society HEALTHIER
- PSYCHOTHERAPEUTIC · to declare that one *is* (rather than *has*) a condition; to assume that WORK, 'success' or 'raised self-esteem' are preconditions for HEALTH or happiness; to deal with unsociety-created UNHAPPINESS by suppressing its effects with NARCOTICS; to declare that violence, confusion, impotence, stupidity or even malingering are illnesses (rather than, say, strategies or consequences) which it is the 'duty of society' to treat
- MANAGERIAL · to assume that the solution to problems of education, health, efficiency or energy is more schools, hospitals, paperwork or power-stations
- SCIENTIFIC · to confuse [the metaphor of] measurement for the reality being measured; to ignore the role of the environment [CONTEXT] in evolution [gene-coding]; to ignore [or gloss over, or hide in theoretical interpretations] the role of [soft] paradoxical consciousness in [quantum] reality
- EDUCATIONAL · the attempt to teach quality (morality, beauty, etc.) by *explaining* it; the notion that 'teaching styles' must be matched to 'student learning styles'; the assumption that syllabuses, teachers, exams, schools or teaching itself are necessary for learning

panjective [pandʒɛktɪv]
adj soft-edged pre-objective *and* pre-subjective awareness (i.e. that which is aware of both THINGS that are 'out there' and THOUGHTS and FEELINGS which are 'in here')
- gives DEEP MEANING and HILARIOUS NUDITY to mere facts, and to mere me
- synonym of QUALITY

pantego [panteɪgəʊ]
adj & n stark and poignant absence of soaps, lotions, pebbles, mirrors, postcards or inexplicable chrome instruments in the bathroom after your wife or girlfriend has moved out

paradox [parədɒks]
n unthinkableness

PARADOX

T O THE MIND this image is either a duck or a rabbit, one after the other, but not both at the same time. Mind may 'know' it is both—but this knowledge is itself a non-paradoxical either-or idea. Every time you  try to directly experience the image as it is, as both things at once, it is immediately reduced to what it partly is, to one thing or another. For a split second you think you've got both the FIRST-IMPRESSION duck and the rabbit simultaneously; but you see that really you are just flashing rapidly between two SECOND IMPRESSION interpretations.[5]

You can only see the image as it is by not interpreting it at all, by letting go of the interpreting mind and, like a kind of vegetable, just witnessing, or SEEING; directly experiencing your first impression. The image then becomes impossible and pure, like the weird sound-blobs of repeated words before you understand them, or like the pure strange form of an object before you interpret what it 'is'.

In the mystery of the direct experience of first impression you perceive two different things at once; not binary *either-or*, but analogue *both-and*. This is intellectually and emotionally impossible (to the self) and, initially, very difficult for most adults; yet strangely pleasant, mesmerisingly agreeable, deeply meaningful, or, when the mind is completely stunned by the totality of what is (in great art and craft, wild nature, unconditional love, death, etc.), literally awesome.

Both-and paradox creates the pleasure of great art—as my non-interpreting paradoxical UNSELF recognises itself in paradoxical metaphors ('Juliet *is* the sun'), melodies, puns, tragi-comedy and mind-stilling masterpieces—and it also creates the strange meaning that science moves towards (but can never grasp) in fractal forms, perennial philosophical problems and the fundamental wave-particles of quantum physics; which are all paradoxical DRABBITS.

Scientismists violently object to such 'populist' presentations of quantum reality (and stridently assert the right to determine the 'correct' definition of paradox, quantum and so on). The egoic scientist is unable to grasp that being able to rationally *describe* the extraordinarily strange and paradoxical behaviour of quantum reality (in, for example, the famous double-slit experiment, which demonstrates that the most basic elements of reality are both waves and particles) does not make *reality* unparadoxical. When pressed on the reality of what Schrödinger's equations and so on are pointing to scientists unwilling to accept the limits of science will exit the discussion. Or get very rude.

The bizarre super-reality that genuine art and brilliant science points to is, when directly experienced, a simple impossible mystery to the scientific mind, but when it is indirectly experienced, it devolves into one duck or another rabbit; the secondary, mind-made idea-tools — or useful scientific facts and techniques — of living.

The hard-conscious mind-self sees (and can *only* see) reality as these either-or, duck or rabbit, idea-tools; while soft-conscious unself EXPERIENCES reality in a paradoxical state of both duck and rabbit at once; then uses its either-or tools to live. If the hard-conscious non-paradoxical self is not subordinate to (doesn't OBEY) the soft-conscious paradoxical unself, its choice of which of any particular either-or to choose (duck or rabbit, relax or tense, act or accept, leave the room or stay in it, black-and-white or shades-of-grey, or any other of the innumerable vital choices I am faced with) will necessarily be self-referential, self-determined, selfishly inapt and contentious (such as the schizoid antipodes of black-and-white SCIENTISM and shades-of-grey MODERNISM, or the black-and-white of ORWELLIAN goodiewinners-and-baddielosers vs. the shades-of-grey holy cause of HUXLEYAN 'equality').

If, on the other hand, the non-paradoxical self is subordinate to the paradoxical witnessing I — if I am unselfishly aware of my self — it will necessarily see and its choices will necessarily fit the extraordinary, or paradoxical, context; be creative, original, elegant and intelligent (*see* SELF-MASTERY).

partnership [pɑːtnəʃɪp]

n the unfathomable and in-destructible experience of being both you there, am I? and me here, you are!

- the most intense, demand-ing and rewarding spiritual training ground in this di-mension; knocks Shaolin monasteries and Vedanta ashrams into a cocked hat
- antonym of RELATIONSHIP

passive-aggressive [sniːk]

adj 1 a vogue word for what was formerly called 'shifty', 'snidey', 'sneaky', etc. used to make these failings sound technical, complicated and medical 2 a catch-all label signifying peace-advocating objects of social threat[6]

- one example of the fash-ionable medicalisation of social or moral problems (*see* PANCULPISM)
- famous 'passive-aggressive' people (sense 2) include Ghandi, Chomsky, King, Pinter and Jesus

pathate [paθeɪt]

vb to delay a freak-out until the danger or the death has passed, in order to not infect others with your personal panic or despair, or to deal straight with the straight fact

A BRANGWEN OF PARTNERSHIPS

LIBELULA (*vb & n*) to curtsy someone's brains out

FLUME (*vb & n*) to tenderly burst through an iron-plate of disconnected EMOTIONAL CRAUNCH by absorbing the gentle wafts of sweetness or presence that your partner emits weirdly by being there

PAMPLEMOUSE (*vb*) to let woo develop organically, without force or stress, yet ready…

YAWP (*vb*) …to stun someone into awe with a fabulous dis-play of bottle

ELEMB (*vb*) to scan the envi-ronment for sources of mu-tual delight

DISCANE (*vb*) to ask your part-ner to help you free yourself of your moody (rather than justify it, lash out or pretend it's not there)

SPANG (*vb & n*) to wake up your fellah by playing *Siki Siki Baba* on the stereo, jump-ing up and down on the bed screaming, handcuffing him to the head-board and then blowing him off

JASSLE (*vb*) to gently bring a fear or desire-altered husband back from the virtual other-world (tax, record-collection, sex, *must-win*) he is lost in, and back to his senses

ALORPH (*n*) the extraordinary transformation one's wife or girlfriend goes through—from misshapen red-eyed she-goblin to speechlessly beautiful irresistible living magnet—upon breaking through the carapace of ego between you

QUAST (*vb*) to give someone a strange, long, intense orgasm through hugging them and whispering strange devotions

OMNILLIA (*n*) the experience of walking around, wishing you could have sex with every woman on earth before getting home, making love with your wife and realising that she *is* every woman on earth

ABELOISE (*n*) a petite wingéd godlette that passes from his eyes to hers, picks up deadly messages and delivers them to guts with trumpets

MELLISANO (*n*) the speed that clouds, and highly conscious penises, move

LARESH (*vb*) to unconditionally forgive (i.e. to completely forget) a partner's darkie

ONEIRIC (*adj*) [descriptive of] bemusement that the realest moments seem like dreams

HEPATE (*vb*) to realise, with mounting horror or éclats of relief, that reality is responding to you exactly the same way as the opposite sex does

REGENDLE (*vb*) to positively renew woo, every day, for a partner that you just believe you knew, thereby making him or her mysterious again

SHILLESCE (*vb*) overcoming PMT with jungle-shuddering love-making, energy-raising baking or ecstatic gardening

SWEETSPOT (*vb & n*) the *precise* point between firm and soft, where clamping, ape-fisted sadism meets feeble, floppy, glad-handing masochism and both dissolve into confident tenderness

SYMPHOLIUM (*n*) the state of being eyes docked and overwhelmed by a silent, impossible-to-describe connection with each other and, through each other, somehow, with all things

AMOPHILATE (*vb*) to surrender *completely*, to give *everything*, *nothing* withheld

SORTALIA (*n*) the good luck of people in love

GALAMANXIS (*n*) a hydrogen bomb in petticoats: A) good for me like my legs are for my torso B) good for me like vitamin C only more so C) looks like G minor and smells like a rainbow D) wakes up, makes up a song and sings the solo E) goes back to sleep and then hits me with a yoyo

peace [piːs]

n I unconditional stillness 2 the insanely reassuring recognition that-which-observes-mind feels when it is surrounded by nothing made by mind 3 the fragrant green foothills to joy's blazing crimson peaks

- you can only find nature violent by A) not living in it or B) ABREACTIVELY looking for violence; peace is *by far* the prevailing experience of nature
- occasionally confused with CEASEFIRE [siːsfʌɪə] *n*

pederate [pɛdəreɪt]

vb to subtly change your life by subtly changing your walk, the tone of your voice or the rhythm of your breathing (especially on June 5th: *see* CALENDAR)

pelk [pɛlk]

vb to check if an error was, in fact, a hidden intention [7]

pemmick [pɛmɪk]

vb & n to foolishly rule out the option of steamed cauliflower for tonight's dinner [wb]

perg [pəːg]

vb to choose to not be embarrassed about it

personality [pəːsənalɪti]

n invisible disguise that you put on to get you through the day but which, because you put it on all day every day, sticks to you and eventually becomes you, so you can no longer tell the difference between it and you

- *imperceptibly* sucks the life out of all activity, injecting frustration, unreality and poisonous discontent into experience
- laughs a bit too loud (or never laughs), complains a bit too much (or never complains), does a whole lot of liking and not liking and *always* has an opinion [8]
- antonym of CHARACTER
- near synonym of EGO

pessimism [pɛsɪmɪzəm]

n the self-indulgent cult of self-doubt, *so-what?* can't be bothered, all is vanity, and everything is shite

- used by excluded cult-losers and ADDICTS to excuse their UNHAPPINESS, enjoy PORN, justify antipathy to change or solicit ego-reassuring MISERY-MIRRORS [mɪzərimɪrəz] *n.pl*
- YAYSAY (sucking up) and NAYSAY (taking the actions of others out of CONTEXT

thereby generating a 'perfectly reasonable' OBJECTION) are synonymous
- antonym of glorious, super luminous REALISM
- synonym of OPTIMISM

phebe [fiːb]

vb 1 to have a sneaky little feed on superiority (e.g. by considering your successes or the failings of others) 2 to make your self feel right by making someone else's self feel wrong

philanthropy [frlənθrəʊpi]

n 1 taking a small portion of the surplus stolen through the ignoble business of the MARKET and giving it to the ignoble business of CHARITY in order to persuade one's customers, one's shareholders or one's self, of nobility 2 'sustainability', 'shared values', 'social responsibility', 'responsibility to protect', and all the radiant, giving *goodness* of the master race

philia [frlɪə]

n a NATURAL expression of natural CHARACTER
- antonym of LIKE

philosophy [frlɒsəfi]

n thought is *never* deep

A GÜELL OF PHILIAS

AVEVAPHILIA · love of uncertainty, discomfort, mortality, nevermind, oh-well and sod-it

STREPIPHILIA · love of distant blue, long grass, ice-cold, fast water, apples, silent hills, solitary oaks, forgotten shacks, shy yellow shards and distant woodpecking sorts of thing[wb]

KONTOPEPHILIA · love of waddling around, hips akimbo, going *'pahkeek, pahkeek'*

NARIBUPHILIA · love of squid-beaks, cats' elbow-thumbs, cock-crests, friendly storks, galaxy-emulating spiders and secret jaguar go-kart tracks

INFINIPHILIA · love of ant's nests softly viewed as a whole organism, woodworm routes, dewy spider's webs, roosting starlings, queen sago spines, blizzards by moonlight, chestnut trees booming in the wind and cloud shadows slipping over distant hills

CALCEPHILIA · a love of footwear which honours the natural shape of the foot

QUIRINDIPHILIA · love of the flaws that make for flawlessness such as endearing fears, font-bleed, QUINK (*see* BODY PARTS) and the 0.5% piss flavour of prawns (*see* SALT)

AMAPHILIA · godlove (sense 1)

PHILOSOPHY

THERE ARE TWO KINDS OF PHILOSOPHY

ABSTRACT PHILOSOPHY was invented 2,500 years ago by three Greek men—Socrates, Plato and Aristotle—who, like the founders of MONOTHEISM, hated anything which could not be neatly thought about or controlled; art, nature, mysticism, children, humanity and the context. These men based their speculations on the abstract ideas of disembodied, egoic thought; such as 'matter', 'truth', 'beauty', and the ultimately illusory divisions which thought creates; such as 'time and space', 'subject and object', and 'nature and culture'. Western philosophers have spent over 2,000 years using their minds to understand the reality of these mental illusions but, despite some useful technical advances, have not got very far.

Abstract philosophy today is carried out in universities by submissive professionals who are contemptuous of ordinary society, who resist non-specialist incursions into their domains and who, like all professionals, can only conceive of repairing mind-made problems by more use of the mind. There is, within the minuscule OVERTON WINDOW of professional Deep Thought, contention and debate; rationalists vie with empiricists, realists with idealists, theists with deists and so on. But they all start with the assumption that mind can clarify the problems and paradoxes that mind creates. For this reason their output is boring, confusing, futile and has absolutely nothing to do with real life.

CONTEMPLATIVE PHILOSOPHY is an endeavour, by philosophers, to *experience* (rather than just think about) the cause of their perplexing mentations; which is to say, to experience LIFE. Because they aspire not to discover the meaning of thought through thinking, but the meaning of life though living, their lives tends to be marked with struggles to overcome self, master [abstract] CRAFT, open themselves up to CRITICISM, free themselves from [institutional] compromise and explore the unknown; and, although their output may sometimes, through *use* of abstractions, be difficult, it tends to be vivid, playful, simple and mysterious.[9] Such philosophers tend to discuss *ways of living* (or perceiving) as a cure to philosophical problems, rather than generate more things to think about.

Abstract philosophy is based on the assumption that reality is a collection of objects perceived in space and time by a subject. Contemplative philosophy expresses the experience that this 'subjective self' is *itself* an object, behind which there is a PANJECTIVE soft-consciousness which precedes both subjects and objects—and therefore spacetime—and so cannot be expressed in spacetime thought; only gestured to.[10]

Those unwilling to follow the gesture and experience consciousness, can never understand reality, truth, beauty and the other subjects of philosophy, no matter how many books they read; while those already familiar with the simplicity and mystery of consciousness—who know that philosophy must be simple and unfathomable if it is to bear the mark of authenticity—find that they are not *instructed* by great works, but inspired and delighted; the delight of RECOGNITION.

phobia [fəʊbɪə]
n an idiosyncratic, secretly nurtured, secretly enjoyed expression of PERSONALITY

phorb [fɔːb]
n a significant look shared behind someone's back

photography [fətɒgrəfi]
n pointing a machine at a thing and pushing a button
- often mistaken for ART
- manufactured with CAMERA [kamərə] *n* power machinery used to certify official experience (e.g. marriage), possess fleeting experience (e.g. FUN) and to fragment [isolate from context; and make possessable] undivided experience[11]
- contributes to the erosion of memory, to HYPERMNESIA and to the belief that a 'moment is lost' if not captured on a poxy camera

phung [fʌŋ]
vb & n to fling your naked, laughing body pointlessly at the black cube

A KITARO OF PHOBIAS

AUCTORAPHOBIA · fear of the competence of one's employees or of the knowledge one's partner has of one's shortcomings

APOMEIPHOBIA · fear of nothing at all; just a residual agitation left over from getting over-excited a few hours beforehand

CHAREPHOBIA · fear of hello / awkwardness at goodbye

GELAPHOBIA · fear of jelly-like consistencies, esp. in pies

APAPHOBIA · fear of sentences which begin *'there's something I have to tell you…'*

SYNANIPHOBIA · fear of meetings, interviews, appraisals, tests and reviews

IPSIPHOBIA · fear of one's own super-powers

CHARISTIPHOBIA · fear of having to express gratitude for something you didn't want

APHAPAPHOBIA · fear of the derisive laughter of schoolgirls

CELERAPHOBIA · fear of things moving with freakish speed or distorted slowness

KREMMIPHOBIA · fear of onions (the shy, haunting notion that they are ever so slightly watchful, ever so slightly 'on to you')[wb 12]

TONSUPHOBIA · fear of a bad haircut

STANAPHOBIA · fear of beaky or astringent words, like *vim, monetize, integrated* and *sustainability*

MANUPHOBIA · fear of hardwork, waiting, dirt and death (manifests as DISORDALIAS; *see* SICKNESS)

CRAICANALPHOBIA · morbid fear of shop-banter

GALLUPHOBIA · fear of men who are rude to waiters, dominate dogs, bully or pander to parents, bite their bottom lip while dancing, wear espadrilles or gab in the morning

OVIPHOBIA · fear of women who reek of perfume, wear pointy shoes, roll their eyes a lot, say 'I was like; *hello?*' or move like a magnet towards the biggest cock in the room

PARVAPHOBIA · fear of small delays or minute changes to your routine

IPSIDIKIPHOBIA · fear of perceiving some dark otherness behind the eyes of someone you THINK you know, or of witnessing a terrifying 'not you' behind your own eyes in the bathroom mirror which watches… watches… watches… then suddenly lurches forward and goes *'boo!'*

LIBEPHOBIA · fear of love; and love's fear of you

physiognomy [fɪzɪɒgnəmi]

  n 1 manifestation[13] of inner state (character, vibe, personality, attitude, feeling) in outer form (body, tone of voice, gait, etc.) 2 the art of judging a book by its cover[14] 3 the art of understanding somebody by PURZING her characteristic expressions

  • the muscle-matrix of the [unself-connected] naturally-grown face resembles, in subtlety and beauty, a natural terrain (e.g. a forest or an ocean), and can express the same natural quantity-range and quality-intensity of mood-hues

  • the muscle-matrix of the [ego-limited] unnaturally-grown face, expressing a thin, vibe-range of stuck emotions (bland, anxious, staring, hollow, etc.) resembles a managed-forest, an indoor-heated swimming pool or a modern carrot

  • the SEEING of physiognomy is both an art—and so betrayed by the assumption that it can be measured (e.g. with callipers or brain-scans)—and a type of AUGURY—and thus betrayed by the assumption that form causes quality (e.g. that a small GLABELLA *creates* stupidity); the art of physiognomy is therefore betrayed by scientism, sexual desire, anxiety, pomo porn and PHOTOGRAPHY

  • the EXPERIENCE of being, or what it FEELS like to be, me is expressed by what I look like, how I sound and seem, etc. Paying soft attention to these manifestations of me is to feel me as I do; such experience is pleasurable to the extent that my me is not controlled by my self... in other words to the extent that I am softly paying attention to *you*, a situation sometimes called LOVE

  • in schizoid societies physiognomy, as well as gently SEEING faces, is TABOO—because the egoroot knows it is exposed in the fruit of the face

  • the deep ability to see faces (gaits, etc.) is an effective defence against lies and tyranny; nobody in a sane SOCIETY would allow themselves to be led by someone with fixed, dry or STARING eye-pellets poked into the pancake of a smooth inexpressive facemask, striated with coarse, stereotypical wrinkles[15]

—— THE PINK TIP AND THE PROBE ——

THE PINK TIP is an ultra-sensitive naked vibe-antenna, a fractal wave upon the vast, blossoming, blooming ocean of the bellymind, reaching out tremulously into the world. The pink tip doesn't just *feel* what is happening 'out there', it *is* what is happening. Inside the body is the colour of this afternoon's light, the crisp ionised vibe of it, the nut-knuckled, honeysuckled, desert-zephyred dewlap of it.

When something particular needs to be picked from the present, the pink tip pokes up into the brain and becomes the probe. The probe is the abstract-making part of the brain, which (as HARD-CONSCIOUSNESS) isolates an object from the context, splits it from its opposite, judges it, names it, fits it into a system, expresses it, or writes a little sub-routine in the internal computer; called a *habit*, a *system* or a *map*.

When the probe listens to unself, it is integrated with the pink tip, and its habits, systems and maps fluid, useful and beautiful. When it is cut off from the selfless pink tip however, one little part of it debating with another, it becomes delayed, confused and stuck; either stuck *in*, unable to think, make a decision or, in extreme cases, insanely unable perceive to timespace at all, lost like a monkey on acid in a kaleidoscope of raw impression; or stuck *out*; compulsively thinking, wanting, worrying and concentrating, the restless turned-around telescope of attention excluding what is happening.

The probe gets cut off from reality by *pink-tip atrophy*— the process of blunting that comes from ignoring the advice of the pink tip or neglecting its perceptions by overly focusing on ideas, emotions and external objects, from shouting down its messages with vibe-corroding stimulants and from allowing fear of losing—status, youth, possessions, ambitions, or even life—to overcome courageous pink-tip instincts.

Systematic pink-tip atrophy, or forcing attention down pre-programmed schizoid probe-paths, is also known as BRAIN-WASHING. Result: *Mind is a brittle mechanism*. Pink-tip cultivation, or allowing soft-consciousness to flourish, is also known as SELF-MASTERY. Result: *Mind is a soft creature*.

pink tip [pɪŋktɪp]
n the softest part of me

plan [plan]
n & vb 1 a friendly liquid iff-
ish-familiar which, if over-
fed, becomes a catastrophically solid life-consuming
golem 2 an item of small,
edible jewellery, something
like a peanut
· extended, time-consuming
BUREAUCRATIC systems *force*
members to plan and to be
bound by plans
· antonym of SPONTANEITY

plasma [plazmə]
n 1 elastic vibe which accrues on objects, clings to
faces or drips off walls and
which makes things seem
weirdly odd, aversive or attractive or comfortable 2 the
atmosphere of objects [16]

platypus [platɪpəs]
n 1 a fact which does not
fit into a neat SYSTEM 2 a
problem which CLEVERNESS
alone cannot solve

play [pleɪ]
n & vb the unnecessary and
free spontaneity of relaxed
EMPATHIC PRESENCE which
connects me with my PART-
NER, my SOCIETY or with my
surroundings, in one tower-
ing, magnificent ÜBERSELF
· synonym of GOD *&* LIFE [17]
· deprivation of free play is a
potent technique of BRAIN-
WASHING [18]
· play with rules is a GAME
[geɪm] *n* of which there are
two varieties:

1. PLAYFUL GAMES (partnership, impro, ritual, sport,
free creation and selfless
formality or conversation)
in which the play is more
important than the game;
and so following the rules
and winning (or achieving)
are respected, adapted or
discarded in order to play
more elegantly, or daftly,
to include less proficient
players or to EXSUPERATE

2. JOYLESS GAMES (argument,
competition, bureaucracy,
blocking, politics, relationships, WORK, power-games,
and 'playing games'—such
as MINGING and PUNGING)
in which victory (or dom-
inance—and therefore in-
tense scrutiny—of oppo-
nents) is more important
than playing, and rules are
either broken or treated
as inviolable scientific or
religious LAWS; so that I
or my team *wins*, or you
or your team *loses*

police [pəliːs]

n 1 PROFESSIONAL standing-army invented to track down slaves, control large, defiant, crowds and protect shops 2 later used for surveillance, intimidation (the threat of violence) and to make life unpleasant for unemployed people on the street 3 bureaucrats with swords [19]

- the PR purpose of police-work—helping old ladies, protecting harassed neighbours and actually fighting crime (rather than enforcing regulations)—was invented to create the impression (in the public and in moral policemen) that police violence is for justice (*see* LAW) and 'the greater good' and not a means to force debtors to cough up [20]

politics [pɒlɪtɪks]

n system-serving opposame doctrines of social-governance fought out within a wee little OVERTON WINDOW

- on the political 'right' is the [pre-modern] ORWELL MODEL of governance; rule by autocratic totalitarian *people*, limitation of choice, repression of speech and repression of minorities, belief in order, routine and rational-morality and control by enclosure, fear and explicit violence
- on the political 'liberal-left' lies the [modern] HUXLEY MODEL of governance; rule by DEMOCRATIC totalitarian *systems*, over-abundance of choice, limitation of access to speech platforms, assimilation of minorities, belief in emotional-morality, 'imagination' and flexibility, and control by desire, the implicit threat of violence and DEBT [21]
- on the 'left' *and* the 'right' is the [post-modern] KAFKA MODEL of governance (rule through intensely objectifying BUREAUCRACY [22])—in partnership with the PHIL-DICK MODEL of governance (rule through TEEVEE / VR)
- all four models are fundamentally identical

pompees [pɒmpiːs]

n.pl 1 the surprisingly honest face that reveals itself once make-up has been scrubbed off 2 the surprisingly innocent buttock that remains when a SEX-ARSE has been unclothed

- pompees are quite unsettling—even horrifying—to COCKMAN

ponvoid [pɒnvɔɪd]

vb 1 to fill the empty areas of one's bedroom with space [wb] 2 to fill the empty areas of one's underpants with cashew nuts

pornography [pɔːnɒgrəfi]

n 1 extremely addictive expression of time 2 a means of concealing one's lack of genius, insight, talent, sensitivity, presence or love with titilating appeals to ego

- art pacifies fear and want, and generates passion and soft-attention, while porn stifles passion, hardens attention and generates anxiety and craving; the point of art is inner stillness and physical energy, while that of pornography is restless inner movement and physical paralysis (KINERTIA); art conveys the genius of UNSELF (coloured with the self of scenius, craft, memory and tradition) while pornography displays EGO, dressed up with ADVERTS; the soft *look* of art is liquid, variegated and engaged, while the hard *stare* of porn is fixed, single-minded and detached from depth, context and experience
- note that expressions of

pornography *resemble* those of ART—and vice versa; a great story may be dark, sexy and use CGI without being in any sense porn
- effects of habitual exposure to porn include: low-lying feelings of anxiety (leading to worry), annoyance (leading to violence), inadequacy (leading to ambition), frustration (leading to masturbation), boredom ('so-what?'), self-disgust, treating unwon women as prey (seduction = defeating a big boss rather than finding another player for a new quest), PORNSTARE, impotence and dulled libido,[23] treating won women (or NATURE, or BEAUTY) as objectified trophies, frustration that one's life does not meet MAINSTREAM-approved standards of beauty and a cynical sense that life is as you thought it was
- vigorously promoted by sexists and FEMINISHISTS, both of whom are threatened by the complementarity of GENDER and neither of whom can perceive the difference between objectifying women and gazing in awe at God's bum
- antonym of OBSCENITY

· VARIETIES OF PORN: dramaporn · newsmediaporn · fearporn gotporn · sickporn · fuckbeatporn · usporn · victoryporn philoporn · pomoporn · factporn · guruporn · tekporn fxsporn · speedporn · ampliporn · dethporn · goreporn mongporn · weirdporn · catchphraseporn · miseryporn revengeporn · fidelityporn · nostalgiaporn · pompporn optiporn · pessiporn · hopeporn · foodporn · cuteporn fashionporn · subporn · domporn · moanporn · meporn

PORNSTARE

A STATE OF STARING-BLINDNESS which systematically replaces soft consciousness with hard consciousness. Pornstare happens, like any other hypnotic trance, when the senses are dimmed (by uncivilisation, by TEEVEE-internet or by any other hypnotism) to a thin beam focusing on an external object, that, through being intensely desirable or undesirable, grips and then monopolises the attention. Perceptual autonomy (the freedom to decide where you place your attention) is surrendered to the authority of the idea or image.

The face of someone in porn trance is a KINERT mix of blank and eager, expressionless and excited. There is a grip around the eyes, but no sense of flexibility or awareness. It is the kind of face you might see on someone who is listening, but not really listening, just waiting for their turn to speak, or on someone watching teevee, or idly trawling through the internet, or playing a computer game, or on someone who is thinking about something they really want, or something they really don't want; it's the kind of look you might see on the face of commuters, on gallery goers at a private view, on people gossiping, moaning or getting excited, on husbands' faces as their wives prattle on about the minutiae of their day, on wives' faces as husbands hold forth on a favourite mania, on pubgoers as a terrifying moment of SILENCE falls and everyone reaches for their pint, etched permanently on the masks of the half-men that run the world and, of course, on the locked-by-the-schizoid fukflesh stare of cockman... on pretty much everyone's face, everywhere, all the time.

postmodernism [pəʊməʊ]

n schizoid refinement of the MODERNIST view that each of our egoic judgements—which (it is claimed) we can *never* step outside of—are but one of a potential infinity of interpretations or 'realities'; none of which truer, apter or more beautiful than any other (i.e. truth, aptness and beauty do not exist) [24]

- a.k.a. deconstructuralism, structuralism and WANK
- postmodernism, or POMO, is the unofficial ideology of the moral-artistic wing of the totalitarian world, for which persona, image and performance must be considered as real as reality; the technical wing of the self-world bases its approach to problems on [official] SCIENTISM (the idea that truth is a collection of rationally-apprehended facts)—the two ideologies seem to be opposed, but this is because they govern separate spheres of activity, not because they are mutually exclusive; both regard truth, reality, beauty, justice and so on as childish fictions, and both are an inevitable consequence of the self-informed SELF

A DRELLA OF POMO-TACTICS

Modern and post-modern artists use a limited palette of tactics in lieu of craft and creative genius:

TITILATION
titilating the senses with gory, warped, sexualised, outsized, bizarre or 'amusingly' useless sights, sounds, smells and tactile sensations

IRRELEVANCE
the trivia of the artist's life or preferences, or the SCHIZOID breaking up of the context into fragments with no real relation to each other except that the 'artist' has decided to mention them

BLEAKNESS
absence of natural fractality, vibe, colour or spectacular enthusiasm (popular in the pseudo-art of PHOTOGRAPHY)

IRONY
using 'ah, but it's not supposed to be taken seriously' as the justification for smearing one's excrement over a potato

REPORTAGE
replicating 'material-reality' precisely (extra points if the medium is soot, dried peas, lego or Elvis Presley's dandruff); includes EFFORT-PORN ('ooh! that must've taken a long time to do!')

A SPENGLE OF PREPOSTS

- the rage and frustration of floating through the painful and incompetent blank of a call-centre, where nobody can be blamed, and the rage and frustration of floating through the KIPPLE of one's own mind, where nobody can be found

- the light of the dawning sun breaking open man's consciousness of the unspeakable Edenic dream-time and a perfect elongated orb of dripped brie fallen on my trousers and glinting roundly in the winter sunshine

- suddenly skiing over an ice patch—cold and hard, all manoeuvrability gone—and suddenly entering a flailing and ELAILING otherword of unhappiness with a partner

- an incredibly long, dull story of a confused hero who, at the end of an unremarkable series of pointless tragedies and transient achievements, just dies… and your life?

- a tyrannosaur enthusiastically but unsuccessfully attempting to play the tambourine to a favourite Motown record and a sparrow hungry for, and frustrated by, a whole loaf

- the growth of trees, fires, skills and babies—all of which need the right kind of attention until roots are established

---

poverty, poor [pɒvəti]

n & adj 1 inability to craft one's dwelling, feed, clothe, heal or entertain oneself, use one's feet, share one's surplus output or live without WORK, access to the MARKET (cars, internet, supermarkets, electricity etc.) or the correct paperwork 2 needing to *get* things (and scores) to be at PEACE 3 having only crap games to PLAY

prain [preɪn]

n 1 polite request with brisk, strained, mouth-only smile, barely concealing a quaking bulk of psychotic rage 2 a 'yeah I'm fine' hastily plastered over a shattered heart

prepost [prɛpəʊst]

n & vb to see, in an electric pikah! of inspiration, what intimate and distant phenomena have in common

presence, present [ˈprɛzəns]
adj & n 1 reality 2 being in the present, talking about the present, accepting the present, paying attention to the present

- while presence chats about banalities we might beam blue navel-lasers around the room as our true dinosaur selves romp and flop on the moons of Jupiter
- creates the only chat-up lines that actually work
- augmented by SELF-MAS-TERY, IMPRO, NATURE, and the ego-suffering of a courageous, painful, grafting life amongst one's fellows
- eclipsed by the EMOTIONAL illusion of time; either past time (thought / sadness) or future time (hope / fear)

primal fear [prʌɪməlfɪə]
n ego's constant underlying fear of reality (UNSELF)

- underneath everyday fear of losing what you have, is the atomic terror of losing who you feel you are; this aversion to the (TEMENOS) emptiedness of unbeing is a permanent background anxiety, tension or boredom which lies at the root of all addiction, violence, hatred and despair

primitive, primal [ˈprɪmɪtɪv]
adj 1 original, mysterious humanity (before the WORLD and underneath DOMESTI-CATION)[25] 2 vibe flares fired from the sea-wreckage of the ship of culture we once waltzed upon in dark combustible joy

- antonym of PRIMITIVISM [ˈprɪmɪtɪvɪsm] *n* the SENTI-MENTAL idea that we should return to the trees, abandon SPECIALISM or never take another aspirin

prishe [priːʃ]
vb to suck bad dreams out somebody's nostrils while they are sleeping

prison [ˈprɪzən]
n & adj an institution that restrains, punishes, isolates, coerces and extracts work from individuals who have shown themselves unable or unwilling to live in a society that restrains, punishes, isolates, coerces and extracts work from individuals

- it is impossible to conceive of what is outside of the perfect prison (*see* VIRTUAL)
- pre-modern *closed* prisons were hidden torture chambers; modern *open* prisons are exposed play pens

privatise [pɹʌɪvətʌɪz]
vb to deprivatise
- by 1) defunding then 2) overloading with BUREAUCRACY then 3) frustrating users and finally 4) handing over to private capital

privileged [pɹɪvɪlɪdʒd]
adj able to 1 avoid the pains and discomforts of development 2 order people around 3 insulate oneself from the consequences of selfishness
- natural consequences of privilege: reduced empathy, awareness, sensitivity and experience of uncertainty and pain; leading to increased cruelty, blandness, crudeness of FEELING (and PHYSIOGNOMY), WAISINESS, stupidity and chronic immaturity

probe [pɹəʊb]
n see PINK TIP

problem [pɹɒbləm]
n not the problem

professional [pɹəfɛʃənəl]
n 1 one paid to treat problems created by the system they serve 2 educated, submissive thinker who does assigned work without questioning its ultimate goals; professionals may complain about *how* things are done (and offer STAGVERSIVE suggestions), but never must they overtly doubt the entire point of the enterprise (or hint that it is endless profit) 3 one who spends their education learning what the system demands and then 'freely' carrying out these demands in their work 4 one given elite (and legal) remit to A) create a need that, by law, they alone can satisfy B) define Q-words that, by definition, they alone can really understand C) deprive humans of the capacity to freely act (walk, heal, learn, cultivate, etc.) and authentically feel (*see* EMOTIONAL LABOUR); and then D) sell those actions and meanings back to the deprived
- if the professional becomes sufficiently CONSCIOUS of the fact that ADDICTION, sickness, insanity, ugliness and crime are caused A) by the WORK-SYSTEM and B) by the SELF, they will be passed over for promotion, failed or fired
- there is a common usage of the word professional which means 'responsible' and 'diligent'—best avoid

PROFESSIONAL

GNOSOCRAT (academic) · massively over-specialised thinker employed to direct his curiosity towards funding.[26]

PSYCHOCRAT (psychologist / psychotherapist) · consciously imprisoning agent employed to redefine certain inconvenient, unpleasant or irresponsible actions and feelings as physical sicknesses; works hand-in-hand with the jurocrat (the lawyer rebrands direct attempts of the powerless to secure power as 'crime', the psychologist rebrands indirect attempts as 'mental illness'). Note that the psychocrat does not make spectacular love or write beautiful melodies, cannot empathically experience animals from the inside, is unfamiliar with the bottomless BLACK PIT, and does not daily break down in demolished awe at the mystery of existence; and yet he or she presumes to make judgements on questions of sanity![27]

BIOCRAT / THANATOCRAT (doctor) · someone employed to sell industrially-produced drugs, patch up broken human-units (fulfilling the subservient role of service-user, patient and client), put them back into productive life ('adjusted' to their powerlessness and confinement) and restrict their access to the straightforward medical necessities of a healthy life.[28]

INFOCRAT (journalist) · an ideological manager paid to corrupt nuance and support the rule of mainstream totalitaria and ego by only writing [demi] intelligently about everything else.

JUROCRAT (lawyer) · one who upholds a series of rules that nobody knows by circumventing them.

PEDOCRAT (teacher) · one employed to develop, take care of, nurture, protect and carefully manage syllabuses.

BUREAUCRAT / TECHNOCRAT (manager) · one employed by the owner class to divest workers of their autonomy by A) proliferating BUREAUCRATIC information and manipulating its flow B) obfuscating class-antagonisms (with notions that 'we are all in this together') and C) paying lip-service to finer instincts (empathy, generosity, freedom, and so on), while stamping them out whenever they actually arise. Handles problems by dithering, hiding facts, avoiding direct communication, deliberately confusing, being a bit creepy or outright sadism.[29]

progress[ive] [prəʊgrɛs]

adj, vb & n 1 the active suppression of genuinely useful TECHNIQUES and expertise 2 the paralysing belief that the more complex and inscrutable a tool is and the more it demands SPECIALISED operators to use and maintain, the better it can serve its purpose (e.g. that hand-held nuclear-powered wind-machines are superior to brooms) 3 ego's ten-thousand year project, now almost complete, to do away with nature and replace reality with itself 4 ugly clothes, shoddy furniture and crappy housing, nutritionless unfood, drug-suppressed sickness, BOREDOM concealed with SPECTACLE, self-loathing concealed with 'career', lack of SOCIETY (and lack of privacy) concealed with 'identity', lack of *original* art concealed with *novel* market pornography; an endlessly proliferating PORN-TRANCED self-world of intense, unconscious, omnipresent unhappiness, run by a cancerous system, owned by a corrupt, psychotic elite, managed by a subservient bureaucratic professional-class, built by a depressed, violent, enslaved, sick and over-worked underclass and built *on* an earth which is *actually dying* [30]

prolail [prəleɪl]

vb & adj 1 to show consideration for a slow-walking partner by walking slowly 2 awareness of those who may be walking behind you 3 good pedestrian ethics

prond [prɛbəl]

adj & n 1 the obscure sorrow of seeing in DREAMS what your future self has become 2 urgent advice from your future self sent back in time to your current one

propaganda [prɒpəgandə]

n 1 an image of reality deprived of CONTEXT in order to reflect contextless TOTALITARIA 2 the simultaneous stimulation of positive emotions (desire, security, sex, power, magic) and negative emotions (fear, death, loss, pain, rejection) and the restructuring of the context in order to associate the former with *us* and the latter with *them* [31] 3 the redefinition or DIGITISATION of Q-words to deprive them of reality, followed by (once the original meanings have been lost) the deeply coercive act of unquestioningly assuming their widely accepted meanings 4 the conflation of antonyms (*see* SYNONYM)

- where ORWELLIAN PROPAGANDA of the [MODERN] right tends to the centralised creation of an illusion masking how things really are HUXLEYAN PROPAGANDA of the [POSTMODERN] left tends more towards structuring society in such a way that members are forced to construct, *through their own addictions and anxieties*, an ersatz media-supported SPECTACLE, before which they have no opportunity to exercise *active* faculties of sensitivity, discernment, creativity or conviviality; which then shrivel up, with MR. CERBERUS standing before reacquisition [32]

prorb [prɔːb]

n a heavy, soddy section of a book that one's straying attention seeks to short-cut

prostitute [prɒstɪtjuːt]

n near synonym of WHORE

- note the crucial difference between the PROSTITUTE— who peddles himself either temporarily or part-time, and does everything he can to escape his slavery and to help others escape theirs— and the WHORE—who has given up and, despite STAGVERSIVE protestations, unlives in a whoredom which he excuses or defends

provulsion [prəʊrɪvʌlʃən]

n 1 [job-advertisement generated feeling of] trying to get a job while, at the same time, being appalled at the prospect of being employed 2 fear of losing a job while, at the same time, desperately hoping that one's factory or office will be swept away in a tornado or hammered into OBLIVION by an enormous fist 3 looking around at what COLLAPSE *actually is*—not a black armageddon of exploding suns and punk anti-heroes, but an eternally proliferating deathless INTERZONE of bored, self-conscious and submissive consumers—and wondering if it might not be better if the seas boil away tonight?

prung [prʌŋ]

n the whiff of slight awkwardness that objects exude just before they become too difficult to hold

pry [prʌɪ]

vb 1 to cram an inner HOL-
LOW with the facts of other
people's lives 2 to invite a
drunk, violent or calculating predator into your EGG
by looking at him 3 to see a
porn-mag / unloaded porn-
vid and think 'I'll just have
one *quick* look'

· antonym of CURIOSITY

psyche [sʌɪk]

n & adj the between-world
of plasma and deep vibe; the
subtlest, most elusive and
strangest PINK-TIP of self

· manifests in the self as the
traditional MYTHIC forms
of society (angels, aliens,
goblins, spirits and gods)

· there is no more TRUTH in
the psyche than there is in
matter or in thought; subordinate to the CONTEXT
and animated by unself,
psyche is the substance of
miracle, augury and deep
insight; informed by self
and cut-off from the con-
text psyche is the source
of PRIMAL TERROR, and the
hypnotic flummery of NLP
manipulators, mystishists,
channellers, pseudo-gurus,
corporate yogis and other
charlatans and priests in
vague touch with the wyrd

pubble [pʌbəl]

n a curious combination of
frustration, sadness, relief
and fascination generated
by the discovery, far too late,
of the unspoken subtext of
a situation that, due to your
overly literal, explicit, verbal
or goal-oriented approach,
you thoroughly ballsed up

p.u.c. [piː juː siː]

ab 1 parent–universe concordance; describes the intimate relationship between
how one's parents treated
you (particularly through
the VIBE-ATMOSPHERE they
pulsed into your hyper-sensitive bab-flesh) and your
deep view of the universe
(as a hostile no-man's land,
an omnipresent tit of per-
petually-dispensing money
or attention, an institution
presided over by a hairy divine tyrant or, beliefflessly, as
it all actually, embraceably,
is) 2 the visceral taste-class
nexus that characterises the
divided (SPECIALISED) social
classes; in other words the
poise, bland assurance, dis-
cretion and living-dead liz-
ardliness of the elites, the
smug, tasteful, predictable,
pretentious and prolix anxiety of the bourgeoisie, and

the immoderate crudeness, violence, honesty, sentimentality, generosity, empathy and augury of the practical classes are not, ultimately, the result of peer-pressure, intellectual conditioning or money, but of the tone, vibe and unspoken communal quality of life that pervades the houses of the rich, the professional and the ordinary worker (*see* TASTE) [33]

- PUC also causes most academic, religious and philosophical attitudes — and, therefore, disputes
- also the cause of PARENTAL POSSESSION [pərɛntəlpəzɛʃən] *n* the mother or father-flavoured quality of emotion that (underneath merely MENTAL rebellion against parents or carers) rises up in times of fear and desire, selects parent-shaped lovers or combats the threat of love with mum or dad's psychic-swords
- operates in concordance with, and blends into, the [maternalistic-paternalistic] SYSTEM which enhances and replicates its effects
- note that although PUC is real, nothing good comes of THINKING about it (*see* SELF-MASTERY)

pugla [pʌglə]

n a fabulously beautiful item of clothing that, the instant it is acquired, becomes hideous and unwearable

purge [pəːdʒ]

vb to stop A) eating, socialising, thinking, working, fun, spreading yourself around or taking any kind of drug then B) doing noble battle with Mr. Cerberus before C) waking without the slightest cling of drear — zesty, electric and flashing — leaping out of bed, kicking the ceiling, lifted by JUVALARMU yet serene, without emotion yet crisply, intensely feeling the tangerine tang of the now

purze [pəːz]

vb 1 to feelingly understand someone by impersonating their posture, tone and facial expression 2 to feel like a cathedral or like a kitten, or like an oil-refinery, or like the poor sod who packed your apples, or like Ludvig, or like a black chanterelle, or like the universe that the stars gesture to, or like a git, or like me 3 to be one's cup of tea, literally 4 to commit her heart's thousand and one crimes; one at a time

Q IS FOR
Q
impossibly
TRUE

R IS FOR
recognising
i am
YOU

Q-force [kjuː-fɔːs]

n the strange field of attraction which draws together 1 hangers-on and quitters, talkers and listeners, hoarders and wasters, the orderly and the chaotic, those that linger and the ever-eager to push on and 2 arguments to the ever-angry, bastards to doormats, faithless to the jealous, foxes to the credulous, sickness to those who take their health for granted, HEARTBREAK to those who take their loves for granted, CANERATION to the inwardly ugly, delays to the harried, stupidity to the SCHOOLED, clots to object lovers, collapse to the self-led SYSTEM, revolution to the dominant class, sickness to the doctor-dependent and an ever deepening trough of despair to those who don't wash the dishes straight after dinner

· a willingness to OBEY and learn from the Q-force is a hallmark of MATURITY

· synonym of NEMESIS

Q-question [kjuːkwɛstʃən]

n an impossible question; expressing some kind of bafflement about the meaning of Q-words, or about why there is anything at all

queerishism [kwɪərɪʃɪzəm]

n crude personality-kit that homosexuals without much character can briskly construct a purposeful and justified ideology with 1

· where CAMP and GAY are characterised by supersane life-pumping extravagance, mysterious sexuality and tactile warmth, queerishism is marked by SENTIMENTALITY, extreme superficiality, order-obsession, cattiness or a middle-class groupthink mentality

quog [kwɒg]

n 1 a magnificent falsehood, engineered in a nanosecond, falling from your tongue in glib, effortless perfection, while a tiny, distant part of your CONSCIENCE whispers *'you lie!'* 2 the fog of justification which descends when accused of a misdeed or when moved to recollect a wrongdoing (works like a magic vain fairground mirror, expanding favourable facts and shrinking or erasing inconvenient implications) 3 the brush-strokes of ego-time slowly covering the flowing sheets of memory with flecks of believable bullshit [wb]

Q-word [kjuː-wəːd]

n I any word which partly or wholly signifies [and so can only be understood by] SOFT-CONSCIOUS QUALITY or TRANSDIMENSIONAL APPERCEPTION 2 any word which *fundamentally* refers to experience outside of self; and so cannot be understood or acquired through the efforts or ideas of SELF

· e.g. god, love, death, life, context, beauty, freedom, truth, good, etc; which are all ultimately synonymous

· such words are co-opted, stereotyped, degraded and DIGITISED by, on the one hand, egos that attempt to possess what Q-words refer to, and, on the other, by egos that are threatened by their referents, with the latter ridiculing the former; mystishists, for example, seize on a word like 'divine' or 'spirit', degrading it, and then scientismists ridicule the result; or goth teenagers seize on 'death' which their 'winner' classmates deride, and so on; all the confusing, annoying, cheesy, sentimental, off-putting, abstract, secondary, quality-denuded or debatable meanings or emotional associations of Q-words are created in this way (*see* STEREOTYPE)

· although the mind craves neat Q-WORD DEFINITIONS, they always sound *'a bit disappointing'* because anything but a *whole response* necessarily falls short of the *whole* EXPERIENCE that Q-words gesture to; which is WHY—although I have given *'a bit disappointing'* definitions to beauty, truth, love and so on—really, the *expression* of Q-WORD I give here, is this whole book

qwoth [kwɒθ]

n I lightning strike of divine rapture that rattles the spine and makes the teeth glow 2 an overwhelmingly powerful inner sensation of galaxy-wide waves of ecstasy; plus astonishment that you can bear so much pleasure

rabia [rabɪə]

n I sadistic fury that hard, armoured selves feel towards the soft, innocent, peaceful and silly 2 unconscious guilt expressed as frothing ire at those who share the *same* basic faults as oneself (directed, obviously, at their *different* symptoms)

- often combines with A) the pleasure that certain egos take in exercising power over others, through hurting them, and B) the pleasure that certain other egos take in being powerless; to produce UTTERLY FUCKED UP RELATIONSHIPS

racishm [reɪsɪʃɪzəm]

n an expedient means of ignoring the friendly tone of an 'offensive' word in order to A) get up in arms about its dictionary definition B) deflect attention away from what your little cult is up to or C) get promoted [2]

racket [rakɪt]

n elite ECONOMIC WARFARE fought to create a world of deprived, imprisoned, *developed*, debtors [3]

- an effective international racket is only possible once certain conditions — egos, laws, states, professionals, techniques and money — are in place, after which it is possible for corp-state racketeers to:
1. force states into massive debt (through warfare, taking advantage of catastrophe, etc.) which are paid (via 'aid' — *see* NEWS SPEAK)

to infrastructure-building, resource-depleting corporations and their local clients (dictators, generals, etc.) but paid *by* the state
2. force states, in order to pay these debts, to PRIVATISE all resources and remove all laws that protect local labour, local capital and the local environment, or that tax corporate profit
3. flood local markets with cheap, massively over-subsidised corporate goods, (ruining local producers) steal (i.e. buy up) local resources and local capital, employ locals at the lowest possible rates and turn the local environment into an uninhabitable wasteland
4. repeat until COLLAPSE

radical monopoly [единое]

n 1 an industry, or branch of industry, which becomes the exclusive means of satisfying needs that it alone can satisfy; needs that previously occasioned a personal or social response, such as compulsory consumption of schooling, high-speed transport, industrial foodstuffs, etc. (a.k.a. TOTALITARIANISM) 2 a self-informed-self which has become the EXCLUSIVE source of the reality, identity, and joyous intelligence which once originated in the context-informed-self

- *'When cities are built around vehicles, they devalue human feet; when hospitals draft all those who are in critical condition, they impose on society a new form of dying; intensive education turns autodidacts into unemployables, intensive agriculture destroys the subsistence farmer, public fora dominated by privately-owned news-media slowly denigrate speech and the deployment of police undermines the community's self-control. The malignant spread of medicine has comparable results: it turns mutual care and self-medication into misdemeanours or felonies... Ordinary monopolies corner the market; radical monopolies disable people from doing or making things on their own'.*
  Ivan Illich

rag'nfrid [ragnəfrɪd]
n & adj the exact opposite of a pineapple

rationality [raʃənalɪti]
n see SCIENCE
- synonym of MENTATION
- antonym of REASON⁴

ravle [ravəl]
n to seek to vent unlimited rage on another (or excuse unlimited, cynical, distrust of THE UNIVERSE) by making deals (or DEBTS) which nobody can strictly honour

realism [rɪəlɪzəm]
n experience of or demand for the 'impossible' i.e. that which cannot be egoically felt or imagined, or is outside INSTITUTIONAL power structures
- a degraded Q-word, which usually means something like 'pessimistic rationalism and a demand for nicer FURNITURE which doesn't upset the police too much'
- antonym of OPTIMISM and PESSIMISM
- REALITY [rɪalɪti] *n* so much better than you think / so much worse than you think

recognition [rɛkəgnɪʃən]
n 1 external experience of inner reality 2 one soft consciousness, shared by two
- great art, comedy, nature, the arrival of an old friend, love-making and communion give pleasure not, *first of all*, through [FUN] stimulation or understanding; but through recognition

FRIENDS OF REG

RICHARD · a little fat man with bulging eyes and thick sensuous lips who rejoices at your friend's failures

ELAINE · white, arch, skinny, sneery femme who suggests you throw yourself off high places, push old ladies into the road or who plants similar visions of intense sadomasochism into your mind

ED · enormous bald bastard who stands at the door of your instincts, and pats them down for traces of carefree abandon; will cavity search on suspicion of revolutionary delight[5]

NELLY · twitchy, fussy, swarthy, gummy old girl who is keen to point out that you will be lonely, unloved, poor or destitute if you leave your partner or your job or your personality

JANET DAVAGE · a tight-necked, menopausal hag [who wears clashing colours] urging you to fling yourself at the most powerful man in the room

JACK DAVAGE · square-jawed hunk (with small GLABELLA) who tries to convince you that using a woman is just 'being a man' or 'will work out *fiiiine*'

DOROTHY · a wet, fishy, felty, spinsterish, weak-mouthed woman who says nothing but somehow manages to make you feel both guilty and furious just by her being there

GERALD · a scrawny, whiney, camp little man who tells you to give up the new activity you've started because you look stupid and you'll never be any good at it

OLLIE · soft, boyish, genial, dishevelled, bearded and jelly-jawed sop who tells you that all your creative efforts are 'absolutely brilliant'

---

reg [rɛdʒ]

n smallish, dark-haired man with an unkempt moustache and a nasally 'accountant' voice who stands invisibly next to you in supermarkets and suggests you fondle a big round bent-over bottom, stuff buns into your mouth until wet icing sugar drools down your shirt or scoot down the aisles on a trolley, erect cock wanging about, going '*wheee! wheeeeeeee!*'

· while reg's salacious recommendations only lead to shame, the rest of his advice is generally sound

· *see* friends of SHANGO

— RELATIONSHIP AND PARTNERSHIP —

THREE TYPES OF RELATIONSHIP

1. The relationship is founded on *sexual frustration / boredom* (usually, but not necessarily, his), *loneliness / neediness* (usually, but not necessarily, hers) or, occasionally, *honour* (to a tradition, parent, etc.). It may begin with a dreary sense of inevitability (and a type 1 KSLI sexual encounter) or with a surge of extreme, anxious, excitement (a type 2–3 KSLI sexual encounter) but in both cases he will soon start to feel restless, or bored, and she will start to feel sad and moody. At first she might not notice her sadness, nor his detachment, but over time post-coital tristesse and a deep sense that she is not really being loved will combine with his increasing carelessness and will deeply injure her; although she'll hide her pain from herself and express it indirectly at him. Eventually her irrational unhappiness will give him the justification he needs to be rid of her, although he may call her up later and they'll repeat the friendly-romantic-sexual wrestling match a few times until his genes have informed him that the job has been done and both can go on to their next superficially entertaining and ultimately disastrous fantasy.

2. Option two is much the same only over a longer period. They'll slowly settle into a ghost world of compromise and familiarity for a few years, have a few romantic holidays and lovely days out, before his lack of interest in her, his taking her for granted, his putting his private interests and sexual restlessness before her and his basic, deep-seated immaturity and fear of love will make her more and more emotional and more and more addicted to substitutes for love, until, a few 'us' talks, some aggressive sexual release or a few surprisingly nice but increasingly rare moments later, they'll break up hideously.

3. Finally, option three; they get married or get a mortgage. Splash out on a wedding maybe, then live in a dreamworld for a bit. If they are rich enough he'll take her hither and

yon and they'll build a home, or they'll struggle together against the world; all told be *a lovely couple* for a while before, again, he gets subtly but significantly bored of her and feels a pressing need for independence, have sex elsewhere or go fishing. He might give her a few kids, which will distract them both from his lack of majesty, before he turns his inner self away from her for good, drives his heart into WORK, or FUN (perhaps attempting to live the parody of the life of a playboy bachelor), but in each case driving them apart, creating a pall of psychic dishonesty and doom over their house and thereby BRAINWASHING the children in a cold psychic world of apparent harmony, but actual separation and emotional cruelty.

There are an enormous number of variations on these three themes and the predictable mechanics of relationship can run side-by-side with the magnificent, ever-renewed super-excellent love of PARTNERSHIP, but, in essence, relationship is doomed to suffering; and, in essence, it is his fault.

This isn't to say that women can't get bored too, initiate a break up, or make living hell of men's lives—and there are many hard cases out there who don't stand a chance of love—but most women only screw up a partnership if *he* does not have the sensitivity to commune with *her* or if (through lack of self-mastery) he lacks the strength to stand up to her tyrannous emotions and distrust of man. If he does not love and delight her every day or work ceaselessly to keep the fire alive, she will sicken and dry up inside. Likewise, if he is a clingy wimp who has sold his balls for an easy life (or can't walk away from her emotionality), he will activate the bitching, calculating and *utterly* unreasonable FIENDESS; the nightmare mirror in her of his cowardly, loveless, self-absorbed self.

PARTNERSHIP

If self is in charge of partner-hunting the attracting principle of the other will be primarily something that (semi-consciously or unconsciously) benefits *me*; either my genes (her youthful beauty, his power) or my psyche (the Q-force attraction of a sadist to a masochist, and vice-versa, or the arrival of someone who fits my emotional idea of what I want; usually some replicated parental poltergeist). The outcome of such union is boredom (*I now need to impregnate / be impregnated by someone else*), contention (*why do you always...?*) or the anguish of the damned and the dis-illusioned (*he's changed! she's really a bitch! woe! love has died!*).

If, however, UNSELF is in charge of consciousness, there will, first of all, be a lack of neediness in looking for another, as the source of what you seek is *not out there*. There will also be something mysterious about a first meeting, an attraction that cannot quite be put into words, a sense of *greet!* and a feeling that, despite what ego might think or want, you have no choice in the matter. Something beyond ego is moving in; the genius of soft, unselfish, SEEING; the fond realisation that the 'out there' of the other and the good thing 'in here' are the same, actual, miraculous (i.e. PARADOXICAL) experience of both being awake, at the same time, in the same dream (*see* zzz).

Even then though, unless you happen to be the Buddha, the habitual urge to fall into the sleep of relationship, is immense. After a few weeks or months (usually after a couple have moved in together) the FIEND, initially stunned into silence by love, gets its act together and launches a counter-offensive. The intensely-desired mask (PERSONALITY or DATE-FACE) of the idealised other begins to slip, dark moods begin to reappear and a nauseating heart-sucking realisation dawns that you have cast your lot in with someone, or something, you don't recognise. You try to do something about it, about this thing in the other you don't like—reason with it, argue, flee, threaten, beg or relieve yourself elsewhere—but all efforts fall short. You're not getting what you want. *What about me?* Super-charged delight, you begin to sense, is just for the first flush of romance. And, as your relationship makes the same weary, inevitable way to the same disaster or the same shadow world of familiarity and compromise as every other since time began, you start to believe that love is an illusion, or a chemical, or just sex, or something for other, *luckier*, people.

Self is defenceless against this failure—against the boredom, anguish, hatred and horror of relationship—because these emotions are caused *by* self; its thwarted expectations, its restless, pornographic imagination, its intense, addictive wanting and its predictable genetic programming cause the problems that self then tries desperately to overcome. Only that within which is greater, or more conscious than self, can see through the screen that the ego pulls over the world, or can admit to feeling resentment or discontent and can allow ego, desperate to get away, to turn back home and dissolve. Only soft unselfish consciousness can really live with (*or* really live without) another and whole-heartedly participate in the only commitment that actually increases love; facing-down together, every day, the emotional suffering that ego generates.

As with relationship there are near infinite variations on varieties of partnership. In addition, selfish and unselfish instincts are, in most people, entwined. What begins as casual, unhappy congress, or even an arranged marriage, may eventually crack open two warring ego-eggs and allow true love to pour out; or a magical romance, blessed by the gods, can slowly slip into the hands of the devil; or the slow, easy, organic coming together of a pair in love can be inordinately complicated or even destroyed by his impatience, desperation or confusion, or by her anxiety, idiotic honour or self-doubt. Even ten minutes in bed can be a four-way war of his and her true and shadow selves.

If they are committed to seeing and dealing with all that arises, eventually relationship becomes PARTNERSHIP.

HOW TO CONVERT RELATIONSHIP INTO PARTNERSHIP

DON'T SUBTLY PUT EACH OTHER DOWN · teasing is an essential ego-corral, and a right laugh, but subtle put-downs—especially with others—build up in the psychic sub-structure between you and rot your vibe-connection

DON'T TALK ABOUT YOUR EX · which summons up their ghost and deposits it in the corner; better to only mention them when a situation or, *perhaps*, an unrelated story demands it

DON'T FUCK MORE THAN MAKE LOVE · you need sweet, intimate generously attentive sex to keep you connected. If hard fuck-energy gains the ascendant, a subtle hardness will slowly sharpen your collective edges

YES AND... · not *'yes, but...'* (i.e. IMPROVISE together)

DON'T BLAME EACH OTHER FOR YOUR MOODIES · moodies can be overcome together by talking about what's on your mind or doing some planet-queen dancing on the sofa and letting go of weird inner grip. Which is to say; be honest (e.g. about your CRAUNCH) and don't sweep emotion under the carpet

MAKE LOVE EVERY DAY, WHETHER YOU FEEL LIKE IT OR NOT · your shared-egg will fade and your connection dry up if you don't bother doing what you don't feel like; love—and making love—has *nothing* to do with what you feel like

DON'T STOP WOOING HER · consider her yours and moods are on their way, take her for granted and she'll soon be off, try and control her and, although she *may* submit, for a while, something truly terrible inside her will not

DO NOT BE INDEPENDENT · that's right; do everything together, because total honesty and exposure only suffocate ego

BATHE IN THE VIBE MORE THAN IN EMOTION, IMAGINATION OR WORDS · underneath all the ups and downs, and the appalling war of ego, is the strange, silent inner plasma that connects you. Lose touch with, lie about or repress that, and you're doomed. Likewise, if you *think* about your lost or absent loved one, you will suffer, whereas if you *feel* your actual love for him or her in the solar plexus, death has no sting

DON'T CLING LIKE A WIMP / DOORMAT OR BE CASUAL LIKE A BASTARD / BITCH · constant soft intensity, combined with courage before the storm, is the way to unlock your loved-other's underground ocean, strafed, of course, with roaring rampages of indomitable joy; desperation—before during or after a relationship—is, like jealousy, repellent at the cellular level, and threats certainly won't help either, alright?

LOVE · works better than contention, effort, imagination, games or that most fraudulent of duties, 'working at the relationship'

If, after all that, it's still not right, leave and don't look back

A LEIGH OF RELATIONSHIPS

DESTINGATE (*vb*) to engineer romantic accidents and coincidences so as to create the convenient impression that 'it was meant to be'

DATE-FACE (*n.phr*) The façade of being a stable, attractive and normal person on a first date; either evaporates after orgasm or three weeks after moving in together

SLIFF (*n*) a feeble pretext to touch someone: e.g. brushing a hair from their cheek or offering a poxy massage

RESCIPISCENCE (*n*) the act of mourning a fluffed seduction

SKOD, GUNGERDROUGH (*n*) an EMOTION-FUELLED own-goal cruise-missile counter-strike custard-in-face wipe-out [wb]

CARNE-VU (*n*) the grim feeling, while having sex with someone you don't connect with, that you are two weird lumps of solitary meat (sometimes manifests as a distant voice in the back your head saying 'there you go, well done, you made it, you're actually having sex with someone').

SECKALGIA (*n*) the raw, hollow feeling of ego-revealed, which surfaces after orgasm; ennui, self-disgust, neediness, confusion or the panicky need to run a thousand miles

HIROKOMPAI (*n*) stifling feeling of intense *coupledom* that slowly fills the room like a humid cloud

MALMORÉ (*n*) consternation, when you tell everyone how in love you are, that they don't seem to care that much

VIMP (*n*) a tiny unconscious gesture, word or BLIP that betrays one's fear of intimacy, EMOTIONAL awkwardness or antipathy, such as a glance away after a meaningful '*yes*', a reflexive swallow, sniff or hand drifting up to the chin

QUAIME (*vb*) to punish your partner, after he or she reasonably asks you to change a bad habit, by carrying out their wishes with martyred, dogged persistence

PRINGE (*n*) brief inner cringe of secret shame as you reuse a romantic gesture that magically doesn't work this time

SHIND (*vb*) losing interest or putting up protective emotional shields as a relationship enters an intimate and vulnerable stage (i.e. a form of long-term date-face melt)

LUNGER (*vb*) to try and deal with a partner's emotion (e.g. over-excitement or moody) with *more* emotion (e.g. anger or pleading)—*see* FUTILE

MENDERSTRIL (*vb*) to glimpse, in a moment of awful clarity, the truth of your 'significant other', your relationship and your ENTIRE LIFE in a trivial physical detail (e.g. spotting your girlfriend in a crowd and wondering *'what is that person?'* or feeling, for the first time, while looking at your husband's hairy toes or the back of his head, the mute block of ignorance he barges his way through life with)

CRID (*vb*) to refer to a nightmare of giddybliss alternating with hateful despair, underpinned by the needy fear of loneliness, as 'love'[6]

KARG (*n*) a hateful argument with a 'loved-one' which, to maintain a public image of togetherness, is conducted through gritted teeth, in urgent, hushed tones

THE ANFORTAS PLIGHT (*n*) *'but why doesn't he speak to me? / ask me out? / help me? / ask me what the matter is? / admit he's wrong?'*

THE GREGER DILEMMA (*n*) *'I can be dishonest and rend my own soul, or I can be honest and rend hers'.*

TEAM-WE (*n*) an advertising campaign for how wonderfully adjusted, enlightened, enviable or electable you are

ASSELE (*vb*) to keep the exposure, sacrifice and ego-crush of committed cohabitation at bay by keeping the partnership 'casual' and 'flexible'

GELPH (*vb*) to further insult someone whose heart you are tearing apart, with that most cowardly, derisory of offers; *'let's be friends'*

UNK (*n*) feigned, pouty, hurt

IGHT (*n*) an UNCONSCIOUSLY shameful (and thus unconsciously concealed) inability to apply the apparent wisdom or competence of one's job, field of expertise or guru-nature to one's bedroom

TWAVLE (*vb*) being unable to split up with her so behaving like a shit until she leaves you [while *you* look on amazed]

STEMP (*vb*) [for the mind] to swiftly connect every random thought after losing someone, to their absence in your life [while *you* look on amazed]

ELAIL (*vb*) to be trapped in a horrific otherworld of suffering and distance from the partner you are torturing for your own weird inner imprisonment [while *you* look on in helpless confusion]

CLUSHE (*vb*) to say *'that's it! It's over! I'm leaving you!'* and walk out the door [while *you* look on horrified]

relationship [rɪleɪʃənʃɪp]

n I a MENTAL—EMOTIONAL—
GENETIC NARCOTIC: initiated
through BOREDOM, loneli-
ness or insecurity; sustained
by ADDICTION, FEAR or the
MARKET; then terminated
in indifference, cruelty or
despair 2 the cult of two

- antonym of PARTNERSHIP
- because profound engagement with nature and with
any meaningful society are
disbarred by the WORLD,
hopes for depth, release,
fulfilment, security, connection, variety and delight
tend to be redirected into
love for another; which *can*
absorb the pressure, quite
easily, but add ego to the
room and the relationship
doesn't stand a cat's chance
on the moon

religion [rɪlɪdʒən]

n a football match with no
teams; instead the referee
dresses up in a flamboyant
outfit and the crowd stands
around hoping *it* will win

- if you judge religion and
SCIENTISM by what they *believe*, they would appear to
be different; whereas if you
judge them by how they
behave—treating reality as
a mechanism (operated by

laws or by gods), restrict-
ing access to knowledge or
TECHNIQUE to the uniniti-
ated, dressing up big men
in gowns, dressing up language in jargon-saturated
scholasticism, taking metaphor (the scientific metaphor of measurement or
the religious metaphor of
myth) as factually true and
being 'outraged' by attacks
on orthodoxy (reason or
God)—they are identical

- religious beliefs are only
lies to the degree that they
A) express commitment to
superstitious facts or B) express allegiance to a CULT;
in some cases though, profession of supernatural beliefs (god, last judgement,
reincarnation, etc.) is not
intended to express loyalty
to cult-approved faeries,
but a commitment to prac-
ticing a certain way of life;
taking such beliefs at their
face value is a [largely ide-
ological] act of literalism
perpetrated by atheists and
theists alike

- n.b. the antonym of science
is not religion, but AUGURY
or SPIRITUALITY, although
the history of religion—a
massively complex, varied
and subtle ten thousand

year old STORY—contains elements of all these things, all five definitions of GOD and god knows what else; another fact glossed over by atheists, scientismists, and culty religionists

rent [rɛnt]
n & adj 1 means of forcing tenants to become dependent on PROFESSIONAL fixers 2 piecemeal theft 3 legalised extortion
· needs, like BUREAUCRACY and DEBT, the threat of violence to be kept in place

repandrous [ripandrəs]
adj descriptive of A) glowing exaltation of affection B) a face hot with absorbed BEAUTY C) joy that can be seen wafting from delighted skin in heaty ripples and D) a gratitudegasm of freedom upon re-realising you *never have to do that again*

requirrel [rɪkwɪrəl]
vb to scrutinise the far side of the universe for a brilliant idea (or QUIRREL [kwɪrəl] *n*) that floated into the mind, lightly landed on the awareness, before flying out for good into the inaccessible vastnesses of the unknown

responsibility [rɪspɒnsɪbɪlɪti]
n it's all my fault
· impossible in monarchic, democratic, capitalist or other totalitarian systems which, via BLAME, substitute responsibility with the guilt of false CONSCIENCE [7]
· in the end though, it really doesn't matter whose fault it is… the only important thing is *what am I going to do about it?*

revolution [rɛvəluːʃən]
n either 1 [futile] changing one set of elites for another, or one system for another (near synonym of STAGVERSION) or 2 [effective] allowing UNSELF to end the rule of ego and world and to organise SOCIETY (near synonym of SUBVERSION)
· effective revolution eventually leads to free, autonomous, classless DUNBAR groups of mutual aid and GIFT-ECONOMY-regulated social activity that gradually take over the activities of everyday life, ignoring THE SYSTEM, until, like a FEAR or a WANT no longer thought about, the world loses its grip, fades from view and comes to seem rather foolish; and people

wonder how on earth they could have bothered with such a silly, silly thing
- *see* UTP and UTOPIA

rich [rɪtʃ]

n & adj 1 [those who] have acquired more MONEY than most people through having destroyed the capacity to creatively or GENEROUSLY spend it 2 able to buy service, favourable attention, access to nature, COMFORT and fine culture; and thus, without the need to create these things, unable to
- synonym of PRIVILEGED

rights [rʌɪts]

n.pl access to professionally administered resources
- the reason why professionals assert that rights can be owned, traded, defended, lost and so on is that part of their job is selling rights to those that the SYSTEM forces to be in desperate need of them

ritual [rɪtʃʊəl]

n a collective play of quality-creation or affirmation which honours the mysterious source of truth and, like tradition, marks a soft boundary of society or self

- the most degraded of the arts;[8] those rituals that remain are *spectacular* (supplying market commodities to deified CHILDREN, or embracing one another at an arbitrary clock-tick, or melding into the hive-mind of a mass sporting event, or watching actors get prizes from their artistic-business overlords) or are *bureaucratic* (receiving documentary proof of subservience to academia, visiting a bank to register a joint-mortgage, etc.) rather than *participatory*[9]
- antonym of SPECTACLE

romance [rəʊmans]

n & vb 1 boy meets girl 2 girl patents diamond-encrusted flame thrower 3 boy puts kestrel wings on his ears and tries to fly[wb]

rubicon [ruːbɪkən]

n the line or point at which you admit something which annoys you and turn to deal with it
- INTELLIGENT YAWP-TRUMPETS and SUPERAPT THUNDER-CUPBOARDS have extremely *low* rubicons
- also known as NEGATIVITY THRESHOLD

RITUAL

SMALL RITUAL (PLAY)

- thanking your legs, thanking your tools, thanking the farmer
- drawing little eyes on acorns, plug-sockets and pepper-pots
- improvised jamming with friends, solitary DANCING in the woods or tightly choreographed movements of many people, all incarnated to the tips of their fingers
- friendly, theatrical formality, passing the jam with outrageous grace and sensuality, richly enjoying the gentle lifting of a sleeping spoon from the boudoir of the drawer, and YUDO
- secretly purchasing a dragon suit, putting it on while your girlfriend is in the shower, then launching yourself therein
- mini-olympics on the green, association solar-flares in the forest, followed by *animal expert, it's Tuesday, death in a minute, pass the fork*, or any other light IMPRO game
- recording yourself singing a sublime 'yes please', overdubbing fifteen or sixteen harmonic variations then playing your recording, at ninety decibels, to an offer of cake

BIG RITUAL (FESTIVAL)

- taking ten-year-olds through some weird, physically demanding nature-based ordeal in order to allow them adult freedoms
- harvest festival that crosses catholic mass with Takeshi's castle [10]
- three day non-step festival of impro, with no sleep
- seven days of incubation in the depths of a chauvet cave
- gathering one hundred and twenty buddha-natured friends together in the woods and simulating death, or…
- re-enactment of the death of the whole world, in a sombre collective midnight chant through the streets, followed by…
- intimate communion with god, through canyon-filling collective song, mad, ecstatic dance and, possibly, peyote

Rituals (unlike playful, but more obviously goal-oriented, games and sports) cannot function without self-handicapping unstatus or with any kind of genetic competitive goal-getting or necessity.

S IS FOR
sorry
an empty
PROMISE

T IS FOR
time
a sexy
GODDESS

sacrifice [sakrɪfʌɪs]

n & vb to accept (apperceptively EXPERIENCE), serve or act regardless of EMOTIONS of suffering, anxiety, guilt, heart-break or *wanty-wanty-must-have* that, since they are caused by *not* accepting, then begins to dissipate like a busted cloud

· you cannot *get* sacrifice
· a prerequisite for the tenancy of MISS GENIUS; who then invites QWOTH, JOY and DRAGON-LEVEL GODGASMS to come and stay
· sacrifice *without* EGO is so effortless as to be invisible
· sacrifice *with* ego is fiendishly hard because HANGING ON LIKE GRIM DEATH and 'me' are synonymous

sallitude [salitjuːd]

n 1 the kind of happiness that enrages [i.e. provokes RABIA in] the insane 2 the kind of sanity that offends the UNHAPPY 3 the kind of not-having-anything-to do that infuriates the boss

salt [sɔːlt]

n a substance, idea, sound or emotion used to intensify flavour

· synonym of sugar, swearing, metaphor, melisma,

tell, imperfection, special effect, excitement, INTOXICANT, SHIT and MIND

· over-use of salt is the hallmark of insensitivity, and consequently of PORN and ADDICTION

sanifection [sanɪfɛkʃən]

n the *client–therapist* game; in which one partner (the 'client') habitually lies, or fakes, and the other player (the 'therapist') habitually accepts the lie, in order for both parties to communicate the implicit message; *'security and mutual dependency are more important to us than the uncertainty of the honesty we both secretly crave'*

satisfaction [satɪsfakʃən]

n either 1 a substitute for happiness purchased with self-hypnotism, consumption or the illusion of security that a rich country can afford to pay its middle class or 2 *ahhhhhhhhhhhhhhhh nice!*

scenius [siːnɪəs]

n 1 collective GENIUS[1] 2 collective [soft] consciousness, room-vibe or social vibe

· the source of genre, style, tradition and APOCALYPTIC WORLD-JOY

- demands [PLAYFUL] freedom [from necessity, from fear and from WORK]
- corrupted by MONEY
- synonym of COMMUNITAS
- antonym of GROUPTHINK / GROUPFEEL (for which it is constantly and deliberately confused by those terrified of MASS INTELLIGENCE)

scentate [sɛnteɪt]
   vb not being able to work out whether the problem comes from oneself, or whether it comes from the situation

- is your sadness the terrible truth and your happiness a mask, or is your happiness the profound reality of your life and your sadness just a selfish episode? Is your difficult relationship with your lover causing you to be unhappy, or is your unhappiness making the RELATIONSHIP difficult? Is it your train that is leaving the station, or another train you can see moving through the window?

schizoid [skɪtsɔɪd]
   adj descriptive of tight-focus EGOIC-CONSCIOUSNESS, turned permanently upon itself and finding nothing but objects—including its own 'subjective' thoughts and emotions—which, because they are without their originating, unifying, UN-SELFISH source, become A) derealised, fragmented (i.e. SPECIALISED) and fixed in a freakishly hyper-real (or hyper-awake) present and B) are experienced as having come either from elsewhere (a.k.a. paranoia; *'my thoughts are beamed into me from Titan'*) or solely from me (a.k.a. grandiosity; *'My thoughts control the moon!'*) [2]

- at the start of the SCHIZOID SPECTRUM is the early EGO; at the end is clinical schizophrenia; in the middle is the detached 'no-I' state of MYSTISHISM, MODERNISM and POST-MODERNISM, all of which display varying degrees of the same symptoms and attributes; distancing irony, passive hyper-focus, shallow absurdity (excessive interest in unexpected combinations),[3] existential instability, hyper-focus on details and, in the hardest, shallowest and most intense sense, *me*
- a.k.a. SELF-INFORMED
- antonym of GENIUS [4]
- *see* SELF

HOW TO INDOCTRINATE YOUR STUDENTS

C HILDREN ARE A POTENTIAL THREAT TO SOCIETY; firstly their free, ungovernable and creative INITIATIVE, and secondly their sensitive, mysterious and alarmingly direct EXPERIENCE. The task of neutralising these cardinal threats begins with the parent or carer (*see* BRAINWASHING) before being taken up by the teacher.

The first thing for a parent or teacher to do is to put their children in a SCHOOL—a mediated environment separate from community, culture, context, society and nature. This simple act of separation is enough to foster confusion, stifle enthusiasm, warp relations between children and make learning a curiously unreal experience. After this critical first step, stunting initiative and denying experience are relatively easy.

STUNTING INITIATIVE

The individual must be dependent on UNCIVILISATION for everything; for his food, shelter, security, knowledge, entertainment, health, transport and energy. The greatest threat to the WORLD, therefore, are people who can grow their own food, build their own houses, protect themselves, educate and entertain themselves, heal themselves, transport themselves around and generate their own energy. Independence, in short, must be utterly crushed.

Such independence is gained through *initiative*, which comes from an interest in or love for uncertainty, confusion and the unknown, into which children are happy to plunge, heedless of consequence. This is not something they learn, but an inborn ability which all uneducated children possess. From a maelstrom of chaotic data and continual failure the child can pick out faint patterns, casually discard ideas and strategies that do not work and blithely continue playing, or doing, undaunted by apparent failure.

Your job as a teacher is to destroy this heedless insouciance and make sure that children approach uncertainty and difficulty with extraordinary trepidation; recoiling, for good, at the slightest failure. They must be taught that the unknown is an intolerable, painful or humiliating experience, and that their instincts to dive into, and master the means to let genius play with it, are deviant, unreal or untrustworthy.

This is done by introducing something called 'learning' into the child's life. This is the belief that in order to *do* something it must first be broken up into a set of abstract laws and skills which the child must intellectually understand, remember and then 'apply'. This approach to reality is so alien to children, so confusing and painful, that they will soon recoil from vast swathes of experience with abhorrence.

'Learning' is combined with three other basic elements of student indoctrination; school, syllabus and teacher. Once children have been forced or tricked into a school, they are then constrained by the SYLLABUS—which has near total control over what they can do, and when and where they can do it—and the TEACHER, whose task is to place a group of children in one room, get them all to do one thing, and then, depending on the strategy the school / society wishes to take, either reward them with positive attention for producing the *right* answer (the competitive ORWELLIAN approach); or reward them with positive attention for producing *any* answer (the 'inclusive' HUXLEYAN approach). In the first case, if students cannot produce the right answer they are *wrong*, do not win any praise and are instilled with terror at the prospect of failure; and in the second case if they produce a wrong answer, or perform poorly, they are—*provided they are obedient*—rewarded and 'encouraged'—thus inculcated with total confusion about, and lack of interest in striving towards, quality.

In practice, these two approaches to teaching, like the concomitant ideologies of SCIENTISM and POST-MODERNISM, are combined, partly because it is difficult to reward a wrong answer in maths or a right one in the arts, but in both cases initiative, the desire to understand or do well for oneself without a need for [explicit orwellian or implicit huxleyan] threats or rewards, is effectively suffocated and the classroom 'experience', becomes so weird, stressful and artificial, that children will have nightmares about it for the rest of their lives.

DENYING EXPERIENCE

To subvert the child's experience, focus first, on the experience of other people, other authorities, external rules and imposed norms. This does not mean you cannot ask children what they think, or permit them to 'express themselves'; in fact this is to be encouraged in a liberal, huxleyan society as it gives an illusion of child autonomy, while, actually, confirming nothing more than the opinions of the child's peers, parents, celebrity heroes or managers of consumption.

After limiting the child's understanding of truth you should go on to curtail its experience of sensory reality. Anything more real than a limited band of ideas, emotions, passive virtual sensations and competitive sports must be excluded from the classroom. Intoxicants, solitude, ecstatic art, quality, death, madness, birth, love, beauty, silence, free meaningful creation, sex, practical CRAFTS, and direct experience of nature are all banned from school. Students and teachers can talk about these things, but they cannot experience them. Children are not allowed to do nothing, be completely alone, see or touch dead bodies, shape their own surroundings, ride horses, farm, light fires or live directly in the wild. Nature must only ever be experienced in the form of passive and sanitised entertainment; ideally film, or, if necessary, the odd carefully structured holiday. Again, you the teacher do not have to do anything to make sure this happens. Being in school is enough to isolate children from active social or natural reality.

It is particularly important that your students hyper-SPECIALISE. The more they involve themselves in a broad range of different subjects—especially abstract study together with practical action—the more they will start to ask themselves what different things have in common and begin to seek out that most extreme and subversive of states; connected sensory experience, or COMMON SENSE, which must be avoided at all costs. Such an interest in the big picture could end up with healers concerning themselves with architecture, carpenters investigating the origin of property or otherwise productive engineers wasting years of their lives staring at dandelions.

UNIVERSITY

Professionals are not told what to do, and so, although they must be clever, energetic and novel thinkers, it must be within strict ideological limits. The most important component of professional university courses therefore is on rewarding ideological subservience. This does not mean adopting a particular (orwellian) ideology, but a particular ideological *discipline*. The 'successful' students are the ones who check out faculty attitudes so they can mimic them, who subordinate their own beliefs to an assigned ideology (whatever it may be), who are happy with being vaguely criticised without being provided the tools they need to correct their own efforts and who subject the focus of their attention to fundamentally obedient styles of work. It cannot be stressed enough that the content of the work can—indeed should—be as radical as you like—it is in the way one is forced to approach the work that the professional student is systematically conditioned.

In sum, ideological discipline must go much deeper than mere toadying—or the status of the teacher as 'objective' and of 'not taking sides' would come under critical scrutiny—so the ideology of the university must be built into the syllabus, which must have no reference to moral, ethic or aesthetic truth and, above all, in the structure of EXAMS, which must:

- be separate from context (lots of tiny little problems to solve, narrowly focused themes to consider and abstract ideas to comment on.)
- involve intense time pressure or monotony, both of which will reduce critical awareness and creativity
- focus on other people's concerns and interests
- contain lots of *tricks* to answer (esp. important in maths and physics exams—which reward memorisers over those with creative or reflective skills)
- demand the retention of huge amounts of information (and thus negation of life for years of revision and isolated study)
- demand unquestioned acceptance of given assumptions (e.g. that a normal approach to nature is domination)
- be, like LAW, ultimately irrelevant if you are PRIVILEGED [5]

school [skuːl]

n & vb 1 proto-PRISON that protects adults — those who have learnt how to do what they don't want to do over and over again — from children — those still SENSITIVE and INTELLIGENT enough to find such anti-experience torture 2 an enforced stay in the company of teachers, which pays off in the doubtful privilege of more such company [6] 3 alienated, contextless and perpetually examined WORK carried out for an extended period of time in order to stunt initiative, punish independence, deny experience, standardise thought and behaviour, instil an acceptance of and reliance on INSTITUTIONS, create the illusion that opportunities are scarce and that 'scarce resources' can only be acquired through a middle-man, create needs, force obedience to authority (an ORWELLIAN dictator, a HUXLEYAN profile, a KAFKAESQUE syllabus or a PHIL-DICKIAN manufactured reality), postpone the entry of workers into an overstuffed labour market, forcing them to accrue debts which can only be alleviated by WORK (i.e. in the MARKET) and to *sit still* 4 a place where one first fights to get to the top of the EROTIC LEAGUE TABLE, and where losers first start searching for substitutes

- GRADE [greɪd] *n* gatekeeping device used to incentivise compliance and generate MARKET-friendly depressive-competitive disorder
- leads to UNIVERSITY
- antonym of LEARNING and DOING [7]

science, scientism [skɪzəm]

n either 1 traditional method of perceiving, understanding and acquiring the timespace craft of life (SCIENCE) OR 2 personification of the egoic opinions of professors x, y and z (SCIENTISM) [8]

- scientism supports and is in turn vigorously supported by the SYSTEM, which A) ceaselessly broadcasts its orthodoxy and B) awards good jobs, promotions and career-making grants to its cleverest and most enthusiastic proponents
- GENIUS without the craft of science is either A) LOVE B) free, childlike RITUAL or PLAY C) mere talent or D) nothing but a good idea
- synonym of RELIGION

- what science is good for:
- KNOWLEDGE · science investigates and reveals the *structure* (the *form*) of life, thought, what is happening in the formal, factual world (of the SELF) and, through abstract-oriented philosophy, colours in the landscape of the possible
- CRAFT · the scientific method is the source of the technical power to create form; all that is great in art and society requires mastery of some kind of science
- STUFF · bags, ball-bearings, pianos, tinned tomatoes, anaesthetic or any other object or system that serves man (within UTP)
- BULLSHIT-BUSTING · science is sometimes the only apt antidote to the lies of mystishism, post-modernism, economics and many cosy emotional insanities
- what science is absolutely no good for:
- UNSELF · TRUTH, LOVE and LOVE-MAKING, the deep REALITY of NATURE, DEATH, the essence of SELF-MASTERY, the depths of VIBE, SOFT-CONSCIOUSNESS, profound certainty, timeless ART or STORY and dancing in a rhythmic brainstorm

scoffon [skɒfɒn]
vb & n 1 to dismiss a thrilling or liberating viewpoint (as unrealistic, pretentious, hippy, etc.) because its proponent doesn't have a family, a mortgage or decades of GRINDING UNHAPPINESS behind them 2 to dismiss a critique of uncivilisation—its professions, cars, money or high-tech—as A) 'angry' or B) 'hypocritical' because its proponent is A) revolted by the horror of the world or B) has been seen to go to the dentist or use computers 3 to dismiss serious talk of UTOPIA as 'utopian'

scondle [skɒndəl]
n & vb a desperate plea for advice or reassurance masquerading as an innocent 'random' question

sconk, ponk [skɒŋk]
n & vb a round pea of good luck that emerges from the belly-button and invites you to pluck it[9]
- you cannot walk with improvised GENIUS, through the world behind the world, without gentle, feral, alacrity and a warrior's ruddy gumption to pluck, unhesitatingly, le ponk

THE SCIENTIFIC SELF

1. ISOLATION: of TIMESPACE objects from context. This is the activity of HARD-CONSCIOUSNESS; the concentrated, focusing, excluding and dividing mode of awareness used to perceive, or pick out, separate bits and isolated things from amongst the bewildering blended totality of what is going on. Stage 1 occurs in the [hard or PROBED] self. It precedes what is known as 'the rational mind', and also preceded, in pre-history, what is commonly understood as the scientific method.

2. REPRESENTATION: the creation of mental REPRESENTATIONS of time-space and of the objects it appears to contain; facts, measurements, symbols and ideas. If the scientist is mediocre these representations will be exclusively those received, or assumed, from the rigid, specialised, TRADITION (sometimes called PARADIGM) in which he works. If though he is at all animated by [pre-stage 1] GENIUS, these ideas will come from other domains or experiences; in other words they will be metaphors which carry science to genuinely new places. Stage 2, part of the rational mind, is proto-science (and proto-history); also undertaken at diverse places and times.

3. RELATION: the systematic relating of these representations with each other ('theories') and the testing of these theories against fact (through experiment) to verify their accuracy. Stage 3 is that part of the process normally called science; the method of systematic observation, measurement, and experiment invented by the ancient Greeks[10] — bless 'em — advanced in the Islamic golden-age, picked up by Western Europeans in the late medieval period and then perfected in the [so-called] European 'enlightenment'.

Although only stage 3 bears the name science, the scientific method is founded on a more fundamental human capacity; the [stage 1] creation of divided up time-space and the subsequent [stage 2] ability to think about these divisions. But when the self is soft, when there is a mind-silent 'witnessing I' experiencing timespace, it becomes *unscientifically* obvious that reality, although experienceable is not, ultimately, mind-knowable or divided; that timespace is, *ultimately*, a creation of mind. This does not mean that time and space are *inventions* of the mind; there has to be something in reality that is timespace, or our thought and language would be gibberish. But *at the same time* (i.e. PARADOXICALLY) there is also something in reality which is not timespace, which the consciousness which precedes the timespace-making self mutely RECOGNISES.

This preceding consciousness, along with the timeless reality it recognises, is unknowable to science, because it can *never* be detected by hard consciousness, or rationally proved or disproved. The rational mind can never literally understand or represent that which precedes itself, or that which is softly conscious *of* its own divisions, representations and relations — any more than a map can literally *be* the terrain it represents. This means that science can never know how timespace began (because science *is* timespace), nor how life evolved from so-called 'inorganic matter' (because scientific knowledge *is* an inorganic representation), nor what soft-consciousness, or truth, really is (because the hard-conscious facts of science are not the truth; they are perceived *by* the truth). All that science can know are the timespace objects that it scrutinises.[11]

None of this is a problem. Science is a tool, and sane people do not expect a hammer to dance. Those who do are followers of the RELIGION of SCIENTISM, which arises from the self-informed-self's inability to still itself and be [softly] conscious of its own operations. Such a self is inevitably committed to using the self to solve the problems of self. This FUTILITY manifests emotionally as permanent, restless fear and desire, and mentally as obsessive worrying, thinking and [modern] MANAGEMENT and PROFESSIONALISM; all of which express the same message; submit to mind, machine and system.

Scientism, therefore, is egotism and ignores, ridicules or attacks the same reality as all egoists — both rational or irrational — fear; UNSELF, which it is inherently unable to recognise.

second impression [daʊt]

n.phr the fluffing agitation, shed-jawed torpor or delayed distracted entry into the present that causes you to break things, forget them, miss crucial clues, fall back on old routines, PRY, GUCK, SWELK, skuff shots, let slip gaffes, miss opportunities, accidentally invite vampyres in and misplace the entire universe behind a particle of KIPPLE

- often leads to A) SORRY and B) the AVAILABILITY ERROR [əveɪləbɪlɪti ɛrə] *vb* the tendency to choose the most obvious, the first or most insistent thought, emotion or limited perception that comes to one's awareness; rather than to perceive and respond to the WHOLE of what is actually happening
- caused by EGO; a.k.a. THE UNCONSCIOUS AUTOPILOT
- antonym of FIRST IMPRESSION

secretist [siːkrɪtɪst]

n one of two kind of dealers in secrets; A) THE HOARDER, who enjoys the long thrill of power B) THE BLURTER, who prefers the quick thrill of *'ooh, really?'* attention

- a.k.a. HIDEMONGER

see [siː]

vb to pull back from habitual looking *for* (picking out one isolated thing after another in the world) and instead, like a kind of easeful swede, witnessing *as*

self [sɛlf]

n antonym and synonym of UNSELF

self-mastery [sɛlfmɑːstəri]

n.phr the overcoming of me, by not-me, with my help

- antonym of SELF-CONTROL [sɛlf kəntrəʊl] *vb* one part of the self—idea or emotion—controlling the rest; leads to effort and suppression

self-shidder [sɛlfʃɪdə]

n.phr not being able to understand what one's earlier self was up to at *all*

self-slagia [sɛlf-slaldʒə]

n.phr surprise and admiration for one's earlier self

- *Brigitte smiled with gentle self-slagia while she read the letter she had sent, five years before, to her ex-husband*

self-swendle [sɛlf-swɛndəl]

n.phr gentle forgiveness for the silliness of one's earlier self

THE HISTORY OF SELF

THE RISE OF EGO

SELF CAN BE DESCRIBED as a mechanism (or tool) which uses calorific power to animate an *organic* apparatus (comprised of interrelated parts) which is capable of A) manifesting reality as sensations and feelings B) structuring reality into spacetime things and ideas and C) manipulating these things and ideas. Everything I physically sense (*matter*), inwardly feel (*vibe*), think (*mind*), and my motivating *energy*, occurs in, or as, the extraordinary machine[12] of self.

Although, to civilised, historical man, this means I am trapped in a me-shaped prison—with no way of knowing what is beyond self, and so what anything or anyone really is—for most of human history it was implicitly clear to men and women that the unselfish *consciousness of self* is not limited in the same way as self is; is not mechanical, divided into parts, describable or limited by spacetime. For most of history the awareness of my thoughts and perceptions provided a mysterious (and pleasant) experience of what the apparent subjects and objects of my experience refer to; a reality out there that, somehow, ultimately (or PANJECTIVELY), I am, in here.

Around twelve to fifteen thousand years ago this mysterious experience began to slip away from mankind as *self took control*. As with the growth or development of any other tool (or system), self has a utility tipping point (UTP), beyond which it begins to A) use more energy and information than it gives and B) take on autonomous (self-governing) functions. When self grew beyond a certain level of sophistication (when man began indirectly thinking and emoting more than directly experiencing) self began to take control of [soft] consciousness, and began to call itself 'I'. Self slowly became EGO and the genuine experience of reality slipped into fantasy.

Previous to this FALL I experienced what self is not; an intimate (which is to say, EMPATHIC) union with a mysterious, generative and intensely felt reality. Women, having softer and more fluid selves than men, had greater access to this reality and so were considered more whole, mysterious and (more obviously) productive than men. Likewise reality itself was considered to be feminine. Men and women did not worship 'a female god', but conceived of the vast, fecund, productive mystery of life as feminine; they were GYNOTHEISTS and expressed their love for this reality in terms of a man's manifest [priapic] love for the female form, or vagina; symbols for both of which litter the early anthropological record.[13]

Man, having a harder, stronger self, was more cut off from life. Just as male art (and the male West) is characterised by a certain abstraction, HEROIC NARRATIVE, culminating payoff and reconciliation with the void, so male experience has always involved a sense of aspiration and need to undergo trials in order to journey back to a supple intelligence and maturity that woman is, along with her eggs, already born with. This isn't to say that women do not develop themselves or achieve things, but that this aspect of self is (or was) for women, less fundamental. It was not she who developed her self-tool beyond her capacity to control it, who left reality and journeyed into history in an attempt to find it again; it was he. Man fell and dragged woman down with him.

This he did partly through aspiration (or wanting), but mainly out of fear. Although pre-fallen man was surrounded by mystery, he DIRECTLY EXPERIENCED phenomena with his own mysterious consciousness, and so was not intrinsically threatened by what he could not emotionally dominate or intellectually understand. After the fall however, ego became afraid of anything in experience which was mysterious to or ungraspable by self (or UNSELFISH); such as death, darkness, loss, paradox, the wisdom of women,[14] the innocence of children, the difference of outsiders and the thoughtless presence of the wild, all of which became a threat. The extraordinary life that I once perceived in and behind all matter (which I gave fluid NAME to) became ordinary supernatural 'gods' (with fixed and superstitiously venerated names), which 'I' had to appease through gifts and sacrifices; and all the threats 'I' now found itself surrounded with had to be manipulated, controlled or vanquished.[15]

The growth of the timespace self provided some technological advantages, particularly for those early civilisations that managed to keep it mastered, but its most conspicuous effect, other than resource depletion and agriculture,[16] was the creation of ANDROTHEIST (the worship of maleness), stratified, concentrated, warlike tribes (proto-Aryans and Semites) which began overrunning the world, overturning its primal cultures (introducing into local myths heroic male gods, or the monotheist God, which defeated and vanquished female 'devils'[17]), corrupting and subjugating its people and forming class-based cults and, eventually, technologically-advanced uncivilisations (esp. the literate—virtual—Egyptian, Semite, Chinese and Greek megacults) which slowly spread over the surface of the earth.[18]

After several thousand years of the growth of ego, direct conscious experience of reality was so rare[19] and attenuated that a group of unconscious abstract philosophers in uncivilised ancient Greece (mainly the nature-, art-, body-, society and children-hating Socrates, Plato and Aristotle) began to wonder what reality really was, or what the matter was that their [self] perceptions referred to (*see* PHILOSOPHY).[20]

For a thousand years or so the problem of matter and reality was largely ignored—or rather assumed to have been solved by MONOTHEISM which preferred bizarre scholastic debates over philosophy—before it resurfaced in the so-called 'enlightened' thought of seventeenth century Europe and the arrival of René Descartes, the first MODERN ego to begin philosophically investigating experience. Descartes, the father of SCHIZOID MODERNISM, concluded that self is just THOUGHT, isolated from an objective spacetime reality which comes to self via the medium of abstract ideas. After Descartes, Emmanuel Kant concluded that spacetime itself—which is to say, the entire knowable universe—is formed (although not invented) by my self, which means that the self-mechanism can *never* know what is really happening 'out there'—what anything is 'in itself'. All it can ever know is its own time and space. True knowledge of the real is ruled out by self's inability to directly experience it, or, consequently, communicate it. Although we may tell ourselves otherwise, speech, really, is nothing more than waving placards around hoping, with a growing sense of futility, that, if there really are other people out there, they can correctly interpret our desperate, lonely, gestures.

It is not just our inability to experience what anything really is that is insoluble to the self-informed-self, but why I am here, what death is, what I should do, if there is a god, how I can create beauty, who you are, what consciousness is, what distinguishes humans from animals, how the universe began, what time is, how I can be more creative, less addicted, more spontaneous, less anxious, and every other meaningful (which is to say ultimately unscientific) Q-QUESTION about what is beyond self. If the self-machine is questioning itself about what is beyond itself—or where self come comes from—no answer it finds, ultimately, is ever going to make sense; and if the self-machine is operating itself no solution, ultimately, is ever going to work; because everything that I say, see, feel and do is, ultimately, motivated by an inapt selfish [genetic–mental–emotional[21]] impulse. Ultimately, the only message a machine can give itself—that can make sense to a machine that creates its own programming, or attempts to understand itself with itself—is 'expand, defend and avoid death'.[22] *Forever.*

THE FUNCTIONING OF EGO

An increase of one part of self means a decrease in another; more energy and attention given to the operation of the brain (for example) means less energy and attention given to the muscles of the body, increased perception in one sense, or faculty, means a decrease in the acuity or sensitivity of the others. This trade-off leads to different selves having different specialities and weaknesses. Although all selves are fundamentally the same, just as all trees are fundamentally the same, each self, having a different arrangement of elements, is also unique, with its own particular SWELLS (sensitivities and strengths) and STUNTS (insensitivities and weaknesses). It is also, like a tree, alive; passing through birth, growth, fructification, senescence and death.[23]

If the life of self is determined by [a part of] the self, it will necessarily direct its attention towards itself—which means towards what it wants, thinks, likes and feels—and away from unself—away from what it does not like, does not want, does not feel and does not (or cannot) think. To the self-informed ego, what I like, want, feel and think are what I am; which must be experienced, expanded and defended. The selfish self must, like the cancer cells it generates, refuse senescence and ceaselessly grow. No other action is conceivable to the self-informed-self but pure self-ADDICTION.

Addiction (or hyper-self-SPECIALISM) can be *physical* (narcotics, over-eating, SALT, loud noise, aestheticism and sex), *mental* (worry, chatter, gossip, theorising, over-thinking, perfectionist ideals, GROUPTHINK and sex), *emotional* (complaint, excitement, drama, attention-seeking, affection, argument, needing to be right, adrenaline, violence, GROUPFEEL, care, mystishism, CHARITY and sex) or *energetic* (blind acquisition, over-work, over-exercise, excessive travel, fidgeting and sex). Which particular configuration and flavour of addiction one is susceptible to depends on one's particular swells and stunts (although sex is usually, somehow, involved).[24]

When ego is forced, by circumstance, to experience aspects of reality that negatively correlate to its swells—when, in other words, it is pushed into contact with the 'I am not', the 'I don't like', the 'I don't believe' and the 'I don't know' MARKERS (acquired through childhood BRAINWASHING) that form the boundary of its self-defined comfort zone—the result is emotional discomfort; first of all boredom (or superficial interest), then [dismissive] irritation or confusion, then agitation, depression and open scorn, before, finally, anger, hatred, insanity, chronic depression or psychotic violence. All of these negative emotions are expressions of ego's primary fear of what it is not, of those particular experiences which represent the polar opposite, or diminution, of one's particular, personal, ego-addiction.[25]

The most intense negative emotions do not come from particular ego-fears however, but from the fundamental existential threat to ego posed by UNSELF; what self is not and can never be; what it cannot imagine, grasp, isolate or control. Ego is inherently threatened by and resistant to silence, darkness, death, mystery, mysticism, Q-force, temenos, the meaning of any Q-word, the intelligence of loving women, the innocence of uncorrupted children, the mystery of the wild, the context, and any meaningful contact with soft consciousness.

The problem for ego is that this, the threat of unself, is literally everywhere and nowhere. The space that surrounds ego, the profound reality of the objects it experiences, the conscious light in the eyes of others, the nature of the body and, most intimately and terribly of all, my own soft consciousness, follow ego even unto DREAM—and yet can never be grasped by it. This engenders a *permanent* feeling of primal fear, a constant background restlessness, anxiety, insecurity, worry, irritation, emptiness, indecision or boredom which—if self softens, if unself gets too close, or if ego's growth-through-addiction slackens—blows up into dread, violence, depression, horror or chronic psychosis.

Ego deals with the threat of its underlying feelings of anxiety the only way it knows how to deal with any problem; with ego; with concentrated, selfish thought, effort and emotion. This perpetual mental–emotional focus DIGITISES [degrades the fractality of] hyper-subtle experience (especially vibe), abstracts reality, OSTAVISES context-signifying Q-WORDS, limits awareness to isolated spacetime objects, representations and emotions, hardens self (making it less sensitive, empathic and aware), corrupts character into caricature[26] (PERSONALITY), and replaces paradoxical reality with a mind-emotion-made simulacrum; a bewildering, threatening, yet plausible timespace dream which the self takes to be waking life.

In this mental–emotional self-dream everything is comprehensible, and therefore seemingly capable of being measured, possessed and controlled; but, for self, forever elusive. When ego possesses[27] freedom it finds its new prize is now bound and not worth having, when it grasps understanding of life it finds it is staring at death and when it thinks it has its body, its wife, its children or its lawn under control, they rise up and brush ego (and ego's world) off the face of the earth.

The self, by itself, has *no way* of effectively dealing with these, or any other fundamental problems of existence (i.e. EXISTENTIAL CRISES). It can only understand what its own self-informed swells report, and so lacks any discernment of the cause of or solution to its suffering. With nothing but its own intelligence, fears and desires—its own self—to guide it, it is forced to swing between optimism and pessimism, mania and depression, subjectivity and objectivity, 'I'm the problem' and 'you're the problem', happiness and unhappiness, feeling special and feeling worthless, acting and accepting, staying and leaving and every other false (SCENTATED) antonym.

All self knows how to do is swap one addiction for another through SELF-ADJUSTMENT, suppress its emotional unhappiness with SELF-CONTROL, work towards abstract futures through SELF-IMPROVEMENT, ponder its own fabulous qualities and achievements with SELF-LOVE, masturbate over its problems with SELF-PITY, pump itself up with SELF-RESPECT, impose its will on the world through SELF-ASSERTION, lose itself in SELF-ABSORPTION, or paper over its mediocrity, dependence and insensitivity with SELF-PROMOTION and, that most fashionable of psychological red-herrings, SELF-BELIEF.

Although the details vary from person to person and although the growth of ego is uneven—with a powerful hold over consciousness in some situations and weaker hold in others—the culminating state is the same; consciousness is cut-off from the unself-context and unable to perceive any experience beyond self; unable to perceive any meaning which can be shared or any intelligence but its own will to focus more and more tightly upon itself, until hard-consciousness becomes frozen in an internal world of petrified *bits*, without even the timespace of the mind to structure it; a perfectly present, perfectly detached, prison of self. Although there are as many kinds of insanities as there are kinds of [extreme] ego—some fuelled by hysterical energy, some sunk in the sludge of depression and most mingled or alternating with the authentic I—all insanity is either a subset of, or reaction to this tendency of the self-informed-self towards total, isolated self-absorption, or SCHIZOPHRENIA.

THE RISE OF THE WORLD

Ego first arose in the Middle East and West Asia,[28] where, a few millennia later, it formed the first uncivilised megacults of Mesopotamia (the Semites) and Indo-Iran (the Indo-Aryans). From here it expanded east to India and China, south, via the Bantus, into Africa, and west to Graeco-Rome, which ceded to the Islamic Caliphate, which ceded (via the Mongols) to Europe, which swallowed the world before ceding to the US and, finally, the modern corp-world and its executive states.

The individual differences and brutal antagonisms of these various pre-modern cults—their peripheral styles and marvellous achievements and their enormously complex histories—tend to mask their shared motivating and modernising intelligence; the ego of their members. Ego has not only had the same ends since the dawn of history—expand (through conflict and subjugation), experience self (through addictive stimulation) and control or annihilate unselfish reality—but it has used the same means to achieve them; a body of virtual-technical knowledge which has been passed on, appropriated, refined and developed by each succeeding (or concurrent) cult (*see* VIRTUAL).

These TECHNIQUES—used to eradicate or control unself (nature, innocence, pain, etc.) and to expand self (through unlimited access to stimulation)—are SCIENTIFIC; which is to say they make reality MANAGEABLY virtual through tight-focus isolation of objects, or from ripping things and ideas from their originating context, which can then be converted into abstractions (such as slaves from communities, natural resources from forests, scientific facts from 'noise', and bureaucratic facts, LAWS and ECONOMIC MONEY-units from society) which are predictable, immune to decay and uncertainty, which can be stored indefinitely, reproduced perfectly, controlled at will and, most importantly, possessed.

The conversion of the universe into an abstract body of controllable, possessable data further requires the interdependent techniques of mechanisation, social-control, coercion, emotional management, urban-planning, opinion-shaping and the threat of violence, which were all refined into their modern form at the same time as philosophy was; around the 17th century, when institutions, serving a totalitarian system, began to take over the role of reality-management from crude, overtly violent and inefficient priestly or royal authority.

The new methods of social-control focused not on disciplining the body, on hiding criminals away or on physically forcing populations to submit, but on controlling the psyche through propaganda, through BUREAUCRATIC surveillance, through the *threat* of deprivation and through powerful appeals to egoic fears and addictions. This was not achieved through the conscious efforts of Machiavellian princes, but through schools, prisons, hospitals, barracks, factories and organs of mass-media which A) were unconsciously structured to select for obedience and submission B) separated individuals from the world C) exposed them to perpetual bureaucratic scrutiny, D) demanded an intense degree of abstraction and rational planning E) divided institutional identity from inner consciousness (and made them mutually antagonistic) F) placed enormous constraints on speech, thought, movement and feeling G) continually stimulated ego through (positive and negative) addictive pornography[29] H) disciplined members to a life of permanent work and never-ending institutional-slavery and I) through taboo and the degradation of Q-words, made it impossible to understand what was happening or directly express dissent without sounding like a nutcase (*see* SYSTEM).

The effect of turning everyone on earth into an isolated, pressurised, examined and assessed mass of observed facts, of suppressing their spontaneity, generosity and initiative, of depriving them of meaningful, natural, communal, physical experience, of continually stimulating their fears and desires, of attenuating their conscious experience to the thinnest virtual stream of abstraction and of never admitting that any of this is happening is, eventually, to make it impossible for anyone, anywhere, to *escape themselves;* to experience what is not self. It is to create, in other words, a global virtual prison of sick, violent, unstable, lonely, confused, touch-starved, anxious, addicted and depressed schizophrenics.[30]

SELF-MASTERY

ELF-MASTERY IS THE ERADICATION OF EGO (or of self-*as*-master), through softening of attention (also known as sensitivity-enhancement) and spontaneous apt-action, until self is in its place; back on the tool-shelf where it belongs. This does not mean, of course, that I have no sense of self—no fear, no thought, no body, no desire—but that I experience, or can call on, an encompassing unself-consciousness that precedes self; and so can act despite 'my' fears, pains, doubts and addictions.[31] There is no other skill as valuable, or as *practical*, as this. All anxiety, boredom, suffering, shame, doubt, confusion, anger and even clumsiness and bad luck are caused by a self that won't fade back into the void of the context.

The discipline of self-mastery is comprised of two components; consciousness-softening and conscious action.

CONSCIOUSNESS SOFTENING

Consciousness softening—a.k.a. EMPATHY-ENHANCEMENT, AWARENESS-WIDENING, APPERCEPTION PRACTICE and UNSELF-ING—is the practice of letting go of self by letting THOUGHTS and EMOTIONS dissolve into soft-conscious union with the CONTEXT, via the nearest thing in existence to the context; the BODY. This is achieved by continually placing attention on the whole self (as opposed to being unconsciously lost in isolated mental–emotional parts) and then slowing that attention down until a void opens up between the thoughts, pains, emotions and other spacetime objects of thinking–emoting self.

In this conscious experience of 'nothing-to-me' (sometimes referred to as stillness or 'the space between thoughts') the ordinary mental–emotional experience of spacetime—of me here experiencing that there—begins to dissolve, and with it, the agitated dominance of ego.

There are two complimentary methods of consciousness softening; HOME *(a.k.a. the degraded Q-word meditation) and, much more usefully,* AWAY *(a.k.a. the equally degraded Q-word mindfulness)*

SOFTENING SELF AT HOME

- Sit comfortably, but upright (not slouching or reclining).
- Take a few extremely slow diaphragmatic breaths into the solar plexus (i.e. by filling the belly, not by raising the ribs).
- APPERCEPTIVELY experience the inner buzz or subtle grainy feeling of life in the entire body (by very slowly moving attention around the body)...
- ...being light and normal about it though—slight smile at the corner of the lips and around the eyes—not all deep and important and *ohmmmm*.
- Feeling where there is emotion (tension, hardness, heaviness or bored restlessness) and feeling the present, pleasant space around the emotion.
- Let the emotion slowly... slowly... *slowly*... seep down into the empty fire of the BELLYMIND. This is not an imaginative exercise, but an inner releasing.
- Watching thoughts, without judgement, as they babble and kipple on the screen of the mind (especially thoughts like *'I can't do this'*, *'this is boring'*, *'I've failed'* or the all-time classic, *'I've done it!'*). This is not 'me' experiencing the present moment—because 'me' is what I am watching. This is the present moment experiencing me.
- Then, letting go completely, and allowing the conscious, witnessing I to slip down into THE BIG BLACK WELL.[32]

BLOWING SELF AWAY [33]

- Pull back from habitually focused STARING and experience (SEE) the whole panorama before you, the whole experience of the light (sound, smell, etc.) of whatever situation you are in.
- Apperceptively feel the proprioceptive quality of your gait as you walk, and the sensation in and about your whole body; become more aware of your posture and your breathing.
- Put your friendly attention on things that reduce ego and thought (that make you neither want nor not-want), such as the sky, silence, birdsong, the ordinary light in the room, the space between things and the cold, white fire of the bellymind.

- Place soft-consciousness upon your fidgeting (leg-jiggling, smoking, snack-grazing, porning, news-reading or obsessive mail-and-media checking). Trying to overcome such habits is megafutile; they are the product of unconscious restlessness and *eventually* fall away by themselves when softly perceived.
- See how no situation is so terrible that some part of you cannot find it interesting, funny or, in some strange way, softly right.
- Watch your body act, your mouth speak, your mind think; see that in such watching there is no need to decide what to do. It all happens by itself. The body knows.
- Let go of (i.e. refuse to dwell on) failure (stupid comments, lack of presence, stumbles, gaffs, moods and angers) instantly admit [to yourself and others] your fluffs, awkwardnesses and conceits, and don't justify them (*see* FENK and IMPRO)
- Constantly feel [and express] gratitude; for your roof, toast, functioning lungs, warm companion, hot water, lack of work (if you've escaped), capacity to enjoy or whatever other conditional freedom and ease you happen to temporarily enjoy.
- Ask yourself who it is that sees, thinks or feels this and experience the hyper-subtle sense of youness, that you've had all your life, that precedes an answer.
- Use the world to defeat the ego; walk without allowing prying egoic attention to unconsciously latch onto porn-verts, or onto shiny-shiny, or onto fertile sexual forms in the street, or onto mindless gossip and gassing.
- Pay soft, silent, absorbed attention to extreme subtlety, such as can be found in the vibe, tone and muscular peculiarity of others, in fields of artistic or natural beauty you have never explored (i.e. in an expanded TASTE-MATRIX), in the particular character of animals, the particular feel of places and objects and the particular vibe of times of the day and year.
- See that your ego thinks, doubts, masturbates, moans, uselessly plots and plans (i.e. with no intention of acting), justifies itself, rises up in CRAUNCH when criticised, when excited about getting something, when anxious in a new situation, when faced with thwarted expectation or with no praise for a good job, and, through this seeing, and through placing awareness in the silent bellymind, either allow it to fall away, or act...

Softer consciousness eventually leads to a greater sensitivity to the context, to beauty, joy, creativity and, crucially, to PAIN; the voice of CONSCIENCE. For the insensitive, unable to detect the early stages of conscience, or afraid to do anything about it, pain is an enemy that, under temporary smotherings of narco-fun, grows and grows until it erupts in appalling suffering. For the wise, pain is a master, the horror of which is copped and the first tiny (painless!) twinge of which is instantly OBEYED, no matter what *'don't like / don't want / don't believe'* no-entry MARKERS it prompts them to pass through.

Through leaving comfort zones, through sordid failures and self-exposures, through knuckling downs and never giving up, through tearing it all up and starting all over again—in short, through making enormous, ludicrous, shameful mistakes and learning from them—it is possible to learn the supreme art of conscious action (a.k.a. SPONTANEITY, NOBILITY and SHLAARG–MAKWANG HOOSH FE'TARP).

CONSCIOUS ACTION

Conscious action depends on the context, which tends to press on the swollen addictions of the individual self. For feckless, overly romantic, adventurous types the context is likely to demand getting a job, knuckling down and staying with one's partner through thick and thin. For dependable doormats and the middle-class security-cocooned, the context is more likely to demand leaving work and walking away from one's family. For sensuous, sleepy types true conscience tends to demand exercise and action, while for the mobile and wired, it asks for idle peace. The young are asked by the context to step forth, the old to step back. What many of the context-prompts of true-conscious have in common is that they eventually cause the true self to come into conflict with the egoic SYSTEM. It is impossible, in other words, to master the self—lead it into the ever more sensitive and empathic unknown—without, at the same time, striving to overcome the restraints or radically help the victims of the WORLD. Conscious action, therefore, is nearly always synonymous with deep SUBVERSION.

FIRST OF ALL *the context puts pressure on to the addictive swells and anxious stunts of the individual self. Such demands have particular, circumstantial variations, but they apply to everyone, putting ceaseless or repeated pressure on all selves to:*

- Face death without imagination or excitement; talk to loved ones about their inevitable death, look at or handle dead bodies, spend time in graveyards, consider your own death and be ready to die (*see* DEATH).
- Be honest in love, be honest with your partner about your anxiety, be repeatedly honest about how much you love them and MAKE LOVE every day.
- Master crafts, especially those that do not rely on perfecting high-tech (post UTP) tools. Do real things, with real things; learn practical skills, work with stuff.
- Work, but without expectation of reward; give up work (as much as you *possibly* can), give up career and institutional ambition; seek huge swathes of unstructured free time.
- Stop deciding. Just choicelessly do what you prefer.
- Raise your expectations of what your life could be to their most fantastic pitch and then ORIENT towards *that*.
- Start something new, go somewhere else, be a beginner…
- …or knuckle down and accept what is, without complaining.
- Believe nothing, including this.
- Forgive those who have wronged you, even as you stand up to—or walk out on—them.
- Cross taste-matrix class-boundaries, on a rocket.
- Act despite fear, pain, doubt and can't-be-botheredness.
- Learn IMPRO. Be a FOOL out there.
- Subvert the system in reckless, creative, amoral abandon.
- Stop looking for the source of satisfaction in fame, money, stuff, power, cult-membership, emotion, knowledge, any kind of addiction, holiness, enlightenment or romantic love.
- See—but don't think over—every negative emotion; and see the attachment or futile wanting that is feeding it. See how the selfish self always calls things good because it wants them, while CONSCIENCE wants things because they are good.
- Live in nature, away from society, if only for a year or two.

- Stop going over the past (telling your *terribly* sad story) and dispense with those that feed it.
- Breathe deeply, and enjoy it. Relax the back of the head.
- Learn to *adore* solitude, [inner] silence, space, darkness and, minute-by-minute, YINYIN (or GOD).
- EXSUPERATE out of comfort-zones and comfort-selves.
- Take massive quantities of hallucinogenic mushrooms and enjoy an explosive fountain of screaming bellowing orgasms in a forest thunderstorm, during a solar eclipse.
- Face the coming COLLAPSE; which means seeing that the world is always ending; now (*see* UTOPIA).
- Convert RELATIONSHIP into PARTNERSHIP.

SECOND OF ALL *context-promptings have a tendency to press on the fiendish pain-body of entire social groups, nations, classes or sexes. The context, for example, has a tendency to demand:*

MEN · contain anger;[34] not with 'count to ten' effort, but by being conscious of the sensation of it in the body, and of your silly EXPECTATIONS · give, over and over again, to woman in love-making · give up putting love for career above love for woman · give up masturbation and porn · give up independent fun · raise your game · tread the hero's cycle (*see* STORY)

WOMEN · withdraw dependence · refuse loveless sex · give up acquired maleness, especially mania for worldly ambition and VR pleasuring · go cold-turkey on the drama-drug · receive love without needing to please, perform and pander to the weaknesses and addictions of men · go foraging

PARENTS · become aware of how your emotions are distorting the vibe of the nursery · stop living your life through your children, and telling them how to live their lives · refuse to allow anxiety (or CARE) to influence your reaction to your child's growing independence · become aware of how you control, put down or violate your children with BLIPS, tone of voice and other BRAINWASHING techniques · spend time with your children and help them with interests that come from their own initiative · provide [soft] constraints—make sure they know the rules of the game of living in the house and

that the rules apply to you too · refuse to indulge the demands
and fears of ego · love unconditionally and physically · show
them in their own experience what emotional possession is
and how it works · take them out of school; join or form a
home-schooling network · make sure they spend as much
time as possible in the wild, with animals, doing real things
with actual objects · let them live with tables that have feelings
CHILDREN · see how your parents' weakness, violence or disinterest has warped your reaction to pain, death, freedom,
uncertainty, partnership or unself and how it has installed a
whispering mini-mum, fascist dictator or corporate state in
the mind · actively, unsentimentally forgive your parents for
this, and take RESPONSIBILITY for *your* problems
THE POOR · refuse constraints · subvert institutions · unite as a
class · take control of the workplace · refuse to gain knowledge
of the world from corporate media · give up trying to rise
out of the corrupt lower class into the more corrupt middle
class (through emulating bourgeois tastes, amassing capital
and career advancement; although there is nothing wrong,
of course, with mastering middle-class arts and refinements)
THE RICH · cancel debts · give your private capital and excess
money away · dissolve systems · leave your class, and work
towards erasing privilege *without taking charge* · clean the bog

To master self eventually and inevitably means doing battle
with MR CERBERUS, which will at times be a god-awful struggle.
You'll want to give up, you'll feel it's all hopeless, you'll be
overwhelmed with confusion and self-doubt, you'll be hated
and you'll lose more than a handful of marbles. But if you
don't bring this pain on yourself, life will; and, as you must
know by now, it will hurt more that way.

Eventually, when self has been mastered, thought, emotion, sex and all the other previously warped activities of ego,
including violence, can be employed without destroying the
bellyverse. SALT can be added to meals without ruining them,
thought can be indulged in without leading to masturbation
or anxiety, and technology—wheels, specialisation, alphabets,
internets, hierarchies and selves—can be kept within its UTP.

semminge [smɪndʒ]

n & vb 1 to repeat a stupid gesture or a weird sound in order to make it look as if it were intentional the first time 2 to cough, smile or scratch your face in order to cover up your awkwardness

senifalgia [sɛnɛfaldʒə]

n [descriptive of] time spent reassuring yourself that you made the right decision

sensitivity [sɛnsɪtɪvɪti]

n apperceptively experiencing what is happening, in the whole body, now

- often confused with EMO-TIONALISM [ɪməʊʃənəlɪzəm] *n* a limited form of hyper-re-activity to the emotional component of ego and its melodramatic reactions to PAIN, CRITICISM and doubt
- sensitivity, like generosity or creativity, is not a *characteristic*, which some have and others don't, but an innate quality of human nature; different selves have different types, arrangements or SWELLS of sensitivities (creativities, generosities) but the insensitive (uncreative, ungenerous) self is corrupt, or knackered
- painful in crowds

sentiment [sɛntɪmənt]

n 1 a fashionable emotional display or reaction used to gain approval, conceal existential doubt or mark group-think membership of a cult 2 a sick, pink dream of love invented by teenagers cor-rupted by the WORLD and by mature women repeatedly deceived by COCKMAN 3 the sticky, sickly-sweet dregs at the bottom of the barrel of EMOTION

- synonym of CYNICISM
- a CYNICAL-SENTIMENTAL-CULT-MATRIX may include pursed-lipped disapproval, effusive hugs, ironic eye-brows or noisy bursts of vaudevillian laughter; gen-uine expression of feeling appears *deviant* and mem-bers will suppress or cen-sor themselves violently to conceal how they feel

sephel [sɛfəl]

vb & n to engage in the sub-tle and affectionate art of deeply insulting someone in a way that entertains them

sepherate [sɛfəreɪt]

vb to wrestle a pioneering question from the path to glory with a marauding pack of answers [wb]

SEX AND LOVE-MAKING

OVE-MAKING is not a soft-focus, buttercup 'union of souls', but an experience of complete self-surrender with another. Not *communication* (the ordinary passing of signals) but an extraordinarily fulfilling *communion* (the bizarre sharing of UNSELF), which generates more pleasure than can possibly be imagined, or remembered, and which leads to soft-edged contentment and clingless creative amazement all day. Love-making, unlike SEX, or fucking, or porn-wanking, *reduces* problems between people.

When self gained control of consciousness and became ego (*see* SELF) the insane joy of love-making became a restless, reality-excluding tight-grip focus on self-created image and emotion. This sex-fucking is no different to masturbation or porn—there just happens to be someone else there.[35]

Being egoic, sex is fundamentally *excessive* (i.e. a bestial sub-dom caricature of naturally gendered animality), *addictive* (i.e. can only be satisfied by extinguishing one's vitality), *temperamental* (leading, after the emotional up of excitement to an emotional down of irritation, apathy, distance, moodiness and inconsiderate disinterest which, in extremis, leads to rabia and hatred), *deeply unerotic* (restrained, indirect, aggressive, genetically-mechanical, unsensuous) and *male*.

The sexual desperation and consequent violence of man makes that of woman—feminine woman—look like a slight itch. Unless male sexuality is suppressed by age, boredom, worry, ill-health or work in the antiseptic, virtual interzone, it is a rampant tornado of fiendish energy, feeding on the male animal self-swelling of projection and forcing him to constantly fantasise, use and make PORNOGRAPHY, use women as a means of self-pleasuring (the pleasure of power over another—of victory), acquire economic fukpower (through going into business, dominating a fashion, or joining the military) and, in extremis, rape and murder. The entire male-created (and, because of its omnipresent pornography and fear, sexually-repressive) world is, in large part, an extension of man's weaponised penis.

Woman, far more receptive than man, unconsciously absorbs the world of his sexual violence and unreality, and slowly becomes 22.5% male herself; tight, predatory, hungry for orgasms (or coldly uninterested in them) and, in the act of sex, eyes-closed, robotically gyrating, tongue lashing around in a ridiculous performance of submission or learnt, teevee-acquired 'nymphomania' while a little voice in her head whispers, *'this isn't how it's supposed to be'*. JOY is not involved.

It is not easy to free yourself from the fukfiend though. Arousal can only occur through sex or love-making. When you decided to transfer your energies from the former to the latter—by being present, looking in each other's eyes (with the light *on*), moving the penis with vanishing slowness (unto complete stillness), apperceptively enjoying the entire body, bringing each other out of the mind and pouring love out into the fantastic multi-sensory mystery that the other really is— you find, yes, Mr Fucking Cerberus is there, and it all seems ridiculous; meat-puppets devouring each other, cockdrop or an unnatural sense of clinical exposure.[36]

As with any metamorphosis—or journey into unselfish new inner territory—you must first pass through the 'don't feel like it' suburban hinterland of the psyche—through chewy, boring oddness—before the GARDEN OF EARTHLY DELIGHT is reached. Then true sexuality—the *what? what? what?* hilarious rapture of self-sacrificed sensuality—reveals itself in PARTNER-SHIP and, one day, in a SOCIETY of genuine sexual freedom.

HOW TO MAKE LOVE

- Sink addictive-unreality by giving up PORN, idle sex-fantasy and snide sex-guffawing, and by daily practicing APPERCEPTIVE BODILY PRESENCE. This will decrease his pre-excited, pre-maturity, release her grip on her tense or dark inner doubter and give them both the power and presence to make überlove.
- Throughout the day self-master emotions or confess them. If there is anything hidden between you and your partner, still-minded riotous-hearted love-making will be impossible.
- She needs self-mastered presence to discern the difference

between the love of partnership and the excitement of relationship; without this she will allow the fiend in and waste her time with cockmen, bastards and wimps who are unable to hear or respond to her weird unspoken wisdoms.

- Foreplay, in the sense of drumming up excitement, is not necessary; delighting her for hours or months before sex and enjoying her subtle sweetness all day, is sufficient.
- Keep each other present and together; eyes docked and speaking. If one goes into the grippy world of pornsex, the other gently brings them back. *Do not think* (*see* SELF-MASTERY).
- He gives to her; sacrificing himself to the superintense pleasure of her body, filling his softening consciousness with her total sensuous physical reality; her scent, skin, sound, taste and, under all, her intoxicating vibe. He must be wholebody absorbed in the apperceptive reality of the experience, or the mental fukprobe will intervene and tense or terrify the penis, which will tense the vagina, or keep it tense, and make it all sordid, frustrating, boring, oddly 'distant' or plain silly.
- The penis enters the vagina extremely slowly. If the penis is present enough, his experience of his self will be on the shifting, booming level of vibe, which will open up her vibe, blending them both in an immaterial [*absolutely*-material] hyper-vividity. He will feel he is entering, and she will feel herself overtaken by something impossibly vast.
- With enough connected presence between them there is, of course, no need to follow any damn rules; passionate movement, [non-bestial] animality, sexy lingerie, devoted oral-sex all contain dangerous fuckery and are best avoided initially; but with enough bananas love, he can tie her to a tree.

---

sex [sɛks]
   n & vb 1 a tight-grip MENTAL–EMOTIONAL [KINERTIAL] focus on a reality-excluding self-created image 2 a NARCOTIC vibe-destroying porn-wank in the shadow of another's company 3 the restless, frustrated foundation of the WORLD, and of vibrating sexual turnips
- used to sell everything but sex itself, which is illegal
- antonym of LOVE-MAKING

FRIENDS OF SHANGO

GORAX · the god that lives in the guts making weird noises

LAZLOID · the god that hides your keys, scarf, nail-clippers, lighter, cork-screw and biro

SASAGÉ · the 'library angel'; she who chooses *just* the right book for you to read next

WEDLEY · a little-appreciated god that prevents text-messages you would later regret from sending, cars to places you shouldn't go from starting, credit-card transactions for useless SHIT from going through and computer files containing work you should redo from scratch to corrupt or get lost in a crash

HIYOKOSAMA · a goddess that sits on hatching eggs whispering encouragement to pipping chicks; also behind the last voice you can hear when all is not yet *quite* lost, saying *'don't give up little man'*

JEEVUS · a bug-eyed god that tempts you to stare at blood, fat and unhappiness; resist

KOGEBAKA · the godlette that watches over the making of mayonnaise, the public playing of difficult sonatas and other DO-OR-DIE finicky actions; brother of GENIUS, but can be a right bell-end

SELEMUS · goddess that gets you home when you're hopelessly lost, or drunk

LUQUENTIA · raucous goddess that sits on the tongue ever-ready to let an elegant flow of astonishing honesty hose down all within ear-shot; usually chained up by ED

GUNGO · a god that sits on [BRUNDLED] leaves broadcasting good ideas via semaphore

DAEMO · a momentary god, or *daemon*, that appears when the attention is blasted wide by something marvellously *here*

THE APPERTROI · a very small chorus of gods that applaud productive mornings, healthy poos, neat lobs, finished laundry, lush bike skids through short-cuts and the like

---

shango [ʃaŋgəʊ]

n 1 vast uncaused QWOTH of electric energy that connects you to all things in a silent DISPLOSION of unemotional enthusiasm 2 a playful but unruly godling who yawps delight through OUTSIDERS from what most people perceive to be the future
· surprisingly cheese-ball
· *see* also REG

share [ʃɛː]

vb either 1 criminalised generosity or 2 legalised theft

shawp [ʃɔːp]

n a sudden spurt of *yeah!* followed with a protracted *hmmm*, and an eventual slipping back into *no, not really*

shem away [ʃɛməweɪ]

vb to slowly creep away and leave somebody talking to themselves

shit [ʃɪt]

n (IAPC) the entire situation; continually emerging from ASS [as] *n* one's entire self[37]
· natural home: the fan

shiticism [ʃɪtɪsɪzəm]

n 1 a gag which is not intelligent, witty or even meaningful but which provokes laughter because it solidifies GROUPTHINK disapproval of an alien, or marks the limits of acceptable depth 2 the opposite of constructive CRITICISM; contains no help, analysis, BEAUTY, authority or experience, just a SPONKY label; 'it's shit'

shneck [ʃnɛk]

n 1 the point when an initial burst of creative energy runs down or hits a grim hurdle 2 the point when the quobbing god which births art, orders down tools and further gestation time
· giving up faced with 1 and pushing and *pushing* before 2 are hallmarks of creative immaturity

should [ʃʊd]

md.vb either 1 an expression of CONSCIENCE or 2 Satan's favourite modal verb
· often used by INFOCRATS, who prefer to *recommend* cessation of self-centredness rather than act—or, in their case, write—without it

shuff out [ʃʌfaʊt]

vb 1 to extinguish one's sensitivity, sweetness or creative fire with comfort, fame, rut, attention or WORK 2 to block the mindpipe to GENIUS or smother the heart from SCENIUS 3 middle class conversion from pseudo-subversive stagversion to smug corpish spoddery 4 to slowly become a sad sunken ghost of one's former self
· the secret purpose of fame; when you are sufficiently separated from genius and scenius, you're shuffed out enough to be truly FAMOUS

A SZASS OF SICKNESSES

PENSITIS · inability to stop thinking; an affliction which is highly debilitating but goes unnoticed because everyone is suffering from it; leads to worry, self-doubt, irritation, insomnia, inability to settle on one activity, lack of spontaneity, guilt, stress-inducing fantasy and low-lying fear of everything and everyone.

PALABROSIS · inability to tell the difference between language and what it means. The palabrotic experiences reality as a series of relative-abstract names, ideas or rules. If something is not relative or abstract—nuance of voice, tone of situation, mystery of love—the palabrotic cannot experience it. Instead he adheres to received or dictionary definitions and so is unable to PLAY with language, form new definitions, metaphors or paradigms. Q-WORDS are translated into understandable definitions. 'Beauty' then becomes a subjective emotion, 'death' is an absence of movement, 'love' something you want, 'truth' a subjective 'myth', and so on.

SYBISIS · the pursuit (or CON-SCIENCE-less enjoyment) of five-star luxury or PRIVILEGE

HYPERMNESIA · the perceiving of blended experience as discrete photographic particles, each of which is judged and compared with other such particles; symptoms include despair at catching one's lover looking for a moment less-than perfect, disapproval at faulty soups and smugness at being granted more biscuits than the dog next door.

GURUITIS · the mistaken belief that one is a spiritually enlightened god-among-us; symptoms include 'above-it-all' vibe, liberal use of Sanskrit terms, beatific smiles and long, serene hugs (especially with good-looking women).

DISORDALIA · rebranding selfishness, laziness, stupidity or WAISY-making INSTITUTION-ALISATION into 'disorders' or 'mental illnesses' in order to dispose of irksome responsibilities or the difficulties of SELF-MASTERY, or in order to control troublesome populations through professional or narcotic dependency; includes the interpretation of tiny quantities of PAIN, when learning a CRAFT, as 'no FUN' **A.K.A. DIAGNOSIA** (*see* MANU-PHOBIA, PANCULPISM, BIOMO-RALITY, DIAGNOSIS *&* SUTTERY)

sickness [sɪknɪs]
  n antonym of ACCIDENT

silence (inner) [məsʌɪləns]
  n the origin of sound [38]
  · occasionally confused with
    its *near* synonym, SILENCE
    (OUTER) [ambɪgjuːɪtisɪŋs] *n* a
    [meaningful] lack of noise

sing together [sɪŋtəgɛðə]
  vb to give voice to ÜBERSELF

slavity [slavɪti]
  n either 1 suppressed self-as-
    sertion; submitting to de-
    cent [ANANARCHIC] leaders
    while nourishing your in-
    decent hatred of their com-
    petence or EXPERIENCE or
    2 the misplaced morality of
    slaves; you shouldn't lie to
    market leaders, steal from
    corps, default on loans, col-
    lectivise the crown estate, be
    RESPONSIBLE or *fight*

sleep [sliːp]
  n & vb 1 the amber crust you
    wake up with around your
    eyes; literally sleep in solid
    form 2 to pass into a state of
    total unbeing (*see* ZZZ)
  · successfully going to sleep
    is achieved by pretending
    to go to sleep; like becom-
    ing a pop-star and, in some
    cases, being in love

snidery [snʌɪdri]
  n & vb helpfulness, chummi-
    ness and [limited] generos-
    ity used as a means to hide,
    and avoid being rejected for,
    being a total git
  · de rigueur for the lower
    manager who uses it to sti-
    fle guilt at being around
    people he has to directly
    oppress and to co-opt their
    sociability into the work
    machine; senior managers
    can (off camera) dispense
    with it, and treat their sub-
    jects with naked contempt
  · *Geoff's 'good-nature' masked
    his sadistic insecurity from
    his 'friends', but the Filipino
    immigrants washing his car
    in the 40° sun weren't fooled*
  · SNIDES [snʌɪdz] *n.pl* are al-
    ways astonished or out-
    raged when treated unfairly

socialism [səʊʃəlɪzəm]
  n either 1 antonym of CAP-
    ITALISM or 2 synonym of it

social media [səʊʃəl miːdɪə]
  n.phr an expensive, heavily
    policed, ad-funded virtual
    graveyard, haunted by fa-
    mous ghosts, with grave-
    stones that display live up-
    dates of the corpses' various
    states of decomposition
  · synonym of ANTI-SOCIAL

SOCIALISM

THERE ARE THREE KINDS OF SOCIALISM

1. AUTHORITARIAN SOCIALISM is identical to capitalism, with the same institutions, laws, money, privileged elite, restless majority, bureaucracy. hierarchy and hostility to nature, wilderness and other manifestations of unself. The only difference to ordinary private capitalism is that the state, rather than private individuals or corporations, controls surplus (and is thus antagonistic to corporate 'capitalists'). Examples of authoritarian socialism (or STATE CAPITALISM) include the Soviet Union, China and North Korea.

2. LIBERTARIAN SOCIALISM is roughly synonymous with ANARCHISM in that no central state or centralised institution organises or owns capital; workers control and own the means of production and, crucially, surplus is shared and controlled by those that produce it. There are few examples of such a system, because, firstly, it is deeply feared and violently suppressed by authoritarian systems and, secondly, it cannot work without constant, active recognition of the fundamental role that context, vibe and unself must play in a free, functioning and pleasant SOCIETY. Nevertheless touches of libertarian socialism appeared in 1640s England, 1870s France, 1910s Russia and 1930s Spain; which is to say in times of authoritarian breakdown, or 'revolution'. Other examples of anarchic libertarian socialism include open-source software development, independent communes, pre-historic tribes, families, groups of friends, lovers and most of nature, including the self; but these groups only succeed when A) they, and not owners, can control surplus (i.e. unlike coops and worker-managed enterprises, where surplus remains in the hands of others) and B) when they are OMNARCHISTICALLY apt and unselfish enough to render this control to the context, rather than to their rational egos.

3. SOCIALISHISM is a blend of 1 and 2 used by middle-class PROFESSIONALS to assuage their guilt, and to further their career. It is synonymous with STAGVERSION.

SOCIETY

HEN ATTENTION IS NOT LIMITED by the rational or emotional prerogatives of the ego, attention flows only to where it needs to go, regardless of what self may want or like. I then find I am fascinated and amazed, not just by where my soft attention wanders, but *what I am* that witnesses and directs this APT growth; a process which sometimes adds to my body, mind or vibe-apparatus, sometimes adds to the world around, and sometimes subtracts everything into baffling empty presence. The weird *what I am* is still naturally attracted to my own unique sensitivities and strengths (*see* TASTE) but it is not conditioned by them; past crises have not MARKERED off inner territory into prohibited and permitted zones; and attention is free to go where ego is not; which allows the tree of me to grow naturally (or GENEROUSLY), forming a balanced structure that can respond immediately (or SPONTANEOUSLY) to unusual situations, and commune with unlike others; growing the most excellent composite-self known as a partnership, überself or society.

Human society, in other words, is comprised of selves that are, first of all, soft-enough to generalise—to do what I can't do very well—and only secondarily hard enough to specialise—to do what I can do better than anyone. If the softness of great generalisation, or free attention, does not come first, specialisation takes over the system, degrading (DIGITISING) co-operative societies into mere TEAMS. These teams are comprised of separate, specialised partpeople who are unable to experience what they are not (each other) and so must rely on their adherence to what they know or feel they have in common; their shared fears and desires. Such a team must compel members who do not share these fears and desires to co-operate through *fear* (of guilt, punishment, deprivation, etc.) and *desire* (for money, power, etc.). The team therefore ends up being comprised of members who are overwhelmed with existential terror and psychotic appetite.

Until they leave the team, that is, and rejoin society, which may also be called HUMANITY.

society [səsʌɪti]
n an überself of SUBJECTIVE selves and OBJECTIVE tools knitted together by UNSELF in order to super-augment the relaxed CONSCIOUSNESS of HOMO LUDENS
- antonym of CULT, 'TEAM', and UNCIVILISATION
- variously defined by the WORLD as 'the public', 'the workforce', 'the electorate', 'the nation', 'the population' or 'the mob' depending on how it is serving or threatening the elite class

soft-consciousness [sɒftmiː]
n see CONSCIOUSNESS
- n.b. *not to be confused with* soft-bodied, soft-minded or bland soft-willed passivity and weakness

solastalgia [sɒləstaldʒə]
n 1 heartbreaking disorientation caused by homelands altered by ENCLOSURE, agriculture and 'development', rendering them alienating and unfamiliar 2 homesickness felt by people who are still at home[39]

sorrow [sɒrəʊ]
n the heart of the self resonating to the state of mortal creatures in existence

- natural reaction to DEATH, loss and the SACRIFICE of others; conducive to love, creativity and self-renewal
- antonym of UNHAPPINESS, SUFFERING & DEPRESSION
- *see* WEPTH

sorry [sɒri]
adj default state of ego

sound [saʊnd]
n ear-vibe

space [speɪs]
n the gap between things, the space between thoughts, the silence between sounds, the nothing between somethings; oh yes
- it is not far mountains or distant bittersweet yesterdays or fiery glad utopias that excite such coil and mighty pudder in the reverent breast, but the space between us here and them there, which the formless mystery within rises up to wordlessly RECOGNISE

spacetime, timespace [stʌf]
n useful illusion generated by the concentrated CONSCIOUSNESS of self[40]

spaddle [spadəl]
n a little spade[41]

AN ENO OF SOUNDS

ORGUE · the unutterable foreignness of certain repeated words, like 'worth' and 'put'

HACKASH · dry woody hollow clacking sounds and shimmery rustling things

CHU-CHU · the quiet sound of gratitude eating anxiety (synonym of NYUM-NYUM)

LUSHINDO · the grinding poff of footsteps in the snow outside, signalling the arrival of a three-month absent lover

PLIB · the sound of little waves lapping the side of a boat or breakwater at night

PLOB · the sound of a heavy FUZZING BUTTOCK vertically striking a village pond [wb]

LUARP · a spider's yawn

QUAP · sounds such as *'brrr'*, *'ugh'* or *'phew!'* used not because you are cold, disgusted or relieved, but to tell someone else you are

CHARG · the sound of walking through the Danish countryside in wet shoes

BLISHINGS · sounds that only lovers can hear

DJELLUCE · the WHISPERINGS of everything; the speech of things, the *'mmm'* of stuff

WEEF · the sublime sound of fannying-around (demands around seven years of dedicated practice to hear)

s.p.c.i. [ɛs piː siː ʌɪ]

ab the shango psychic civility index

specialism [spɛʃlɪlɪzəm]

n either 1 use of one's favourite tools to express the big picture (which one can put one's tools down to SEE) or 2 a technique, label or other element of self, used to avoid the big picture (to feel special or expect special treatment) and protect the institutions of the world against *common* sense [42]

· SPECIALIST [spɛʃəlɪst] *n* either A) (obeying UNSELF) one who crosses fields and gardens on a clumsy whim on their favourite bicycle; characterised by an interest in cross-disciplinary insights [43] or B) (subservient to SELF) one whose paid identity depends on psychotic over-focus on and jealous guarding of trivia; characterised by fear and meticulous contempt for the non-specialist [44]

· the variegated GENIUS-SOCIETY of 1/A becomes the divided-labour HORROR-TEAM of 2/B when specialist powers are not subservient to hyper-generalist LIFE

· *see* SCHOOL

- reasons used to feel special, expect special treatment or exemption from *offensive criticism* include:
- having a serious disease, being disabled or having a tragic back-story
- being from another country or having connections to another culture
- reading big books, learning long words or having a special qualification
- odd sexual preferences
- being old, rich or having symmetrical features and a standardbeauty culturally approved body-type [45]
- belonging to a moral social group (eco, religious, political, etc.) or to a minority (don't forget: bonus points for persecution!)
- appearing on the TEEVEE screen, earning a few attention-credits on an internet FAMEMONGER or having access to talented people
- having had a strange, gruelling, *important* or mystical experience
- having WORKED or 'lived' somewhere for five minutes longer than the new bloke, or just being old [46]
- having a special title, need, PHOBIA, ability or car
- being an expert or a parent

spectacle [spɛktəkəl]
n a means of suppressing antagonism or tranquillising atomism through deploying enormously powerful techno-displays, collective cultic groupfeel and extreme porn in which SPECTATORS do not actively or fully participate
- the largest spectacles (new year's eve, the world cup, eid, general elections, etc.) are always presented as an antidote to all suffering, with dissent represented in HUXLEYAN societies as 'griping' or 'cynicism', or, in ORWELLIAN societies, as 'heresy' or 'conspiracy' [47]
- a vast species of FUNSHISM to be creatively subverted at all costs

speed [spiːd]
n 1 ego's rational response to the threat of stillness 2 an extremely expensive means of stupefying consciousness used by the POOR

spenth [spɛnθ]
vb 1 to gently cement someone's nascent inclusion into a social group by lightly taking the [TABOO] piss out of them 2 to cool far-hearted ZEEDLING ego-bulge with the balm of gentle ridicule

THE SHANGO PSYCHIC–CIVILITY INDEX

The PANJECTIVE SPCI *measures how psychically civilised a region is; how easy it is for sweet-natured, mystery-loving, soft-selved fools to live there. Physical uncivility— such as the kind of threats and abuses members of concentration camps, ghettos and fascist dictatorships have to put up with— are not included in the SPCI. The SPCI of a region is based on it's aggregate performance in the following 25 Basic Psychic Civility Indices (0–4pts per item);*

1. Freedom given to children / the degree to which children's opinions are respected when making big decisions

2. Depth of love for animals and nature, access to and desire for protracted experience of the wilderness

3. Excellent PROLAIL, widespread ability to have a versatile conversation, 'decisions' reached gently (without overt debate), disinclination to STARE

4. Freedom to [JAY]WALK

5. Freedom to SCHOOL at home

6. Freedom to die at home; recognition and familiarity with TEMENOS and DEATH

7. Freedom to exact community justice and live by— and break— communal traditions

8. Freedom to heal one's friends

9. Fluid ego of average person

10. Lack of predatory sexuality and sex-violence; combined with non-SEXUALISED nudity and abundance of outrageous sexual intercourse

11. Status, freedom and love for women; along with lack of dominating male-made systems for which women must deform their innate femininity in order to achieve status, freedom, love or a wage

12. Toleration of FREELOADERS

13. Abundance of leisure time

14. High empathy, wide attention span, slow pace of life and soft CONSCIOUSNESS

15. Identification of and refusal to cross UTP of group size, speed of transport, use of self, use of commons, tool sophistication or power of system

16. Genuine freedom, diversity and general gloriousness of dress — master sempstresses and tailors everywhere

17. Experience understood to be a consequence of consciousness and context (rather than of wealth, race, sexuality, age, genes, blind luck, MONOTHEISTIC god-made destiny, etc.)

18. Tolerance of ambiguity and silence, appreciation of irony, love of the surreal, playful formality (as opposed to rigid formality or lack of formality)

19. Visible conscious glow

20. Scenius vibrating in the skies

21. Opportunities for GENIUS-play everywhere (waltz-partners in the spinney, chess-masters on the bus, etc.) and extremely high regard for CRAFT

22. Acceptance of outsiders, service to others, generosity

23. Love or acceptance of madness, waiting, pain and sorrow

24. Universal appreciation and knowledge of mushrooms

25. Gay disco

The maximum SPCI of a country or region is 100. The current highest score, shared by forty one regions around the world — such as Extramadura, Spain; Ishikawa-ken, Japan; Campbell River, Canada; Kerala, India; West-Cork, Ireland and a few working-class or deeply rural pockets of Ecuador, Poland, New Zealand, Ghana, Senegal, Greece, Indonesia, Turkey, Hungary and Mexico — is 8.5... UTOPIA swings between 100 and, ooh, 80?

spirituality [spɪrɪtʃʊəlalɪti]
n millennia-old expressions of heartbreaking PARADOX and intimate techniques for widening awareness, overcoming ego, accepting pain, listening to the body, subverting the world and loving the void
· spiritual techniques must be divested of conscience, spontaneity, service, practicality and radical creativity to work for the ego or in the MARKET, where they can then be profitably employed (by MYSTISHISTS) to get promoted, advertise an ethical body-lotion, invent a more ADDICTIVE smartphone app, or feel dreamy, SUTTERY and *ever* so special

spit in your face [spɪtɪnjəfeɪs]
vb the direct reaction of anything or anybody you don't love in existence
· propelled by Q-FORCE
· *Christopher's own legs spat in his face*

sponk [spɒŋk]
n an anecdote / story which amounts to something happening which was liked or disliked (i.e. that was positively or negatively exciting); frequently concluding with

'*...and it was really good / it was really weird / it was really bad...*', etc.
· sponks always fall flat on their face, leaving the audience suspended in an awkward collective *so-what?*

spontaneity [spɒntəneɪti]
n yes-flavoured, now-blended first-impression flow of deep BODY-INSTINCT into a free flowing world
· deeply threatening to the SELF-WORLD; curtailed by GROUPTHINK gossip, TECHNICAL SPECIALISM (which introduces ponderous time between managed decision and front-line act), the VIRTUAL world / SOCIAL MEDIA (which force all acts to be competitively and self-consciously assessed; and so pre-emptively styled) and all the spontaneity-BLOCKS of egoic self-doubt
· near synonym of IMPRO

spoonduel [spuːndjuːəl]
n a duel with spoons

sport [spɔːt]
n 1 a physical game 2 an enjoyable way of pretending or practicing to do something meaningful 3 a means of SOCIAL CONTROL through

the sanitised satisfaction of blood-lust, strict rules and huddling groupfeel
* three types of sport:
1. SOLO [səʊləʊ spɔːt] *n* enjoyable play fight against a bit of wood or leathery sphere, or somesuch
2. TEAM [tiːm spɔːt] *n* temporal semblance of blended togetherness (all strapped sweatily together roaring in an hilarious ÜBERSELF)
3. SPECTATOR [spɛkteɪtə spɔːt] *n* standard means of assuaging collective impotence and / or a pervasive death-wish with surrogate manliness; prevalent in UNCIVILISATIONS that are losing their grip (Late Rome, Mexico under Montezuma, Nazi Germany, etc.)

sprile [sprʌɪl]
vb to openly respect leaves

spring [sprɪŋ]
n 1 a short time of the year when trees are not static, but erupting and flowing; expressively twisting hands offering oranges up to lovers in balconies above, like energetic Russian brooms sweeping cobweb-free the ceiling sky, or like spurting fountains dripping puppet branches down to the grassy stage; when sticky buds are born, ten winters-all in unhappy love affairs, pulling themselves free like faeries from cracked godheads, exploding into an orchestra of skirts and trumpets, dancing and swelling in a green universe of delicately chaotic clusters of floating firebright branches revolving past orbiting hearts burning hot lemony yellow 2 a permanent state of mind, an ever-green, ever-present garden of the SOLAR PLEXUS

sprunt [sprʌnt]
n one who 1 tells anecdotes that always seem to amount to his own wondrous excellences 2 cannot experience pleasure without congratulating himself 3 cannot undergo unpleasure without blaming others 4 admits to doubt, poor memory low esteem, failing eyesight, clumsiness or phobias but never to being mean-spirited, inflexible, narrow-minded or lacking humour
* yes! you sir!

s.(s.)o.d.s. [sɒdz]
ab the sorby scale of displeasures

— THE SORBY SCALE OF DISPLEASURES —

I. TUT-INDUCING · sneeze that won't come · trying to get into an unopened pistachio, box of condoms or find the end bit of the sellotape · overhearing a conversation in which strangers are struggling to recall a name that you know but cannot correct without sounding like an interfering know-it-all · a cheap JOOF at your unusual name · trying to wash your armpits in the sink or getting the ends of your sleeves wet washing up

2. GRITTED TEETH, GRR INDUCING · shoelaces snapping while in a rush · trying and failing to change a duvet cover · being lost in an infinite automated switchboard loop · helplessly watching someone miss a bit cleaning something · turning up an hour late because the clocks went back last night · red knickers in with the bastard whites · a bit of nail at the quick which keeps catching on fine cotton underwear

3. CUSS-INDUCING · fouling up your chances with someone you fancy · tennis net · fenton · dropping your dinner over the floor · chronic constipation, itchy, heaving, puuush... nothing, *nothing* · extended bureaucratic QUEUE-RAGE · MANAGEMENT

4. GNASHING OF TEETH, LASHING OUT AT WALLS-INDUCING being stuck in the hands of an incompetent storyteller [tailor, lover, masseur, etc.] · massive accidental deletion of unsaved work event · waking up after a sleep that does not refresh in order to travel for over an hour in the miserybus to spend the day in alienating activity · waking up to discover that your shame is plastered all over the internet · the realisation that something somewhere has gone terribly wrong, followed by relief that actually it hasn't and it's all okay, followed by the further realisation that, no, you really *are* fucked

5. TRUTH-INDUCING plunging into TEMENOS · realisation that you are dying *now* · facing the fact that the end of the world is actually happening · the perfectly awful, perfectly still, *all is lost / this is the unthinkable* timeless MOMENT OF TRUTH

stagversion [stagvəːʃən]

n 1 FUTILE protests (marches, petitions, votes, strikes) or attempts to reform the world through participating in it[48] 2 hating the world or moaning about it, blaming it for your vices or directing all your rebellious energy, *first of all*, at 'them' instead of at the 'I' that is angry (*see* FALSOLIS) 3 cynically knowing that the WORLD is a lie, or that its WORK is a prison, while wearily, sardonically, ironically participating in it 4 HUXLEYAN journalism and academia; promoting MYSTISHISM, ECOSHISM, FEMINISHISM and SOCIALISHISM while working for a TOTALITARIAN, corp-funded UNIVERSITY or NEWSMEDIA CULT 5 anarcho-punk groupthink rebellion-consumption

· stagversion is not just effortlessly subsumed by the world, the world actually *requires* stagversion to effectively operate; without the eco, female, 'radical', artistic and philanthropic veneer created by PROFESSIONAL stagversives (esp. journalists) the entire system would lie exposed and threatened

· antonym of SUBVERSION

stare [stɛː]

vb & n 1 to create [a semi-illusion of] frozen spacetime through isolating the sense of sight from other senses 2 to HYPNOTISE oneself by filling up the field of hard, stuck-PROBE consciousness with an isolated thing 3 the first step towards a SCHIZOID society of perma-KINERTIA

· antonym of the soft GAZE
· godfather of the SMIRK
· privileged by TECHNIQUE
· sometimes useful

steef [stiːf]

n the atom-thin veneer of psych-varnish and ego-inflating self-conscious coldness layered over women by the PORN-STARES of desperate, *desperate* men

· does not just cut women off from men, but from soft reality, making them harder; i.e. *more like men*

stereotype [stɛrɪəʊtʌɪp]

vb & n [to make] SELF-directed — and therefore fixed and inflexible — motorways in the GARDEN of the mind which, like physical motorways, force attention down common and predictable, pre-programmed (i.e. laid by *other people*) routes and restrict free attention from wandering on impulse into the wilderness of the gut, the unforested grassland of the knee or the pine-bound mountains of the feet

- stereotypical reactions and opinions are those shared or created by CULTS; if you are reluctant to share an instinct, a feeling or an idea with your family, friends or WORK colleagues, it is either a shameful symptom of your ego-madness, or a truth that you have freely discovered beyond the stereotypical boundaries that mark the limits of the surrounding groupthink
- dependence on stereotypes leads to A) unquestioned comfort with SPONTANE-ITY-eroding habits B) acceptance of predetermined ideas and feelings (routes through the GARDEN) and C) an unconscious resistance [irritation, boredom, etc.] to dissent / low-tech depth (going off-road, on foot)
- near synonym of CO-OPT
- antonym of GENERALISE

stillness [stɪlnɪs]
n a jungle-path to nowhere, UNSELF and the root of all blasting pleasures

stimulus [stɪmjʊləs]
n the opposite of STILLNESS, and great, yes, but, honestly, still; nowhere near as good

stingo [stɪŋgəʊ]
n a conversation which gets derailed from a subject that you wanted to talk about, but which you cannot return to without looking like you care about it a *bit* too much

stions [ʃtjənz]
n.pl a series of supporting lies required by a principle lie, such as the 'sick-voice' and symptoms that must be invented to support an unflu
- stions are more unpleasant to utter than principle lies

stoph [stɒf]
vb 1 to insanely sit through a film you are not ENJOYING 2 to insanely sit through a LIFE you are not enjoying

story [stɔːri]
n 1 a pre-conscious picture of the dreamlife of the world 2 an image of the psyche
- good stories reveal subtle psychological VIBE-REAL-ITIES, masterfully arrange events so that the external world mirrors the internal world or force characters

we RECOGNISE or LOVE to overcome the self through making difficult choices that lead to archetypically satisfying self-sacrifice and total change; all of which produces, in the listener or viewer, tender reconciliation with a friendly UNIVERSE, enhanced EMPATHY, the laughter of RECOGNITION or HEARTBROKEN awe

· in other words; all GOOD stories (an accurate image of the psyche) are true stories and 'true stories' (factually accurate accounts) that are not faithful to the inner world are false

· good stories are only possible by using imagination and craft to *show* reality as it is—imagination without reality results in PORNOGRAPHY, which *tells* people what to think and feel by A) using an excess of gossip, metaphor, CGI, music, surrealism, sex and other SALTS or B) manipulating characters into situations which are supposed to be funny, touching, deep or inspiring; holding up, in effect, mood signs saying 'cry' or 'laugh'

· MASCULINE-WESTERN stories *tend* to emphasise the hero's active, linear, archetypical journey through a fantastic world of conflict

· FEMININE-EASTERN stories *tend* to emphasise the heroine's passive, polychromatic EXPERIENCE of real events which are slowly revealed to be an intimately recognised whole

· naturally though no story can be completely masculine or feminine without being dull or clichéd; just as no person can

· synonym of MYTH

strikhedonia [strɪkhɛdəʊnɪə]
n the potent, liberating joy of saying 'sod it', giving up, and walking away; and *never* looking back

strub [strʌb]
vb & n to freeze in momentary godhorror upon realising that your STRIKHEDONIA was founded upon an insane illusion... before realising with profound relief, no, no, it's all alright, you made the right decision after all

stunk [stʌnk]
n the appalling realisation that you are no longer carrying the valuable thing that you've had on you all day

stunt [stʌnt]

n a branch of self that 1 is *naturally* smaller or less sensitive than one's swells or 2 through lack of use or attention, has *unnaturally* withered, hardened or digitised

stzog [stzɒg]

vb & n 1 to demean a dog by dancing with it 2 to dignify a lizard with a novelty hat

subjective [səbdʒɛktɪv]

n led by—or viewing reality through the filter of—emotions, thoughts or ego-conditioned addictions
- near-synonym of OBJECTIVE
- antonym of PANJECTIVE

subversion [sʌbvəːʃən]

n unselfish, social, conscientious, creative UNWORLDING
- antonym of STAGVERSION

succeed [səksiːd]

vb to achieve CRAFT-mastery, MARKET-independence, or freedom from FEAR
- often confused with SELL OUT [sɛl aʊt] *vb* to achieve—through skilled, sustained WHORING—the power to give more orders than are received, a big bank score or maximum dependence on the SYSTEM

suffering [sʌfərɪŋ]

n 1 not wanting sorrow 2 not liking [straining away from] PAIN 3 not accepting what is [50] 4 constant experience of self clinging onto itself
- accrues in the body, forming a living archive of compelling but completely useless advice; and tending to produce a veritable litany of ghastly *can'ts*

superstition [suːpəstɪʃən]

n 1 prayers for forgiveness, immortality or personal success engendered by a self which perceives the life of objects, while being afraid of the DEATH they may bring [51] 2 the compulsive 'reading' of signs, omens, facts, data, statistics, and coincidences to see what might be in it for *me*—or for what I BELIEVE
- the religion of pre-modern PROTO-HISTORY (*see* GOD)
- synonym of MYSTISHISM, RELIGION, SCIENTISM, SORRY and THANK YOU

suttery [sʌtəri]

n 1 a sense of superiority founded on cleanliness or weight [52] 2 capacity, confidence or 'character' which is founded on belief in the safety of one's surroundings

SUBVERSION

- REFUSAL TO COOPERATE *as far as your situation permits;* with-drawing children from school · growing your own food replacing time spent on bureaucratic credentialising with time spent actually *doing* (mastering physical tools and CRAFTS or just unhurriedly pottering) · refusing to WORK; ABSENTEEISM; not turning up, PRESENTEEISM; just turning up bodily or OMNARCHY; taking [worker] control of your institution and its surplus · occupying land, vibe, factory and free time · participating in a permanent international strike (contributing to an international post-WORK UTOPIA) paying no rent · paying no tax · deleting apps and profiles
- UNPROFESSIONALISM · breaking down pro-dominion through free skill-shares and omnarchic unions that provide edu-cation, health, construction, transport and companion-ship to each other; all knowledge, energy, clothing, food, medication, entertainment and shelter gained outside of prof-corp-state power structures is yours, and feels good
- TABOO-BUSTING · A) conscious, friendly, free, contextual use of taboo expressions (racist, sexist, ablist, etc.) B) non-emo-tional readiness to engage with taboo subjects (sex, death, madness, the thinker of thought, the seer of sight, class con-sciousness and questioning belief *itself*, rather than the silly objects of belief) C) exploration of all unspoken OVERTON assumptions through judicious use of 'why?' and totalmind being of 'what'; includes occupying ENCLOSED emotional space, common Q-WORDS and co-opted expressions
- SITUATIONISM · breaking down MONOCULTURAL porn with reality-rupturing acts and artefacts of genius · unstatused IMPRO · devastatingly honest public speech · subversive the-atrical pranks · high-quality choral volcanoes · SUBVERTISING ('culture-jamming') · massively, *massively* beautiful art [53]
- SPANNERISM · slowly, subtly, imperceptibly (PABULATING, leaking secrets, surreptitiously injecting truth serum into the water-cooler, etc.) and, where possible, vastly and with enormous obviousness, bringing down the company or institution you work for (opening prison doors, giving

away stock, levelling bank accounts, collectivising factories, etc.). Digital disobedience (hacking states, infecting corp systems, destroying files etc.) is particularly effective these days; naturally you should restrict your attacks to property, systems, accounts and so on though—physical violence for any other reason than self-defence makes you a conspicuous, tractable and easy-to-defame target; and a twat.

- FREEDOMING · the defiant insistence on acting as if one is already free; leaving work or leaving the MARKET, frauding, foraging, poaching, sharing, downloading and stealing (from institutions, corporations, the dead and the hyper-rich—not from small bands, family stores or the little fella!), organising gift-economies and workers' councils and doing whatever you have to do—as far as your situation will *possibly* allow—to live with independent dignity.

- FREE SPEECH · the system relies on the manufactured con-sent, class-ego-reinforcement and context-erasing brain-washing of the media; but the media itself, unlike other institutions, is fragile—word of mouth can destroy it. It is the Achilles heel of the entire system. Genuinely inde-pendent media-outlets and free communication forums broadcasting übernews, teeth-in-the-marrow truthmusic and timeless masterpieces of personal, social and universal gutwisdom are a realisable early step in bringing the entire pyramid of evil crashing into the Nile.

- SELF-MASTERY · the first step in subversive utopiary is using conscious acceptance and action to overcome ADDICTION to the world and fear of reality, because: A) the violent, needy, anxious and emotional ego is easy for the system to control B) it is FUTILE to use a moody, angry, anxious, bored, addicted or shuffed-out self to create a world that is SENSITIVE, free and selfless C) self-mastery leads to finer dis-cernment of tone, vibe and physiognomy and, therefore, to immunity to deception D) attempting to live independently of the system leads to fear (*'how will I survive?'*), self-pity (*'I'm a nobody!'*), anger (*'they're all bastards!'*), futile effort (*'I must change the world'*) and cold-turkey (*'I need a fashionable bag!'*); all of which demand self-mastery to overcome.

- NEVER GIVE UP, NEVER COMPROMISE · the only way to be free of the world is to be free of the unlife of the ego and the work of the system. Not at all easy. Takes a long time, great persistence, help from fellows and resilience to abuse. Ways of giving up, getting lost and SHUFFING OUT; very many. Ways of winning the unwinnable game; *one*. And between this sweet fig, and the root of the sick world tree, stands MR CERBERUS in his most awesome of bignesses. But when you cry true BASTA! draw a RUBICON feet-width-wide and do real battle with him, you find that the BIG BOSS is not the world elite, or the system, or capitalism, or technology, or even my stupid, damn, self. Mr Cerberus—with all his PAIN—works for the most subversive power in the universe and the only thing that can change the world, bring the WORLD to an end or built UTOPIA…

- UNSELF · the system is constructed by and upon self; all my thoughts and emotions, my material body, everything I perceive and do, any part of me—can be seized, measured, bought, sold, controlled and co-opted by the self-made-system. Any unselfish techniques, artefacts, criticism or revolutionary actions that enter from without are *automatically* co-opted by their entry into the self-system, and assimilated. The only thing that is immune to this, is that which is *not* self; that which is softly conscious *of* self; which is nothing that the self can ever *quite* define. This means that unself-directed subversion is *ultimately* without [i.e. only conditionally with] fixed central direction or stated aim, fixed labels ('isms') or symbols, fixed formal rituals, plans, demands, professionalism, violence or *ultimately* ego itself. And *this* means that *ultimately* there are no leaders to arrogate power or be killed; no context-independent ideas to be co-opted; and no 'movement' that can be threatened, compromised, 'reasoned with', or even *found*.

- It also means that there is no need for 'me' to do anything. I have already arrived. I can put the feet of my self up on the dash of the carriage and let the most subversively alive cabbie in the universe drive ten thousand flaming horses through the houses of parliament… or do nothing at all.[54]

swelk [swɛlk]

vb & n I to avoid the difficulty and exposure of directly encountering another via a pre-programmed greeting sub-routine—or 'hello' 2 to speak rapidly or ironically, hiding meaning from one person whilst communicating it to another

- [sense I] swelks can range from frantic name-forgetting blurs to big 'dahhling' hugs, through a range of cool (i.e. cold) 'I'm in the band' postures, to bland mechanical bonhomie, to the classic grunt of 'you do not exist', right up to blatant toadying

swell, swelling [swɛl, swɛlɪŋ]

n see SELF and STUNT

swiddle [swɪdəl]

vb & n to enjoy looking at a group of people or animals that are standing about dispersed and all looking intently at something else in the distance

swuff [swʌf]

vb to try and solve a problem that can only be solved by action, by hoping, wishing and thinking—in other words, by magic

synaesthesia [sɪnɪsθiːzɪə]

n innate [common sense] ability to smell words, taste ideas, vibrate to the grey-red geogravimetric majesty of Keralan pheromones or register sighs as the muted, musical hums of ferromagnetic orientation

- the origin of apt metaphor, paradigm-smashing scientific intuition, marvellous art and the bright power to enjoy and express feelings that cannot be put literally into words

synonym [sɪnənɪm]

n different words that mean *fundamentally* the same thing

- synonym of *antonym* of AN-TONYM [antənɪm] *n* similar words which mean *fundamentally* different things

system [sɪstəm]

n a collection of integrated ideas, people, tools, objects and techniques

- there is, naturally, nothing wrong with a UTP-limited system (a.k.a. HUMAN SYSTEMS), which serve UNSELF (through us); beyond the UTP however, systems become tribes, cults, institutions, ideologies, states and, finally, THE SYSTEM

SYNONYMS AND ANTONYMS

HAVING ONLY ITS OWN EXPERIENCE AND LOGIC to judge by, self cannot distinguish between experiences which are motivated by self, and those that are not. Self therefore views emotions and ideas as essentially opposites which, viewed from the perspective of unself, are fundamentally the same (fundamentally egoic) OPPOSAMES.[55] For example:

FUNDAMENTAL SYNONYMS

pessimism & optimism
work & play
capitalism & communism
death & life
subjective & objective

hope & fear
mentation & emotion
left & right
religion & science
me & you

These illusory—or at best secondary—self-divisions are created by ego in the same way that waves and particles, or ducks and rabbits, are abstracted from their both-and unselfish source (*see* PARADOX). Ego, and its institutions, then zooms in on the superficial differences between its invented terms or, more commonly, implicitly accepts a cultural tradition that uncritically assumes these differences as absolutely real.

Ego also views as synonymous—basically alike—experiences which are antonymous—essentially unlike. For example:

FUNDAMENTAL ANTONYMS

uncertain & precarious
art & pornography
character & personality
offence & abuse
sorrow & unhappiness
feeling / love & emotion
earth[ling] & world[ling]
generosity & profligacy
pain & suffering

idleness & boredom
partnership & relationship
love-making & sex
spontaneous & reckless
intelligence & cleverness
self-mastery & self-control
originality & novelty
empathy & care
freedom & rights

Fundamental opposites relate to experiences which are either unself-motivated or self-motivated; a distinction that self, by itself, is not just *unable* to perceive or acknowledge—it automatically conflates opposites into one idea—but frantically *unwilling*—for acknowledging that there is a *qualitative* difference between work and activity, or education and schooling, or anger and [passionate] ire, or bestiality and animality, or even between being asleep and awake, is to acknowledge the existence of a reality that the *quantitative* self and its institutions is absolutely unable to perceive, possess or control; and, consequently, must define negatively as 'extremist', 'unnuanced' and, most tellingly, 'black-and-white'. Ego sees all fundamental antonyms as 'shades of grey', just as it judges all fundamental synonyms to be 'black and white'.

To complicate matters further there are two different kinds of antonym, or opposite. BASIC ANTONYMS, such as 'cold' and 'hot' or 'extroverted' and 'introverted', which mark out the natural space within self or between self-SWELLS. John prefers reggae, and Jane prefers disco, or Jane prefers Chinese food and John prefers Indian, which enables them to complement each other. The FUNDAMENTAL ANTONYMS here mark out a radical difference in kind between unself and ego. If John prefers hip-hop, fast-food and fucking and Jane funk, slow-food and love-making they are headed for divorce. The difference between horizontal antonyms and vertical antonyms is, therefore, *itself* a fundamental antonym, and, like all such antonyms, ego systematically blends the two into one.

But of course there is no reason, in ordinary speech, to make all these careful distinctions; who cares, really, if we call it love-making or sex, or if we make a reasonable distinction between death and life, or sex and fucking, or blur everything into a mashed up word-soufflé? The point here is, regardless of what words we use, that there are vital differences or similarities in experience that ego cannot perceive and, when it sniffs out threat, seeks to obscure by unconsciously using language to blur distinctions and to create illusory divisions.

HOW TO INSTITUTIONALISE THE WORLD

THE MOST IMPORTANT PHASE OF BRAINWASHING occurs in the home (*see* BRAINWASHING) and at school (*see* SCHOOL). After leaving school the young adult is ready for PROFESSIONAL EGO-CONDITIONING, and is handed over to the institutions of the world, also known as THE SYSTEM.

This vast mechanism of interlocking institutions, tools and techniques was originally created by and is continually powered and informed by the addictive PRIMAL FEAR and the self-informed mental–emotional momentum of the egos of its individual members (*see* SELF). Because it is a manifestation or reflection of the self-informed self, the only purpose of the system is to serve itself. It will feed, house, entertain and care for its members, but only while they are useful to it; i.e. while they are egoic. If an individual is not sufficiently ambitious, mean-spirited, cynical, violent, addicted, subservient, selfish, inhuman or lacking in fundamental dignity she will be discarded from the institutions of the world, prevented from rising through its hierarchies, ignored, ridiculed, exiled (into poverty or precarity), imprisoned or killed by its authorities.

This is not a conscious activity. Nobody is consciously exterminating dissidents, and there is no illuminati ensuring that only system-subservient mediocrities get admitted into prestigious universities, get the highest-paying jobs or get elected (*see* INSTITUTIONAL ANALYSIS). There is no conscious conspiracy because ego *is* unconsciousness. Conscious awareness of what is really going on, is a threat. *The* threat.

In the early [pre-modern] days of the system this threat was eradicated through direct human agency (the will and *overt* violence of individuals in power), but, as flesh-and-blood human intervention contains the seeds of consciousness, it became necessary to abolish humanity as soon as rational technique was advanced enough to create a modern system that could run without it; automatically, and thus, *covertly*.

Without the possibility of selfless human interference the system uses its own mechanical-egoic 'intelligence' to manage its operations; which means that it follows the only

directive it can possibly understand; expand (or 'profit') forever, infinitely beyond any human (UTP) limit. This leads to
excessively large institutional structures which A) cannot run
without bureaucracy B) prioritise abstraction and specialisation C) manufacture nothing but shoddy porn and D) hollow
out culture, destroy nature and generate inequality and waste.

Because human beings do not enjoy living in a sterile,
unreal, unnatural, bureaucratic virtual prison of proliferating
bullshit, and will instinctively subvert any attempt to enslave
them, all institutional processes must be directed through a
set of [interlocking and mutually-reinforcing] FILTERS:

THE FIVE SYSTEM FILTERS

1. RELIANCE ON SELF · the egoic system can only perceive and
therefore function through what can be imagined, possessed,
measured, described, controlled, desired, feared or rationally
used. Everything else—originality, responsiveness to the context, *genuine* mysticism, profound love for humanity and for
nature, outrageous generosity, genius, death and revolutionary
beauty—must be ignored, exterminated, controlled, outlawed,
ridiculed or suppressed from nursery school.

2. RELIANCE ON TECHNIQUE · consciousness is, a priori, ruled
out by the modern system. Its only comprehensible values are
rational action, logical thought, technology, and the ordering
of linear timespace into discrete objective parcels (money,
countries, classes of people, etc.) for technical processing in
service to the system. This technique, however, does not just
demand *more* technique (a machine which produces more
raw material needs more machines to refine and distribute
the surplus, more technical labour, which must be pacified
with more propaganda, etc.) but demands *total* technique (a
technical police force, for example, must constantly observe
everyone to be 'perfect'[56]); there is no other value as comprehensible, to ego-technique, as 'more' and 'total'. 'Different'
or 'nuanced' or 'truthful' simply do not, or cannot, exist and
any suggestion of them must be eradicated.[57]

3. RELIANCE ON THE MARKET · the institutions of the world must all be subservient to the needs of the profit-oriented property-economy. They must be run by corporations that *must* put profit above every other consideration (through fiduciary duties to shareholders and through operating in a cut-throat competitive system). This permanent market-expansion creates distances which can only be covered by the system, waste which can only be disposed of by the system, sickness which can only be cured by the system, futility which can only be made meaningful by the system, helpless stupidity which can only be educated by the system and loneliness which can only be filled by the system. Man is crippled and deformed by the market, and then sold crutches to complete himself.

4. RELIANCE ON OTHER INSTITUTIONS · all reputable information, opinion, authority and, should the system ever struggle, the support of tax and armed-intervention, can only come from institutions (and their professional representatives), elite graduates or agents of power. No other source is as corrupt, as indoctrinated or as submissive; i.e. as 'credible'.

5. RELIANCE ON OBJECTIFYING EXPOSURE · from cradle to grave individuals must be under continual BUREAUCRATIC surveillance so that A) they can be measured, recorded and 'known' and therefore controlled or filtered out; and, more importantly, B) they will place themselves under their *own* SCHIZOID, spontaneity-suppressing self-conscious scrutiny. For the first objective—of CONTROL THROUGH MEASUREMENT—it is necessary that individuals are monitored by those in institutional power (doctors, social-workers, teachers, spooks, etc.). For the second objective—CONTROL THROUGH SELF-CONSCIOUSNESS—the identity or motive of the observer is irrelevant; TEEVEE viewers, neighbours, social-media friends, comments-page peers and some chap with a camera-phone can all enhance the inherently passive, predictable, ADDICTED, anxious and self-referential qualities of the objectified self (PERSONALITY or mask) when it feels like it is being watched, named, rated, judged, defined and recorded.[58]

These five system filters [59] are not consciously put in place by an evil cabal, they are created *automatically* from the expand-and-profit priorities of self, and they *automatically* result in the creation of artificial (VIRTUAL) environments which are separate from nature and society, which force members into subservient roles, which punish independence, which honour only those activities which the market can make use of and which devalue and suppress honesty, generosity, innocence, beauty, soft-consciousness and even masculinity (through rewarding inaction, obedience and wordiness) and femininity (through rewarding ambition, rationality and insensitivity).

Although the system runs automatically, there still has to be human-shaped entities in authority who work, while *at* work, to personally eradicate the threat of independence, but their actions are always within the framework of the system. If they were not—if they were not sufficiently egoic—they would have been caught by system filters long before they reached their position of power. Everyone, for example, who reads submissions, applications, references, progress reports and the results of MERELY OBJECTIVE tests knows the unspoken code by which system-friendly psyches are to be welcomed and those who 'are disruptive', 'have a relaxed attitude', 'cannot concentrate', 'are not team-players', 'are not technically adept', 'have strong opinions', 'are not working to full potential' and other euphemisms for *'reject!'* [60] are passed over. And everyone who holds the keys to elite positions of authority can sniff out the right attitudes, the right ideas, the right 'work ethic' and even the right tone of voice for the job (*see* TASTE).

This is how psychopathic [61] CEOS, ambitious interns, hollow politicians, system-friendly bosses, SHUFFED-OUT professionals, living-dead billionaires and the favoured cultural elite can all claim, with total—factually accurate—sincerity, that *'nobody tells me what to think'*. Nobody has to tell them what to think, because the system would not have allowed them to reach the top if they had to be told. They have learnt—long, long ago—to internalise the values and priorities of the system, and have repeatedly demonstrated their willingness to do so. This is why they SUCCEED.

taboo [təbu:]

adj & n an unspoken law or limit, informally thought-policed by the outrage and offence of egotists, which A) prevents any foundational GROUPTHINK or GROUPFEEL emotion being made light of (or even mentioned) B) conceals power-relations behind gentility C) eradicates the threat of non-verbal or non-literal communication

- A) some taboos span most HISTORICAL (post-FALLEN) cultures—such as DEATH, DEPTH and innocent physical SPONTANEITY (usually described as 'madness')—while others are restricted to particular groups which rely on TOTEMS [təʊtəmz] *n.pl* ideas that are believed to have 'spiritual' significance; the MARKET totem of 'equality', for example, results in taboos on 'inappropriate' terms such as 'chick',[62] 'gaylord', 'spade' and 'spazmo', whereas the RELIGIOUS totem of 'purity' leads to taboos on poo (*see* TASTE and notes to APT)

- B) eventually the boss who abuses the blackfella discovers that his position is better concealed and secured by not being 'racist'

- C) offense, like friendship, is not in words, but in context and tone; which the literal, vibe-blind ego can never understand

- synonym of OFFENCE [əfɛns] *n* an unconscious STATUS transaction (*see* IMPRO) and DISTASTEFUL [dɪsteɪstfʊl] *adj* social marker used to internalise control over others

- antonym of INSULT [ɪnsʌlt] *n & vb* a dickish vibic-tonal attack on the heart

- some taboos cover all situations—questioning belief itself, rather than belief in specifics; death, unfettered joy, touch, nudity, SEEING each other and, that most subversive and awkward of topics; true love—while others are site specific, e.g.;

- LAB · questioning the foundations of science

- NEWS · talking about the profit-motive behind state slaughter or exposing the play instead of the players

- RELIGION · investigation of sources and reminders of the humanity of masters

- WORK · pointing out that we're doing all of this for some wanker's share dividend, making serene love on the reception desk and 'INAPPROPRIATE LAUGHTER'

TASTE

T ASTE IS THE NETWORK OF SENSITIVITIES (swells) that forms in the whole growing self. It does not just apply to the surface aesthetic opinions of self—your choice of music, furnishing, dress, food and films—nor just to your career, romantic inclinations and religious preferences, but to your sensitivity to the vibe of the day, to the feeling tones of your fellows, to the character of animals, levels of cuteness, physiognomy, unspoken understandings and countless other subtle spheres of soft-life discernment.

Although the NATURAL, unselfish self *primarily* enjoys all natural, unselfish experience—natural food, weather, art, etc.—it has a *secondary* tendency towards those experiences that correspond to the unique TASTE-MATRIX (or swell-matrix) of its own specific, innate, self; which changes or evolves over time and place. So, for example, young children are naturally averse to strong, fermented flavours, geriatrics steer away from thunderous dance-beats and everyone tends to expand and refine those elements of self connected to their unique character, and to their unique SCENIUS or 'local style'.

If, however, the growth of self is conditioned by the selfish ego of its parents or by the UNHAPPY SUPERMIND of the self-world, its surrounding vibe-milieu will press upon the most intimate level of psyche during the critical crises of early youth (*see* BRAINWASHING) and force attention into self, creating a self-informed PERSONALITY which is pathologically averse to *primary* unself, causing the tree of the self to grow unnaturally, lop-sided and stunted; either limited to a shrinking range of *secondary* flavours, genres, styles, tones, attitudes, likes and dislikes; or sucking in everything, natural and unnatural, in bland, indiscriminate consumption. The fruits or such trees are flavourless and bitter, and so must be slathered in neon-crude SALT (*see* SELF).

The wider determinants of taste-corruption, after parent and vibe-milieu, are wealth and class, which is to say, FORM and FUNCTION. The richer you are, the less you have to deal with function; actually perceiving [or actually doing things with] actual stuff. You pay other people to really experience, or do, things for you, while you spend your time playing the games, climbing the institutional ladders, doing the accounts, designing the logos, interpreting the laws, diagnosing the problems, thinking about the theories or gadding about enjoying the pleasure of the more comfortable cells in the prison; focusing, in other words, on form. To the extent that your self runs your life, you begin to feel an unconscious *distaste* for function — collective, physical work with sensory objects — because function, for you, equals unself.

In art this might manifest as disdain for a beautiful picture of an apple by an unknown artist. The picture might be beautiful, but it doesn't *quite* count as art because, for the upper-classes, art is not about representing something real, that you would actually look at, or eat, but is an opportunity to talk about the materials the artist used, other artists, the price-value or authenticity of the piece or, if the work is pornographically titilating, applying a few laconic adjectives to the sensation ('moving', 'profound', 'playful', etc.). These are all assessments of form, fine discernment of which is picked up, through vibe-conditioning, in the vibe-milieu of the 'tasteful' middle-class kitchen, in the refined plasma of the drawing room and the bland Voice-of-Authority of a rich father; long before any intellectual model of the world is grasped or any overt indoctrination occurs.[63]

The formal-functional divide finds its way into every social activity; including literature, philosophy, sex, politics, religion and art. The ludicrous fashion, anti-human architecture, inaccessible politics, ivory-tower science, abstract philosophy, meretricious modern novels, decadent modern abstract art and snobbish or subservient journalism of the formal upper or middle classes elicit feelings of frustration, incomprehension and anger from ordinary working people; just as the gaudy fashion, lack of 'learning', crude physicality, sentimentality and taboo directness of the prisoner class elicit feelings of condescending contempt from their guards.

These constraints and freedoms are the SOCIAL MARKERS which keep the classes apart; which is to say, keep the essential psychic structure of uncivilisation—founded on the separation of the classes—intact. It is this structure, or implicit system, which is the ultimate cause of the deep-seated and unconscious rules of uncivilised etiquette, taste and taboo, and its development can be clearly traced in uncivilised history:[64]

Initially courtesy, modesty and discernment arose naturally from the extreme SENSITIVITY of unfallen people. As ego grew, and established itself socially in early cults and pre-modern civilisations, so did insensitivity, SELFISHNESS and outstanding levels of greed and violence. Initially this was dealt with in kind, but as powerful cults gained a monopoly on violence and their elites managed to cut themselves off completely from functional and physical activities, so physical work became, *along with all individual displays of physicality and violence*, DISTASTEFUL. In one sense this 'improved' people, who were forbidden, by the new unspoken rules of taste, from seizing wenches, thumping sods, gobbing mead and such. But the new rulers of manners were unable to distinguish these repulsive habits from childish displays of physicality, sexuality, nudity and wild filthy foolishness, all of which were *also* ruled inadmissible in the new game of modern life.

These new rules were also essential for governance. As uncivilised society grew so did stratification, specialisation, and long, indirect chains of dependence which—instead of the direct and open *control* of pre-modern populations—demanded indirect and concealed methods of *self*-control through the brainwashing, institutionalisation, self-consciousness and altered tastes of its members. First its elites, and then society in general learned to instinctively recoil from world-threatening displays of irregularity, spontaneity, innocence, death, sexuality and physicality, all of which became offensive, were hidden from view or were unconsciously suffocated by the now self-regulating individual in her predictable, restrained and polite social actions (or in those of her conditioned children).[65]

The result of this millennial modernising process is a post-modern, scientismic system that has it that taste is an arbitrary matter of opinion acquired from 'culture' and 'inclination', or that takes 'good taste' as an unquestioned given.

That taste (like art) expresses personal fears, that it is related to social inequality and that it is distorted by cutting individuals off from universal NATURE, can never be intelligently addressed by the impersonal, anti-social, unnatural WORLD, which would prefer that you didn't breach the walls of ego, of class or of reality, and will do everything in its power to stop you from striking at the root of taste in self-mastery, subversion, deeply distasteful spontaneity and *outrageous* courtesy.

❦

taste [teɪst]

n 1 sensitive (and, eventually, miraculous) unselfish discernment of vibe-quality (especially of one's unique swell-matrix) 2 priorities of subtle attention determined by wealth or class and used to sell one's self 3 physiognomy of the psyche

· skipping through restrictive TASTE-MATRICES is an important component of SELF-MASTERY, entailing:

· A) learning, when possible, to live with genuine quality in experiences that lie outside of your social class (seeking out the creative qualities of cultures and styles far distant from your own, patiently exploring strange genres, giving up EXCLUSIVE privileges that your class confers)

· B) discerning cross-class quality in experiences that lie outside of *all* social class (PRESENCE, WILD NATURE, SILENCE, LOVE-MAKING and other aspects of UNSELF)

tather [taðə]

vb to think about another person, why they are as they are and how they are different to you, in order to later present them with a gift of new self-understanding

tax [taks]

vb & n ingenious means of forcing poor people to supply armies, support criminal financial institutions (esp. banks), pay bureaucrats and run up DEBTS

technique [tɛkniːk]

n an interlinking system of tools (TECHNOLOGY), skills and methods which either A) is used by human beings or B) uses them

THE FUTURE OF TECHNOLOGY

Here's a little of what we have to look forward to:

- pay-per-use body-organs
- for the masses; clothes, furniture and tools so shoddy and synthetic they must be re-printed weekly (for a fee)
- for elites; shelves made from moon rocks, milk from real cows and the inconvenience of consciousness erased by uploaded minds to the cloud
- fridges that spy on you, or that refuse to discharge your pizza pills if you're engaging in pernicious thoughts
- state-administered key-cards to use mouths in registered conversation shops
- vast mirrors in space directing reflected sunlight over the surface of the earth, eradicating night forever (with drugs that suppress both sleep and anxiety compulsory)
- police drones to immobilise bridge jumpers, laser-whipping offensive comments and tractor-beaming any minds improperly logged off
- rose-tinted VR contact-lenses
- everyone rated by everyone for *everything*, with low score defined as mental illness
- ten-storey strawberry cubes

- if technique is kept within its UTP, and man is capable of using the tools of self and technique, rather than being used by them, technique can be used to build UTOPIA; if not—if technique is SELF-informed—it *has* to become a TOTALITARIAN, SCHIZOID, over-specialised, CANCER covering the world and corrupting awe, innocence and communion [66]
- any CRITICISM of technique (such as industrial drugs, literacy, industrial-military intervention, surveillance, division of labour, cars or smartphones) is instantly and violently rejected by AVERAGE-MAN, who necessarily makes an extension of himself into his tools, his pleasures and, consequently, his SYSTEM
- self-informed technique, like self-directed ego, *automatically* CO-OPTS Q-words by measuring them; when you go looking for beauty, truth or consciousness with a tape measure, you find nothing but porn, theories or brain-scans; when you go looking for the universe with a telescope, you find only floating rocks
- *see* SYSTEM [67] and SELF

teenage [tiːneɪdʒ]

adj descriptive of either 1 sweet superconscious explosion of the TRANSDIMENSIONAL self in natural life, symptoms include: A) QWOTH B) SHANGO C) OSCAVINE displosions D) a new kind of genius trumpet-blast E) new soft-conscious awareness of just how fucked-up it all is and F) intense erotic joy or 2 the growth of the usurping ego, symptoms including: A) deciding 'from now on I'll be…' B) annoying restless behaviour and then, when told to stop, doing it once more, just so ego can feel that it is choosing to stop C) perversely refusing to do what you enjoy in order to make everyone concerned D) latching onto any reason to feel SPECIAL (no matter how tenuous or sordid) E) being governed by terror of the laughter of peers[68] F) not feeling alive when alone and the conviction that everyone else is having a good time G) aggression under the guise of 'honesty' H) insane self-consciousness (for boys of EGO, for girls of BODY) I) extreme TOGGING J) total VR-PORN induced social and psychological paralysis

teevee-internet [tiːviː]

n 1 sense-dimming narcotic with motor-impairing properties 2 convenient means of deadening the inner core of your being in order to make a day suppressing your finer instincts bearable 3 a tightly-focused square of light beaming suffering-and-excitement-manipulating pornographic PROPAGANDA into an immobile, sense-dimmed body; i.e. indistinguishable from HYPNOTISM 4 a place to *watch* DEMOCRACY

· highly ADDICTIVE; moderate use results in aggressive forms of dependence

· SIDE-EFFECTS include depressed mood and numbness, irritability, reduced attention-span, inability to discern variation and nuance, limited vocabulary, violence, STARING, drained feeling after prolonged use, decreased physical performance, reduced alertness, sapped drive and impaired ability to learn, unpleasant or trivial dreams, clumsiness, increased conformity to established opinion and subservience to legitimate authority, fear of life, diminished self-restraint, less patience with the normal delays of daily life, dependence on the techno-market, a decreased tolerance of unstructured time, suspicion of love (and of the good in people), distorted view of reality (skewed towards vested interests of media-owners), degraded creativity and delusions of culture

- tolerance to the effects of the drug occurs through regular exposure, leading to extreme empathy-atrophy, inability to perceive genuine, natural harmony and the development of a fat, rubbery arse
- *yeaah*, but sometimes it's alright isn't it?
- part of the wider HISTORY of LITERACY-TEEVEE-INTERNET-VR software development, with literacy allowing the most independence (and reverie) and VR the least, and the internet (a 'diverse', 'deprofessionalised', 'democratic', 'sharing', 'gift economy' run by a uniform, PROFESSIONAL, autocratic, secretive, market economy) just the latest stage in the PROGRESS of mankind towards a state of total bodiless subservience to a phone (*see* VIRTUAL)

temenos [kɑːli]

n I the pitiless exterminating angel of brooding annihilation and total, consuming darkness that lies deep in the void of nature, in the strange intelligence of woman and somewhere in the dark, at around 3am 2 the anxiety the average mind [of the AVERAGE MAN] feels when it is surrounded by nothing made by mind 3 to realise while walking around a large empty house, with dread growing from unease to horror, not just that there is no furniture there, nor that there is nobody else there, but that *you* aren't there (this is the night-time counterpart to the day-time misery of changing your life completely or going somewhere new, only to find that you *are* still there)[69]

- also present before DEATH, total loss, utter COLLAPSE and HEARTBREAK
- big sis of MR CERBERUS

thist [θɪst]

n an access of primal fury occasioned by banging one's head or stubbing a toe

- thists are usually of such primitive immediacy, that they propel one back into an animist state in which cupboard doors and table legs have secret and sadistic agendas

- but do note that although thists are often immature and indiscriminate, occasionally objects *do* secretly move to unexpected locations (door frames shrink, table legs shift a bit, cups swap sides of the desk) in order to sadistically mock your lack of awareness
- *see* ECTOMONISH

thought [θɔːt]

n I tiny invisible tube leading out from now and into what is not 2 a useful abacus in a useful storeroom tucked in the mansion of the heart which can be found down a long back-road in the empire of the senses 3 super-addictive ever-shifting teevee-screen stretched over the self; with power to birth new vibes and worlds, but as superficial as a soap-bubble-skin, as stable as a stickleback's shadow and as destructive as a megacluster of exploding hypernovae

thunder–cupboard [jɔːpə]

n I one who, upon arriving at the unknowable, heads *straight* towards the unknowabler 2 one whose motto is *'better dead than worried'*[70]

thunt [θʌnt]

n one who takes a lift to go up a single floor or who prefers travelators to feet

tibling [tɪblɪŋ]

vb.part persuading oneself that a long-hoped-for event which has suddenly become impossible to attain would have been harmful or wrong and in fact you didn't want it anyway

time [tʌɪm]

n I a useful-dreadful clock-made illusion 2 a sexy goddess on a park bench

- madame time treats men as a woman approached by a suitor: if he (or if his culture) treats her like an obstacle to be overcome, believing that if he hits the right combo he will win, she will walk away, freeze over or annihilate him; if he tries to buy her, she will, at best, only give what can be bought; but if he seeks to involve her in what is actually, scriptlessly, happening, she will take off all her clothes

- time (sense 1) experienced via the HARD-CONSCIOUS EGO-PROBE is a three dimensional substance that, like money, can be spent, saved, lost, given, wasted and taken... communication *through* such timestuff is a matter of packaging information into boxes and sending them over to an unpacking mind-machine at the other end of a long, long language-pipe
- time (sense 2) experienced selflessly, via the PINK-TIP, is a continent of ever-varying feelings, seasons and intensities that ebbs into walls, flows through noses, floats and bubbles over the balcony and dissolves into a soft-edged TRANSDIMEN-SIONAL übersoup... communion *as* such timelife is a Q-question of inhabiting the one CONTEXT we share, *instantly*, and allowing it to radiate through the doors of the senses, blown open

tog [tɒg]
vb 1 to unconsciously put down same-sex rivals in a mixed-sex interaction 2 to crawl across a three-mile-wide river of excrement to fuck someone you despise

tomawari [tɒməwɑːri]
n a detour taken to avoid having to say 'goodbye' to someone twice
- *After Akihiro bumped into Mr Akutagawa in the supermarket cereal aisle he was forced to take a somewhat ridiculous tomawari through feminine hygiene*

tomo, ovo [təʊməʊ, əʊvəʊ]
n the combination of sound and movement in novel [especially fantastically grandiose] ways while performing minor chores, such as cleaning, shopping or herding
- part of the secret ART of making great art from insignificant acts
- *see* YUDO and RITUAL

totalitarian [təʊtalɪtɛːrɪən]
adj descriptive of a system which demands complete subservience to itself—not to a particular state, group, ideology or leader (which may, nevertheless, exist and direct attention); but to the reality-denying system itself, to its structure, its priorities (e.g. profit) or to its ideological discipline
- compatible with fascism, democracy, communism, monarchism, corporatism,

feudalism and CAPITALISM; terms which describe local varieties of totalitaria
- the perfected totalitarian system does not have totalitarian theories, there is nothing arbitrary or cruel about its operation, nothing useless or overtly unfair; such practices are part of the [pre-modern] formation of totalitarianism
- drearily literal
- *see* SYSTEM

tradition [trədɪʃən]
n 1 (plus UNSELF) the soft, permeable cultural boundary of a healthy society (a.k.a. GUIDELINES) 2 (minus GENIUS, SCENIUS and CONTEXT) either a postmodern (left) world of rootless 'realities' or a fascist (right) world of monotheist / monocultural TOTALITARIA (a.k.a. LAWS)
- when guidelines becomes divorced from the context (especially when they are written down; *see* BUREAUCRACY and VIRTUAL) they become LAWS which then rule [future] contexts to which they are totally, and often ridiculously, inapt; except, of course, to the priests and professionals who uphold them

tragepalm [tradʒɪpɑːm]
vb & n a fundamentally disappointing [or desaphoric] prize, victory or promotion
- complement of EUPHIASCO

transdimensional [ɪtəːnɪtiː]
adj TIME *as* SPACE

triumfire [trʌɪʌmfʌɪə]
n an inner furnace of reckless despair while at work, inevitably leading to A) running a herd of sheep through the manager's office B) running bollock-naked through reception with a ring-binder on your head bellowing *'I am the sun-god Ra!'* and finally C) turning to your fellows with a jaunty *'see you on the beach colleagues!'* and calmly strolling out
- realising your life-story is one you couldn't be *paid* to sit your way through, tends to generate a veritable volcano of triumfire

tround [traʊnd]
n the surprising discovery, after having been 100% sure that you could not possibly give more than 70%, that, when you have no choice but to do more than 140%, there was at least another 180% left in the tanks

--------- TRANSDIMENSIONAL ---------

A THREE-DIMENSIONAL OBJECT—for example a hand—entering a flat two dimensional world is perceived by a flatlander as five separate disks being born, joining together, then separating and vanishing. The flatlander, with a two-dimensional mind and body, cannot mentally or physically experience the hand as it really is; undivided, in three dimensions. To the flat-lander three-dimensions are a myth which may be dismissed as heresy or mystical nonsense.[71]

That in the flat-lander which is conscious of the time-space mind and body, however, precedes two-dimensions. To the extent that the flat-lander is conscious of his two-dimensional self and his two-dimensional reality he will *intuit* three dimensions; just as, if I am conscious of separate selves in three dimensions, I can unselfishly intuit the entire transdimensional organism they are unthinkably, mysteriously, a part of; a UNIVERSAL living tree of matter, thought, vibe and energy that, seen as a whole, this little me flows in and out of.

Intuition of this enormous transdimensional organism, leads to INSPIRATION that somehow seems to come from nowhere, spacetimeless creativity that somehow seems to pre-empt the future, miracle instinct that somehow knows what plants (or people) are pleasant or poisonous, deep reconciliation with a universe I know is not an alien no-man's-land, and a bright sense of insane adventure which intensifies the mystery of the moment, making so-called 'ordinary' sensations of colours, sounds, flavours and vibes, an intricate and infinitely bizarre madness of quality that you and I share, shape, metaphorically map, play in, love, eat... *are*.

It also superficially solves the problem of free will—there is freedom in the lower separate-dimension, but not in the higher connected one—the problem of evil—isolated dollops of excrement on an otherwise integrated übertree—and the problem of entangled particles—which are only separate in spacetime. Although, of course, these problems—*who's in charge here? why does shit happen?* and *what is reality?*—are far too deep—which is to say real—for thought to do away with.

truth [truːθ]

n I the non-factual experience of the experiencer as the experienced 2 what is actually happening, at the moment 3 an intensely perceived seems-to-be

- first *absolute* (because there is nothing in the universe that CONSCIOUSNESS can possibly be compared to) then, according to context, DUCK-RABBIT *relative*
- because the truth is both A) real everyday experience and B) the extraordinary experience *of* it, truthful accounts seem, to people having ordinary (UNPARADOXICAL) experiences of their own unreal lives, to be either boringly obvious or threateningly bizarre
- ego and its world are *extremely* hostile to the truth and either co-opt it into a cult, or reject it as illusory, relative ('just a matter of opinion') ridiculous, 'mystical' or 'too deep for me!'
- near synonym of MYTH

tufo [tjuːfəʊ]

n I a mad thought, swiftly dismissed, that actually holds the ego-threatening secret to which way up to hold the strange instrument called 'life' 2 an obscenely trivial or irrelevant thought (FESQUE) at a critical time

- e.g. imagining launching yourself in front of a passing train, idly considering never coming back from the paper shop, thinking of marvellous thighs during tea with the queen or thinking of the queen while stroking marvellous thighs

turbulate [təːbjʊleɪt]

vb to nebulously downgrade or vibe-smother someone through irony, smirk, supercilious micro-expressions, STARE, FRINK or other schizoid techniques of distancing and subtle objectification (such as that most sadistic of questions, *'what do you do?'*)

turm [təːm]

vb to obsessively and morbidly verify that one exists by checking every reflective surface, or selfie, one passes

twilt [twɪlt]

vb & n to imperceptibly wilt when blocked by a literal response to one's playfulness, when forced to play a professional part or when confronted by ludicrously shaved genitals

U IS FOR
unversation
rapport
DESTROYED

V IS FOR
vagina
to cuddle
THE VOID

übernews [uːbənjuːz]

n news from the big room

- e.g. man gets tone of hello slightly wrong, chicken in man suit robs other chickens, gene found for slight confusion over rust, ashes scattered on people waiting in supermarket checkout queue, cow's milk opposite of bullshit, etc.

überself [uːbəsɛlf]

n a big person, made up of little persons, made of up littler persons, made up of littler cells, made of up of littler atoms, all able to commune with each other by not being themselves

- antonym of CANCER

übertree [uːbətriː]

n compressed ball of white-hot lightning which flares up through layers of rock and, when it meets the surface, extends fractically outward, tearing through timespace in a gobsmacking existential vent which we occasionally register and refer to as 'tree'

- mega-detonated into this dimension with UR-BOMBS [ʊəbɒmz] *n.pl* seed-grenades which, upon striking soil, explode like geysers, fracturing the frozen air with thick-fingered full-crested knotted crowns, interlocking into the cloud-canyons of the sky

- *the tree does not yes, does not no, but bruises, or provides, a plum*

uncivilisation [ɛːstrɪpwʌn]

adj see WORLD

unconscious [ʌnkɒnʃəs]

adj & n either 1 the WORLD of SELF or 2 the UNIVERSE of UNSELF… blocked out or excluded by the reverse telescope of tight consciousness

- soft-consciousness of the whole is impossible while areas unpleasant to enter are markered off; you can't, in other words, abandon the compulsive, brightly lit, highway of the self while the darkness is labelled 'do not enter'

- the self-informed self will do whatever it can to keep unself out of its life, but it can *never* be conscious of its defences (of the lies I tell myself, of the real reason for my anxieties and fears, and so on) because that which is TRULY CONSCIOUS of self is UNSELF

- COLLECTIVE UNCONSCIOUS = GROUPFEEL

underpriviliged [ɪksklu:dɪd]
adj necessary complement
of PRIVILEGED

· unprivileged LOSERS who
refuse to WORK have three
choices to secure privilege;
1. *don't bother* (in which
case they will be ignored)
2. *shout* (in which case they
will be defined as criminal)
or 3. *speak metaphorically*
(in which case they will be
defined as insane) [1]

ung [ʌng]
vb to continue explaining
after your point has been
made

unhappy [ʌnhapi]
adj happy, unhappy, happy,
unhappy, happy, *unhappy…* [2]

unhappy supermind [makʌɪ]
n collective [UNCONSCIOUS]
psychic nightmare of living
death that hangs over planet earth and imprisons its
inhabitants in a hypnotised
mass-psychotic hallucina-
tion of three-dimensional
time and space comprised
of separate bodies and isolated self-instructing egos [3]
· the unhappy supermind, or
ZONE OF EVIL, is occasionally glimpsed when you SEE
where your burger actually

comes from, or your milk,
or when you see the lives of
the people who made your
door-handles, t-shirts and
pen-drives, or when you
see the deep physiognomy
of the eyes of people passing in cities and malls, or
when you hear the sigh of
the lovesick soil, or when,
very occasionally, a sucking sense of sadness and
dread and helpless horror
overwhelms you and you
experience the appalling
horror and SUFFERING of
the WORLD, as it is

· the unhappy supermind is
created by the unending
misery of ego in the work
world, but it feeds from the
acquisitive power-sex-food
reptile-brain of the free-
time world

· inhabits the CRAUNCH of
the chest and neck, feeds
off of the EMOTIONS and
daily deposits its parasitic
eggs in the right frontal
lobe, which hatch into the
mental KIPPLE of money,
success, bums, fragments
of films, dreams of power,
news-gossip, plans, what-
about-me, what-can-I-get-
out-of this, if-this, if-that
and endless, endless, endless, *endless* worry

unism [juːnɪzəm]

n not taking seriously the use of holiday-travel, religion, WORK, art, NARCOTICS, sex, food, sport, war, ideology, fun, cult or shopping to fill a hole inside

· persecuted everywhere

unitree [juːnɪtriː]

vb to impersonate a tree so well that birds land on you

universe [juːnɪvəːs]

n I living breathing organism that already is what it seems to be gradually turning into 2 a sacred enormity made up of laughing miniscules 3 the BIG ROOM

· touch it, and it will touch you, recognise it, and be recognised

· never mentioned by politicians; for all we know, they don't know it's there

university [juːnɪvəːsɪti]

n a gatekeeping device to A) maintain existing socioeconomic boundaries (an elite or postgraduate university degree is a class marker) B) prevent those who cannot afford college from enjoying the economic advantages that white-collar jobs provide C) throttle lower class access to power, science and art D) proliferate BUREAUCRACY (credentialism) and E) weed out dissent, integrity and self-knowledge through examination (*see* SCHOOL), specialism,[4] huge quantities of WORK, implicit pressures to conform to faculty groupthink and by separating the campus from society

· motivated by groupthink fears, adjusted-curiosity, venality, MARKET-discipline (COMPETITION), continual BUREAUCRATIC assessment and cloaked in a language of creativity, entrepreneurialism and jargon

unlanguage [ʌnlaŋgwɪdʒ]

n see UNVERSATION

unself [ʌnsɛlf]

n I the point where the annihilating mystery of silently witnessing soft consciousness behind 'me', meets the context (or 'thing in itself'[5]) 2 the root of darkness, the innocence of children and animals, silence, sacrifice, intense femininity, the wild, true love, great art, effective subversion, the sweet, contemplating eye and all EXPERIENCE when mind and emotions are soft or silent[6] because language is part of self—which is to say a manifestation of unself—it can only represent unself *indirectly* (through PARADOX) or *negatively* (through what it isn't); this is why art is *inherently* more truthful than science, why the bad guys are frequently more attractive than the goodies, why philosophy is *usually* more interesting when diagnosing PROBLEMS than when providing solutions, and why guides on how to write, draw, have fulfilling relationships, etc. focus almost exclusively on CRAFT or TECHNIQUE, and ignore preparing the bridal chamber for the genius source of creativity and fulfilment to flounce in and waltz you off the balcony

- although unself is the basis of MONISM [mɒnɪzəm] *n*—the PHILOSOPHICAL IDEA that, *ultimately* there are no distinctions in reality—it *falsely* suggests [to the self] DUALISM [djuːəlɪzəm] *n* the idea that reality is constituted of 'stuff' (or self) and some kind of spiritual or psychic 'unstuff' (or unself); but this is only because the unparadoxical self cannot conceive of a completely physical *and* conscious experience. In fact the [scientific] self has no idea *whatsoever* what stuff really is; the assumption that we somehow understand physicality, that matter is solid, or that it is unconscious, discrete, or entirely mind-graspable is the groundless—not to say very silly—foundation upon which all the fruitless, FUTILE mind-body debates rest, along with the consequent MYSTICAL-POLITICAL allegiance to the idea that consciousness arises from this body, or, even more stupidly, that it can be detected in neural activity[7]

- synonym of VOID & GOD[8]

unsolate [əʊldgɪtəri]
vb to revile a vice or crime that one has not the energy, opportunity or capacity to commit

unversation [ʌnvəseɪʃən]
n a compulsive, protective, hollow, self-ratifying, vibeless system-sustaining empathy-depth-blending-shutdown through TURBULATION and constant lingua-BLOCK
- easily commodified

UNVERSATION

U NVERSATIONLISTS DO NOT REALLY LISTEN to the conversation tree—or even to each other. This involves the 'listener' adding a certain number of headnods, 'uh-huhs' or 'wows' while—eyes flat and inward, or restlessly wandering around looking for something more interesting— he jitteringly-thinks about what he wants to say; comments out of step, clumsy, mechanical or jarringly forced; building a stunted, lopsided or over-swollen tree; a tree as drawn by a manager; scratchy, straight and strangely flat.

Some unversationalists are afraid of (or offended by; *see* TABOO) what their conversations may become. If it seems to be leading towards markered-off branches, towards CRITICISM or the unknown, they attempt to drive the structure out into a familiar branch; or—blunderingly unaware of the intricate structure just created—they will, like a fat kid kicking over a sandcastle, crush the entire thing with an argument, non sequitur, BLOCK, SPONK or FALLACY, in order to build their own tree, on their own terms.[9] Such comments feel unnecessarily emphatic, weird, pointless or naff. They create secret body-cringe[10] discomfort as the comment shuts down or jolts the flow of speech, and the conversation that grows is like every other controlled tree; spindly skeletons hung down with tasteless plastic fruit-boobs. Or they might not enter into the stream of speech at all, and—all distanced and enigmatic— avoid the silent, chaotic, unpredictable and dangerous game of *communion* (or SPEAKING TO THE BELLY); unless they know they can play it according to familiar rules.

urban-planning [panɒptɪkən] *n.phr* I the use of enormous windows, open-plan offices and bright lighting around living, WORKING and consumption units in order to turn the world into a 'you are being watched' environment, producing a feeling of total exposure and inducing introjection of the surveillance apparatus[11] 2 the use of confusing, disorienting layouts, sense-overloading sounds, advertisements and over-choice in zones of consumption in order to stimulate people to buy more [12]

urticles [əːtɪkəl]
n.pl 1 an insatiable desire to pick stickers off things 2 the magnetic pull of crumbs clinging to a stranger's lips

usury [juːʒəri]
n 1 lending at interest 2 the foundation of the MARKET 3 extortion 4 sorcery [13]

utopia [juːtəʊpɪə]
n full manifestation of the unselfish self
· an accurate description of utopia does not accurately present what it will look like—a recipe for totalitaria—but what it *feels like*
· '*A map of the world that does not include utopia is not worth glancing at…*'
                    Oscar Wilde

u.t.p. [juː tiː piː]
ab utility tipping point

vagina [vədʒʌɪnə]
n a dark, mysterious space designed to bring life into existence (*from* the void of

the womb) and to accommodate, give pleasure to and mysteriously commune with a flaming love-penis (*into* the void of the womb)
· different to ANUS [eɪnəs] *n* a tube designed to expel shit

valley [vali]
n an invisible upside-down mountain [wb]

vantasy [vantəsi]
n 1 failing by inadvertently enjoying victory before it has arrived 2 paralysis by analysis 3 snatching defeat from the jaws of victory 4 '*I've arrived! I'll be happy now*'

velm [vɛlm]
n the network of muscular tensions in gait, eye, facial expression, tone-muscle and attention which express the inner EMOTIONAL-ARMOUR and a resistance [14] acquired during early childhood to protect the suffering vibe-and-touch-starved self from pain and pleasure
· understood in others via PHYSIOGNOMIC PURZING, SEEN in oneself through AP-PERCEPTION and overcome in both through LOVE
· *see* BRAINWASHING and VIBE CONDITIONING

———————————— UTOPIA ————————————

U TOPIA IS—without law, police or central control—
ruled only by the SENSITIVE and contextually-aware
intelligence and fluid TRADITIONS of human beings
in DUNBAR GROUPS free to do what they like, howsoever they
please, governed by fluid traditional custom-boundaries and
the passion, excitement, vague, whiffling whims and subtle
sense of obviousness which wells up from bellyminds run
rapturously asunder—without ownership—except for what
you can carry and what you are actually using and so—without
class—where all the surplus from all productive work is just
given away (and where all activity, productive or otherwise,
is done just because it is enjoyable)—without destroying the
wild—in fact, using techniques already well understood (low
energy living, soil restoration and carbon-neutral agriculture,
zero carbon building, permaculture, rewilding, etc.) along
with a few barmy ways yet undiscovered (of communicating
with forests, taming mastodons and forming enormous trampolines out of mushrooms) helping the wild to flourish (and
so helping people to become wilder, more temperate, more
self-sufficiently forage-confident and more able to recognise
fractal harmony)—without ego—and so without porn, without shame, without guilt, without fear and with, with, *with* a
monstrous range of heart-rending and hilarious improvised
dramas, recognition of eyes that meet you in the street, thundering swing jams and dangerous festivals of strange, mad,
shattering joy of worship for *watankatatanka*, the ineffable
pulsating electric jellyfishgod which periodically rises above
the clouds, lashing out its fiery white limbs, pinning uto-
pians, howling with delight, to the sky—without a medical
profession—because without much ill-health; where people
are, as they were before the FALL, almost never sick, and with
the means of diagnosing and healing those that are ailing
available to every community—without over-specialism—
where everyone can do a huge number of things pretty well
and a few rare things (such as surgery) extremely well[15] and
therefore—without a teaching profession—because CHILDREN

can [where possible] join in with real social life; those that know more can, *without 'teaching'*, show basic skills to novices, and craftsmen who host genius can help journeymen became virtuosos—with genius everywhere—everyone is, in a healthy society, outstandingly good at a lot of things, and so opportunities for consummate tango, grand-master chess matches, full-speed horse-races, dark operas of death, intoxicated 'naked cluster' paragliding, mind-bending maths chat, ultimate-ninja assault-running, advanced pâtisserie, and the most enjoyable conversations men and women can possibly have are also everywhere, and what's more—with ten thousand years of technique to call on—and with human technology put to its proper use (i.e. play) just *think* what roller-blading bridges we could be radically frolicking across the Thames on, what jungle-libraries we could be swimming through, what solar-powered buses we could be making ten-thousand years of godlove on, or what—bio-fractal homes—we could be living in; with no time-constraints, no money-constraints and with INFINIPHILIC Gaudían intricacy guiding the wood-carving, buildings (from palm-shades to adobe-mud-lounges, to hazelnut-villages right up to lake-submerged domes of iron and oak, fancy-dress-pool-and-jam clubs and forest-city-canopy-cathedrals of living roof-beams) would all be as if grown from the ground, with towns more closely resembling coral-reefs—in which every sane human society could fit—with unself at the helm it is not just *possible* to allow the forest and plains to flourish, peppered with free hunter-gatherer societies that allow children to become friends with THE OTHER and to become, through active physical experience, unspecialised friends with their own illiterate nature; and it is not just *possible* to allow clean, white medieval-style farming hamlets of unalienated free mastercraftspeople neat in nearby hills, nestled against intricate and extensive forests of civilised study and inefficient industrial production slowly growing through and from local woodlands; and it is not just *possible* to hear the BRUNDLES of oaks, and to pay such soft adoring synaesthetic attention to the world that robins will tell you the weather and beavers will stop to admire you headwear... it is *necessary*.

UTOPIA AND DYSTOPIA

The Q-word utopia, like 'perfection', has been degraded by self, and the modern system it serves, to mean either an airy-fairy, unrealistic dream, or a form of DYSTOPIA; which can mean either rigid ORWELLIAN and KAFKAESQUE subservience to an objective idea or plan (the pre-modern or 'socialist' authoritarian 'utopia'), or flexible HUXLEYAN and PHILDICK-IAN subservience to ego's subjective fears and desires (the post-modern or 'capitalist' systemic techno-'utopia').

Both dystopian visions arise from ego and so both lead to a world that is superficially 'perfect' (i.e. on paper), monot-onous (predictable) and that leads, inevitably, to both violence (as the gods of chaos will no more be restrained and made to fit a describable aim, or world-order, or market-system than next week will, or your children, or your own nature; and must be forcibly boxed up) and horror (for as we now know, nature caged will eventually mutate into floods, fires and the insane, world-eating überselves of the suffering mass, unmasked).

The purpose of describing a real utopia is not the orwel-lian aim of describing a world we SHOULD create, nor is it the huxleyan nightmare of just allowing ego to run the show (and disparaging higher expectations of collective life as 'hippy' or 'fascist'), but to point (or ORIENT) towards the EXPERIENCE of an inner unegoic reality that is a prerequisite to creating, not just paradise, but anything other than hell. To put this another way, marking utopia on a map is not so that man changes his own country to mimic an ideal, but that he feels the exquisite need to set sail towards god-knows where.

YEAH? HOW?

Utopia—and not just the fruity oohs of *The Apocalypedia*, but the simple proto-utopia that most people want to see—of everyone having food, shelter and free-time enough to live well—cannot *primarily* occur from organising the world is a certain way, because the fluid, context-sensitive intelligence it is based on comes from the free human being. Utopia, like anything else worth experiencing, can only occur *naturally*, of its own accord, from the innate generosity, innocence, spontaneity, empathy and intelligence of *human nature*.

And how is this to happen? How are people to radically change? Anyone who has radically changed, who has seen their unnatural ego-world for what it really is, knows that the only answer that can be put into literal words like these, is SUFFERING.[16] Nothing changes man *quite* like the god-awful realisation that he is in the worst hell he could ever have imagined—and that it's all his RESPONSIBILITY.

So what are you going to do? Make people suffer? Only the sadistic ego is up for that one. But even if you could, it wouldn't work—man only changes when he sees that it is *his* responsibility, not the fault of some insane psychotherapeutic wizard. What's more, even if you were screwed up enough to want to 'teach mankind a lesson', you still couldn't do it half as brilliantly as man does it himself. Ego (or capitalism, or virtuality) *automatically* creates its own downfall. It contrives to hide or tranquillise the painful effects of its reality-destruction, or pass them on to its servants or, via DEBT, on to the future; but that can only work for so long. In the end the effects become so hard to ignore that even wealth, privilege and power don't work. Even madness itself becomes no place to hide.

The effects of the disintegration of ego's dystopian madness—crime, war, mass-starvation, genocidal corporate police-states, pain and the death of the earth—are now breaking out all over the world and will continue to do so until they are impossible to ignore. There is no need to fret about this. The crime, the crashes, the droughts, and the rising sea-levels are all symptoms of DEATH, and we know what death is. We pretend we don't; we pretend that the deaths that inspire us in stories, are just stories. We pretend that the heroine miraculously back from the grave has nothing to do with winter, or sleep, or our own miraculous recoveries from the dark horrors of the pit, and we pretend that the hero's unexpected but convincing resurrection was all about him; and certainly has nothing to do with the death of the whole earth, or with all the societies that live upon it, with great, collective, joy... or with *me*.[17]

This isn't to say that the world falling apart is a splendid larf, or that world-shaking subversion is not vital, or that we mustn't collectively (classlessly) design our environments for our own greater good. With the soul-raking pain of COLLAPSE it is now more necessary than ever to master self, detach it from the zone of evil and learn to live with uncertainty; free to discover for yourself what is behind pain and death, and in love let it out. This sacrifice is the only thing that has ever changed anything, or ever will. This is the utopia of everyday life, the bedrock of human goodness that lies under broken worlds, pavements and hearts, and the eyes-on-the-mighty conscious experience of *this* that creates, that is creating and that already is the utopia to come. It is also known as BEAUTY.

UTILITY TIPPING POINT

T HE UTILITY TIPPING POINT is the point where mainte-nance of a tool (or SYSTEM) begins to exert a RADICAL MONOPOLY over its users, demanding more energy, time and freedom than it provides.

There are two kinds of UTP; objective and subjective. OBJECTIVE UTP is the point in the growth of locomotive speed, calorific input, technology-use, energy consumption and cen-tralised INSTITUTIONAL power beyond which technical / struc-tural processes begin to dictate social relations, creating a class-structure of comfortable winners and stressed, hungry or exhausted losers, paralysed subsistence activities, perishing equity, withered joy and rampant egomania.[18]

When the component elements of a society grow beyond their UTP limits, tools cannot be mastered by craft, houses cannot be fixed by their inhabitants, roads slow people down, schools make them stupid and institutions begin to appear to manage 'disruptive individuals' (those who react against systematic dominance) and to direct their energy and atten-tion along 'socially acceptable' (i.e. INSTITUTIONALISED) lines. Such institutions include asylums, prisons and schools; all of

SOME ROUGH UTP LIMITS

Detecting UTP *limits—knowing what they are and when they should be temporarily exceeded—is not, nor can be, a scientific question of fact, but of personal (and occasionally collective) sensitivity to being out of balance. Nevertheless, a few soft guidelines are possible:*

SPEED / ENERGY
around 20 kph; roughly half-way between the horsepower used by half of humanity and the power of a red and cream 1970 Vespa '150' VBA scooter

INVIOLABLE OWNERSHIP
that which can be carried or directly used by an adult or, in COMMON, her community

TECHNIQUE / TOOL
that which can be understood and repaired by independent people, and [dunbar] groups

COMMON LAND
how much wood can be re-moved from a forest, or fish removed from the sea, (etc.) before the 'resource' declines

INTOXICANT
once every seven months for cannabis and alcohol, once every seven years for LSD and magic mushrooms [19]

SELF
that which can be let go of / changed *immediately*

FOOD
two handfuls per meal; or up to the point where the belly registers '80% full'

DUNBAR GROUPS
between 120 and 250; with reps in larger, but *powerless*, dunbar confederacies (ANAN-ARCHIC SOCIETIES, and inter-national SUBVERSION, require some mediated hierarchy [20])

---

which existed in rudimentary forms in societies past but, as the world began to unite into a single, global, organisational structure, began to link up into the MONOCULTURAL WORLD.

This world originated (and continually originates) in egos that have passed the SUBJECTIVE UTP: the point in self-use when free attention begins to be monopolised by restless-compulsive thinking and emoting; when journeys through the mysterious wilderness of consciousness become confined to [socially] reinforced pathways that proliferate in the inner world until it is completely overlaid with rigid, stereotypical, mental–emotional superhighways marked off by addictive 'like' placards and agitated 'don't like' no-entry signs (*see* GARDEN).

verigag [vɛrɪgag]

n an unconscious truth or desire manifesting as a weak joke; normally of a sexually suggestive nature

vibe [vaɪb]

n universe of pre-feelings dripping, wafting, babbling, gushing, seeping or sweating through the apperceptive experience of the PRESENT moment

- antonym of EMOTION
- between 70 and 96% of the meaning of a spoken message, or of the behind-the-scenes processes between people, inheres in vibe of voice (i.e. MUSIC), body-language and BLIPS
- self-knowledge, like 'being a good person', is superficial and thoroughly useless (when, for example, facing genius, indecision, uncertainty, love or death) compared to self-aware sensitivity to [one's own] vibe
- note that the EGO is threatened by vibe-communion because vibe demands a softening (or diminution) of self to be perceived
- a persistent resistance to vibe leads to VIBE BLINDNESS [vaɪblaɪndnɪs] *n.ph* an inability or unwillingness

to perceive the *silent* flavour (or BELLY ART) of a situation or utterance; common amongst men, mandatory for clever people

vibe conditioning [triːstʌnt]

n.phr 1 subtle but immensely powerful means of BRAINWASHING babies and very young children through giving and withholding subtle pleasure and saturating the air with stress, anxiety, irritation or sucking, monotonous torpor 2 the creation of a WORK atmosphere that fosters GUGGERSTRASSE

- vibe-conditioned PUC feelings, attitudes and tones are the discrete adamantine barriers between the prison classes (*see* TASTE)

vilicise [vɪlɪsaɪz]

vb 1 to automatically assume that other people feel and act the way they do because of how they *are* (rather than how the environment influences them) 2 to automatically assume that other people's mistakes and problems are because of their character ('*he slipped on the banana because he is clumsy*')

- a.k.a. THE FUNDAMENTAL ATTRIBUTION ERROR

VIBE CONDITIONING

VIBE IS EXTREMELY SUBTLE and so it tends to go unnoticed. Babies, wide-awake lovers, genuine ascetics, the psychologically exposed, the unarmoured and the extremely sensitive (or extremely soft) can feel it. In fact everyone can feel it, on *certain days*, when there is something strange and beautiful in the air, and we hear the under-music of speech, and feel the light of the evening silently breathing its agreement. But for most people, this doesn't last too long.

The vibe-life (or sensitivity to it) is the first experience to be corrupted by the unhappy, egoic parent. Long before actions, emotions and thoughts are manipulated, the baby is shaped by the vibe of its carers; meaning, in most cases, wounded. Like all scars the repair hardens and desensitises the child and warps its awareness down safe but rigid attentive channels. The young child learns that certain kinds of playful exposure are painful (or *wrong*), she learns that many expressions of vibe will be ignored, and she learns, on the subtlest level imaginable, that she is living in a world in which people do not experience each other's inner life; that she is alone.

The child deals with her aloneness by substituting the real pleasure of selfless, physical, present-moment immersion (which is now painful) with addiction to derealised emotional excitement. Parents feel the effects of this substitution—the screaming fits 'for no reason', the moronic attention-seeking, the restless irritable squirming and the insanely demanding 'possessed' selfishness—but they are unable to discern the moment when the child gets lost in self, because they cannot discern it in their own bodies.

Total vibe-blindness is rare though, and there is almost always *some* freedom for the growing child, some mother's love, father's delight or shared family physicality, which doesn't depend on *getting* things, that the young child's subtle self can flow into; and it is in these permitted vibe-pleasures that the subtlest layer of TASTE (and, consequently, class) exists, both pleasurably healthy, or, as the self of the growing child seeks refuge in what it knows, pathologically ADDICTIVE.

The world that the upper class child grows up in, for example, is full of the rich beauty of things, the easy confident tone his parents use with guests and servants, the refined or discerning touch given to meals, and so on. But all this is not, for the young elite, primarily a material experience. It is incorporated on the level of his vibe, and for his whole life he will *pre-consciously* respond to its tasteful manifestation in quality objects and elite attitudes. He will 'recognise' this right thinking good taste, or the lack of it, intuitively, but because his life is funnelled—narrowed and repressed, cut off from function, from uncertainty and from vibe-freedom—this recognition will be corrupted by attachment. He will literally be addicted to good taste and terrified of 'quality' deprivation.

This process is more or less the same throughout the prison-hierarchy. You are not conditioned by learning to *believe* things, but from the imprint that the encircling vibe-life makes upon your subtle body, how it swings you towards certain kinds of experience and away from others.

This is why poorer-class prisoners feel uncomfortable in the reception rooms of their users, why the rich speak with bland, tenderless confidence, why the intellectual bourgeoisie value 'purity' and 'space' and are so easily offended, and why even young children will tend to play with their social equals.

VIRTUAL REALITY

THE TECHNIQUE OF THE MACHINE, or HARDWARE of the world, was first developed through early experiments with the highly-specialised and standardised land- and monument-shaping megamachines (or überselves) that structured early uncivilisations. These were further developed in the middle ages, through the development of specialised time-machines (clocks) and conquest-machines (armies) before—via the enormous work on technics that characterised the enlightenment—coalescing, during the industrial revolution, into the physical form of the modern world.

The VR of the machine, or SOFTWARE of the world, developed (from its superstitious beginnings) into its modern form around the same time as the hardware. It first manifested as science and literacy which replaced reality with digital virtual images that were thinkable and recordable, and therefore DISCRETE (divided up into bits), BINARY (non-paradoxical) and RELATIVE (meaningful from the internal relations of their parts). These virtual images (ideas, alphabets, symbols, etc.), by their nature, devalued soft conscious sensuous inspiration, enhanced hard conscious concentration, fostered a private (reader-text) interaction with society, created the illusion that language is a *thing*,[21] that meaning can be stored, owned and perfectly duplicated, that elite-language is *standard*, and, through the power of the word-image to organise vast numbers of people, generated the proto-VR of Mesopotamia, China, Greece and Rome that led to the virtual revolutions of the renaissance, the enlightenment and, finally, the modern world, which, feeding from and evolving into industrial hardware, has now succeeded in the unconscious mission of ego; to create a 'perfect' image of itself; a dystopian world that can replicate a world in which ego can live without threat, with perfect confidence that nothing has been lost; a 3D simulation of reality, in which imagery, tactility and playability replicate reality exactly, but without its mystery, fractal physicality or death.[22]

The final stage of this rational process, currently being unconsciously carried out, is to conduct all activity through virtual reality; for classrooms, offices, prisons, shops and all social spaces to become 'immersive' on-line holodecks which control and reward participants through permanent, perfect surveillance, the stimulation of positive and negative emotion, offers of godlike powers, and threats to nonconformists of either narco-withdrawal or banishment to an off-line reality now so degraded by the demands of manufacturing an entire artificial UNIVERSE, that only hellish production-facilities, shoddy living-units and prisons can materially function there.

To the virtual egomind, this total (male / masculinising) VR is most attractive; because it *seems* to be perfectly secure. No intrusion from the non-relative, paradoxical UNSELF can make any sense within its rational, binary and relative confines, because the virtual mind, having only its own virtual consciousness to check experience against, has *no way of knowing* if what is happening is real. It cannot perceive paradox, infinity, vibe or the absolutely conscious context, and so digital sensation seems [relatively] real; a limited range or subtlety of virtual movement seems [relatively] fun; literal, vibeless VR communication and information seem [relatively] true and artificial intelligence seems [relatively] alive. If the egoic man had some way of knowing for sure he was living in a simulated world of androids, he would lose the plot. All he can know— and, in VR, know with reassuring immediacy—is 'that does not make sense', or 'that is a non-standard thought'. *Reject!*

While self feels safe and comfortable in the self-made world, the unselfish consciousness that precedes it finds VR at best monotonous and, at worst, freakishly, nightmarishly, unreal. To the extent that the authentic I is forced to operate virtually it is forced to gripe about it, adopt an ironic distance towards it and CO-OPT non-virtual sentiments for solace or for promotion. Eventually, however, after enough dead time of virtual unlife—earning points, dodging people carrying weapons, covering space with structure, solving puzzles, wandering around corridors looking for keys, filling in forms, designing frankenshielas, constantly competing and MASTURBATING to pornography—ego effaces consciousness completely and pure SCHIZOID virtuality, or de-realised living death, sets in. This unnatural state of dead time is something like a cross between the KINERTIA of precarious office work, ordinary, hard-focus schizoid madness and a PORNOGRAPHIC superhero musical; permanently porn-fixed, permanently anxious or depressed, veering between megalomania (or intense specialness) and paranoia (or intense worthlessness), obsessively, anxiously addicted to v-reality, v-power, v-speak, v-god and v-theory, permanently threatened by ambiguity (non-literal criticism or 'offence'), uncertainty (insecurity) and mystery (the unthinkable context), and ever-ready to leap to and cling to fallacies or violence in order to avoid self-unknowable states, such as love, or the terrifying appearance of reality.

vilicuse [vɪlɪkjuːz]

  vb 1 to automatically assume you feel or act the way you do because of an objective reason 2 to automatically assume that one's own mistakes and problems are due to the environment (*'I slipped on the banana because some damned fool put it there'*)

  • a.k.a. THE ACTOR–OBSERVER BIAS (*see* notes to EMOTION)

vilipand [vɪlɪpand]

  vb 1 to automatically assume you feel or act the way you do because of a subjective cause 2 to automatically assume that one's own mistakes and problems are due to one's personality (*'I slipped on the banana because I'm such a loser'*)

  • complement of VILLICISE and VILICUSE; all three are, of course, endemic to ego

viph [vɪf]

  n a word or phrase with the supernatural power to suck all the connected intimacy out of a moment leaving you and a loved one falling away from each other into a cold, bleak void of infinite separateness

  • 95% of viphs are uttered by men

virtual [vəːtjʊəl]

  n unreal, illusory, false

vision [vɪʒən]

  n antonym of DELUSION

void [vɔɪd]

  n impossible-to-describe or imagine point where UNSELF-ISH CONSCIOUSNESS meets the mysterious CONTEXT

  • located in the BODY; not in the body which I observes, but in the body which is observing I

  • only 'known' through DI-RECT EXPERIENCE

  • antonym of HOLLOW

vote [vəʊt]

  vb to demonstrate the legitimacy of prison warders

  • voting for someone who puts the FEAR of GOD into the elites and their professional lackeys, who puts an extra sandwich into the hands of the deprived or who softens the blow of the current collapse *might* be a good idea—but essentially it changes, and can change, nothing of real importance

vulnerable [vəʊkeɪʃə]

  adj politically correct term for the oppressed, used to mind-delete the oppressor

VISIONS

THE PARKER VISION · the conviction that you are sprouting small mushrooms all over your ecstatic, vibrating body.

THE BRIND VISION · that your limbs are a ganglia of light-years long ribbons fluttering from a gigantic '360° vision' eyeball, set slack in the dead-centre of the UNIVERSE.

THE VIND VISION · the practical conviction that you are made of glass and running through a storm of bowling balls.

THE CHICOT VISION · of being a tiny oiled homunculus sliding over and under and round and round the warm gelatinous folds of an massive naked, fat woman, who is laughing madly.

THE GREGORY VISION · that you are currently being worshipped as a god by the peanut-people of Titan.

THE FOSTER VISION · that you are just your head sitting on a small toy car operated by the direction and feeling of the eyes (sly glance to the left drives seductively leftward, lazy-lidded wry grin creeps forward in second, shocked eyebrows raised straight up brakes sharply, etc.).

THE ORGANUM VISION · to see people in their true timeless forms; *apparently* blending back into all the food, light and experience they 'have had' and *apparently* flowing out into the infinite events which they think they are 'going to have' but *actually* mad electromagnetic fractal vibe-ribbons cobwebbing the arboreal multiverse in superluminous strings.

THE JIMM VISION · the belief that an ancient civilisation made you from cheese, stored you deep underground for many thousands of years, where you could ferment and mature, until you were ready to be brought up to the world, and everyone could eat your delicious 'cheese body', and rejoice.

THE TURLEY VISION · also known as *'back to the atom'*, the self as a terrifying super-dense spherical or torus-shaped singularity—frequently perceived in the BAND OF DEATH (*see* zzz).

THE EVOLIAN VISION · to see a world where all the buildings were made, with your own hands, to delight a girl you've just fallen in love with again; more or less a cute, cathedral world.

THE BOEME VISION · to SEE the world; never having seen a thing before.

—— A VOTE FOR THE APOCALYPARTY ——

N O MORE TAX, wealth redistributed, all assets of the rich confiscated, all debts abolished, banks abolished and national debt-money replaced by local currencies, abolition of privilege (all positions of influence accrue zero or negative benefit), abolition of rent (homeless allowed to move into unused homes), all medicine and educational resources free, businesses, utilities and services handed over to employee-control, land distributed to anyone who wants to farm it, job-sharing and job-rotation (same job, same pay, third of the hours and no paperwork), end of the military, no weapons anywhere, and defence budget redirected to stables, all prisons emptied, police abolished (communities self-regulate), abolition of work, production-for-profit, 'career' and 'occupation', abolition of 'experience' and 'qualification' as precondition for activity (unless, perhaps, and only initially, if it is for the use of dangerous machinery), abolition of exams, league tables, enforced academic specialism and syllabuses, abolition of deciding for others what they are, from birth, able to decide for themselves, abolition of schools (replaced by informal skills-shares, apprenticeships, expanded libraries and participatory intellectual workshops), abolition of professions and specialised professional power over life and death (specialist test and surgery clinics maintained but with essential medical and funeral services combined with local post offices; and with care-homes combined with local farms), abolition of all surveillance and bureaucracy, reintroduction of the wilderness and the commons, abolition of long-haul flights, cars, personal phones, high-speed rail, petrochemical-based products and reintroduction of human-level UTP-limited technology, replacement of totalitarian mercantilism with liquid OMNARCHISM (leaders who give orders or seek consensus are handed over to the care of young children until the jib-jab has left them) conducted in DUNBAR GROUPS. All which leading to UTOPIA; the end of money, class, ownership, the letter of the law, democracy, progress, superstition, religion, scientism, WORK, TIME, EGO and, finally, the WORLD.

W IS FOR
woo
inexhaustible court

X IS FOR
x
THE PLANET
OF DREAMS

Y IS FOR
yinyin
of the last resort

Z IS FOR
zero
NOT WHAT IT SEEMS

waisy [weɪzi]
n & adj overprotected child prevented (by parent or system) from becoming fully independent or pain-aware; gelded, effeminate men and needy, anxious women

walport [wɔːlpɔːt]
adj the acidic strawberry of ill-timed irony[wb]

want[ing] [wɒnt]
vb & n a huge black implacable and idiotically grinning whack-a-mole which slowly rises, itching and pressing, until it has filled the entire universe
- synonym of FEAR
- antonym of DESIRE (but interchangeable; *see* SYNONYM)

war [wɔː]
n rational means of acquiring raw materials and using up products
- carried out with BOMBS — expensive to make, used once, destroy lots of stuff that needs to be built or bought again — and SOLDIERS — expendable, deeply indoctrinated murderers with flawless TEAM-SPIRIT, paid to consume a vast array of high-tech products

- recent and permanent[1]
- synonym of MARKET
- why go to war?
- OFFICIAL REASONS 1) compassion, or spreading the good (DEMOCRACY, civilisation, etc.) 2) justice, law, or fighting the bad (terrorism, communism, 'them') 3) self-defence or security 4) honour, glory and love
- ACTUAL REASONS 1) pouring money into the [military-industrial] economy,[2] opening up new markets, controlling areas of strategic importance, stealing resources 2) annihilating the threat and embarrassment of a square millimetre of the globe being free of state control or private ownership 3) groupthink (fear of the unknown) and groupfeel (attachment to the known) 4) boredom, sadism and primal anxiety
- not very popular, so INFOCRATS (when not exhorting consumption, WORK and EGO) must drum up support by ignoring context, suppressing or denouncing dissent, distorting history, exaggerating threat and uncritically 'reporting' official pronouncements
- very, *very* rarely necessary

weal [wiːl]

n the feeling you are being adored; that someone somewhere loves you, or that a dead loved one is telling you that there is *nothing* to fear

wellness [wɛlnɛs]

n a strenuously promoted moral obligation to be OPTIMISTIC, HEALTHY, HAPPY and have FUN, in order to WORK, CONSUME and SUBMIT
· produces ILLNESS[3]

wepth [wɛpθ]

n 1 the weeping of SILENT, empty emotionless tears of total psychological rupture 2 shattered, void; yet overwhelmed with an immense outpouring of unspeakable knowledge 3 rending your heart, sending LOVE down through the centuries and bathing in the gratitude of no-one yet living 4 devastating empathy for the condition of creatures in existence

whelmsop [wɛlmsɒp]

n one who wears the same expression in every photograph

why [waɪ]

adv what's feeble, intellectual little brother[4]

· very useful for uncovering new problems, useless for completely solving them
· the solution to any significant problem is through three or four trapdoors of 'why', leading down to a cellar called 'what is'
· '*…that consideration which acquaints us with the inner nature of the world and thus takes us beyond the phenomenon, is precisely the method that does not ask about the whence, whither, and why of the world, but always and everywhere about the what alone*'.

Arthur Schopenhauer

wisdom [wɪzdəm]

n 1 the quietest voice in your awareness 2 no, not that one, quieter than that 3 nope, quieter still 4 yes, that's it

woo, court[ship] [wuː, kɔːt]

vb & n either 1 an unpredictable, dramatic, tender or vivid romantic encounter followed by unpredictable, leisurely and organic FOREPLAY or 2 a planned, abstract, market-exchange of VR profiles, followed by a short, predictable exchange of likes, followed by rapid fucking—depriving woman

of her spontaneous instincts, and of the time required to see if a man's DATE-FACE will melt away (after orgasm or after the genetic-robot fuck-self feels that she is probably impregnated), depriving man of the sublime opportunity to overcome himself; and depriving them both of the delightful unfolding of the genuinely new together
· *see* RELATIONSHIP

work [ðɪgnəʊbəlpɑːθ]
vb & n 1 spirit-draining process of forced cretinisation, to which the moronising processes of child-raising (*see* BRAINWASHING), SCHOOLING, LAW, SCIENTISM, RELIGION the NEWS-MEDIA and FUN are directed; the UNCONSCIOUS purpose of which being to absolutely annihilate human nature forever 2 the renting of one's freedom (near synonym of SERFDOM: the selling of one's freedom) in order to subsidise the marvellous activities of the RICH (works together with tax, debt, rent and forced consumption)
· for most people 'work is hell', because work and hell have so much in common; discomfort, meaninglessness and eternity

· in a HEALTHY SOCIETY the word work is, like PLAY (or free-time) almost meaningless; in a sick society it is synonymous with TOIL, SLOG, LABOUR and TRAVAIL
· communism (*see* SOCIALISM), fascism, democracy, modernism, postmodernism and demagoguery all have *exactly* the same attitude to work, technique, nature and progress; because all are basically egoic and / or [quasi] rational, and where they are not, they lose ground to their competitors [5]
· the ego-world requires and generates the belief that work is a moral value in itself, that people unwilling or unable to SUBMIT themselves to intense work discipline deserve nothing, that everyone must work for most of the week (with just enough free time to prevent them from blowing their brains out, but not enough to be creatively idle or to contemplate revolution), that good-judgement is compliance, that healthcare and retirement benefits require a lifetime of this work which is practically synonymous with survival

- leads to A) cramming the honest, creative and madly generous part of your psyche into spare time (your life's work is just for evenings and weekends; and even those are not really yours any more) B) using these microns of free time to pursue fun, sex, NARCOTICS, family and tribal bonding (which again are increasingly folded into the totalising COMFORT-ZONE of the friendly, fun, sexy, spiritual and 'social' workspace) C) ill-HEALTH, frustration, GUGGERSTRASSE D) replacement of craft-development (and the concomitant inability of ordinary folk to meaningfully shape their physical world) with the development of TOOLS and E) forced productivity... *unless* you are insensitive to all this pain, in which case; leads to A) SATISFACTION B) 'SUCCESS' C) PRIVILEGE and D) RICHES
- as the WORLD spreads over the earth, so work spreads over the psyche; forcing individuals into a permanent state of WEISURE [wɛʒə] *n* a parody of ludic freedom with added precarity whereby now, thanks to the internet, the workplace is transformed into ceaseless 24/7 work[6] (continuous activity, EMOTIONAL-LABOUR and availability) until you *are* your work—just as you *are* your debt, your belief, your name or your profile—which means, of course, that eventually *you* are not real; nothing is left—and so, unless you practice, in SELF-MASTERY, being who you are, and practice SUBVERSIVELY freeing yourself from being constrained by these co-opted personality-fragments, you are worse than imprisoned—because there is no outside to escape to—you are the whole insane, suffering, SCHIZOID-capitalist universe
- note the *profound* STAGVERSIVE FUTILITY of demanding, or trying to negotiate, higher pay, better working conditions or, most ridiculously of all, workplace equality for your favoured minority; which makes as much sense as demanding more freedom, peace or reality from pac-man
- antonym of ACT, PLAY, DO and CREATE
- synonym of THE IGNOBLE PATH and LIVING DEATH[7]

───────── DEAR OFFICE DWELLER ─────────

Y OU MAY HAVE NOTICED A PEACEFUL PATCH of distant blue through the window, or a small triangle of light that managed to squeeze into the upper right corner of the stationary cupboard, or a strange instant of peace just as your hand reached down for a door knob, or the warmth that a mailed message of beauty spread through your cramped legs, or the lovely colours that Susan from finance has chosen to wear today, or the bizarre clarity of the sunshine after you turn away from your computer screen, or a ghastly yet quite unexpectedly interesting quirk you notice about some stiff's facial geography, or an unprofessional moment of honesty that, for a split-second, nobody knows how to react to, or the pangolin in the canteen, or a sudden realisation—a thought that is so pristinely *there* before you—of being immeasurably powerful and calm and quite above all this nonsense?

Well that was me. I just dropped by to say hello.

All my love, Freedom

world [wɜːld]

n 1 an alliance between the self and exploitation-ena-bling TECHNIQUES in order to create a perfect replica of EGO (a CANCEROUS, INSTITU-TIONALISED, SCHIZOID, MO-NOTONOUS and sense-dulled, virtual mechanism devoted to personal egotism and to endless proliferation) which cannot be perceived as such without a feeling of PRIMAL ANXIETY 2 a gigantic ponzi scheme to pump more and more wealth and power into the centre, until one man (the *winner*) is left alive on a ravaged wasteland, plugged into a VIRTUAL REALITY por-nograph 3 an immense pris-on which isolates inmates from wild NATURE, authentic CULTURE, DEATH, DARKNESS, SLEEP, SILENCE, each other and their own experience, and then makes them de-pendent on the prison for their stimulation, comfort, identity and survival so that they love the prison and de-fend it against criticism or attack 4 an unloved woman 5 a box-ticking exercise

- the three pillars of uncivilisation are ego, separation and ownership, which lead to law, SLAVERY (classic or wage), CLASS, suppression or annihilation of UNSELF and the moulding of the self into a deathless mini-world of stress, loneliness and violent effort
- the oft-vaunted advanced TECHNIQUES of UNCIVILISATION (BUREAUCRACY, LAW, SCIENCE and TECHNOLOGY) are used to protect people from the disastrous effects of its *own* early cultic stages (superstition, sex-violence, slavery, peasant-mentality etc.); *see* BIASTIFY
- created RACISM and SEXISM, by making the work of women and of the conquered uneconomic (and then created FEMINISHISM and RACISHISM to re-incorporate the DEPRIVED into the factory system), created SLAVERY by demanding agricultural surplus (and then abolished slavery in order to create industrial surplus), divided men and women from themselves through division of labour (first peasant from hunter-gatherer, then artisan from peasant, then slave from tribe, and then the whole world into a million lonely little human-silos) and then finally made the non-specialised nature and boundless potential of each of us a terminal threat
- looks like SOCIETY to EGO
- antonym of EARTH

wotnog [wɒtnɒg]

n 1 inability to say 'pardon?' a third time, and so anxiously proceeding as if one had heard and understood 2 not quite understanding what someone is saying but smiling, nodding and 'yeahing' your way through, in the hope that you'll get the point in the end, which turns out to be mistaken as you find you *don't* understand, but you can't now *say* you don't understand because that would mean confessing that all your understanding sounds were tiny little lies; forcing you to press on, not really understanding, but tense, tortured and snared in cringe 3 being trapped in a tiny mind-made infinite-interaction loop of inner confusion which is founded on not being able to be honest about something very small
- *see* JINK

PLANET X

W HEN RELATIONSHIPS END, ex-lovers all fly off to live together on a beautiful planet with all your lost biros, peanuts, pieces of paper with important information, beloved shirts, misplaced umbrellas and scarves left in restaurants. All the perfect fruit you've ever eaten, that made your eyes pop open—the complex, fragrant lemons, the watermelons that were sweet right down to the rind, the buttery mangoes that dribbled jungle gold—it all grows there, on that planet. The vague, freakish, sweet, wrenching flashes of youth and winter sunshine, and the fizz of long-ago thunderstorms, and the voices of long-dead friends—everything good that is lost forever to you lives there still, on a beautiful planet, far away, which, not long ago, collided with a huge asteroid and exploded. Gone *forever*. Okay?

wub [wʌb]

vb to speed up the healing process of broken bones by strapping purring cats to one's crippled limbs

wubular [wʌbjʊlə]

adj descriptive of dense or spherical words, such as *bullion, moose, cow* and *roman mambo*

• antonym of PILTIC [pɪltɪk] *adj* descriptive of hollow or conical words, such as *october, beaker* and *hygienic midget*

x [ɛks]

n the planet of the past

yawk [jɔːk]

vb & n one whose speech-volume is calibrated to cast beyond their immediate listeners and rope in other victims

• never worth overhearing

yeng [jɛŋ]

n sickening realisation that 1 life does not treat you the way your mother did or 2 after graduating from nineteen years of schooling, that you know and can do next to nothing (i.e. are FUNCTION-ALLY ILLITERATE)

• those who are passed from the care of institutional-ised parents to the care of institutions do not get the opportunity of feeling this instructive PAIN

yes [jɛs]

vb to see all of LIFE, all of its fruity sugars and rooty SALTS, all its new-born for you nowness, all its apparent horror and uncertainty, sickness and unfairness; to face death—the end of all your memories and possessions—and the inevitable end of the world; to face the sagging bums and the sodding stains, and to accept it all, as it is, the *lot*

· not an answer, but a state
· the bigger the yes you give, the bigger the yes you get
· a glorious, dark and serious WORLD-detonating *no!* is impossible without the fearless diamond STILLNESS of a sun-in-the-grave-of-the-gut *yes*

yinyin [jɪnjɪn]

n 1 mysterious muse at the heart of the VOID, silently beating in the bellymind of all absolutely present, beautiful and terrible women 2 the ineffable source of all inspiration, all joy, all pain, all soft, spectacular creation and all the death-or-glory triumphs of true love 3 the hips of the world

· does not need to create art, because she *is* that which poets write of

yudo [juːdəʊ]

n the art of making everyday gestures conscious, and therefore BEAUTIFUL; especially those that serve

zeedle [ziːdəl]

vb to absorb all the energy of the room into your swelling supermassive black head

zoil [zɔɪl]

vb & n the straining game of striving well to hold up things that must fall [8]

zoltan! [zʌltan!]

vb & n to build up appetite for risk by standing for three minutes like a superhero

zum [zʌm]

n a vast relief-eliciting observation which voices everyone's secret feeling

zzz [zzz]

n & adj for she who experiences, in the marble of her bones, that she is dreaming, this is the blasted door to mad, miraculous awakeness

---
ASLEEP

ORDINARY DREAMS are organised KIPPLE; directed, as porn, news and average stories are, by want and fear. Want usually means wanting connection, security, or satisfaction—looking for daddy, trying to make it with someone, buying a loaf—and fear usually means not wanting exposure, confinement or death—naked, at school, dead body in the back garden, bits of the body falling off.

This goes on and on and *on*, stumbling around a shoddy, partially formed, 3D-printed world, from one maze to another, running from out-of-focus horrors, lost in forests, *why's he doing that?* crumbling corridors, penis is a lettuce! putting down a dog in Hawaii and not only not knowing why, or what is going on, but not even stopping to wonder.

Occasionally something else seems to happen though. Something deeper, more ridiculous and vivid—and therefore more memorable—rises up and clothes you in sun-god robes while women throw pickles at you, or sends moonwalking cats to keep you company on THE BEACH, or gives you a huge pair of 'robo-trousers' which you use to charge through The Kashmir Tandoori on Palace Street, wrecking the 'as much as you can eat' buffet, before your dad floats in on a cloud.

Or you might touch the BAND OF DEATH,[9] the annihilating TEMENOS of unbeing, which may appear to your self as a supersolid monolithic form, or the screaming horror of the world-building collapsing or a being of such pure eyes-white evil that you can somehow still feel it, awake in the dark.

Or perhaps you find yourself in, or as, the nearby BAND OF LOVE; the dream-feeling of a love *so good* that on waking you know it, or he, or she, to be realer than the real world.

And then sometimes in this haunted universe you *do* stop to wonder. You might be falling from a cliff or cycling towards an oncoming locomotive and think, *'so what?'* or really notice that nothing is really connecting up, that nothing is really secure, or that *'this isn't right'*. You might say to yourself, *'I'm dreaming!'* and the excitement, the very seeing of it, takes you out, back to the bed.

Or maybe there is no emotion, and you simply, directly, SEE you are dreaming, that you are awake in the dream; and so can do anything. With the power of a monogod you bring on the dancing girls, of course, or the spod-rockets, or the private floating islands, or the screaming crowds, or the respect of hallowed beards, or the power to fly, or the talking pillows, or the underground caverns of warm pink snow, or the mile-high sky-rides, or the chocolate furniture…

But eventually *that* gets old. You live several lives as a swallow or a nematode, bounce around with Perky Pat and smoke sheesha with Genghis Khan, and it's all so god-damned delightful, to be sure… but in the end; so what? What is the point? Who is in *charge* here?

Eventually you realise that dreaming is *all you*. It seems that there are people and things out there, but in truth they are all happening in, or made by, you. You are the projectionist, scriptwriter, actor, viewer *and* cinema… and sooner or later, you're going to want to know, what isn't you, or where all this is *coming from*… and, most importantly of all; if it's not you, then how on earth could *you* know it?

If something is to give you the answer to this—and it wants to—it's not going to just *tell* you, because that tell-knowledge would also be you. Instead, it will split you into parts (or characters) and construct a story, or MYTH, in which those parts cooperate and contend with each other, leading you to a self-made point of no escape, where all that you have gained, made, learnt or become, is lost forever. Then *you* stop.

The experience of this is the greatest relief you can possibly feel, and you feel it every night when your mind melts into the still blue-welcoming sea of deep, dreamless SLEEP. Then there is no time, no space and so; no you. To *you* this is nothing, the VOID, but to that which is conscious of you, it is the unspeakable experience of something as it really is.

And there the mystery remains before rising once more, out into the timespace world, to play again the game of realising it… that the end of time and space is not the end of you, that the end of *you* is not the end of you, that the end of the world is not the end of the world.

INTO FLAMES
of desire
I *threw*
MYSELF
and on my
CORPSE
grew
MUSHROOMS

NOTES

A & B

1. Pasted upon the foundation of SCIENTISM—the ideology that quality can be measured (see SCIENCE)—and WORK—structuring productive life in such a way that the necessities of life can only come through the MARKET.

2. See Darcia Narvaez, *The 99 Percent*, Stanley Diamond, *In Search of the Primitive* and notes to FALL.

3. See Ivan Illich, *Silence is a Commons*.

4. APPROPRIATE is a system code-word which means 'market-friendly'. 'Inappropriate' language and behaviour is that which threatens profits, GROUPTHINK TOTEMS (see TABOO) or the repressed, and continually assessed, EGO.
   For the ultimately fluid nature of distinctions like this see SYNONYM and notes to EMOTION. See also TASTE.

5. e.g. A says something witty (perceptive, deep, beautiful, etc.) and B responds with either *'that's witty'* or *'that's not witty'*—result; A is either flattered or annoyed and conversation breaks down.

6. Children who are treated like children grow up into adults that treat adults like children, just as sycophants usually turn into sadists when they have enough power to demand sycophancy... all top rank management material.
   Also note here that an excellent 'moral' brainwashing technique is to massively over-praise your kid for being clever or smart so that it becomes terrified of making a mistake (i.e. of being exposed for *not* being clever) rather than for making a good effort, or for not giving up.

7. Of course you could also physically abuse your child, but this is not just unnecessary—subtle conditioning is

far more effective—but terribly out of fashion—you're unlikely to advance very far in the world these days if you use such crude tactics.

8. *When you don't trust the people enough, then they are untrustworthy.*
    The Tao Te Ching (23).

9. In the academic, legal, corporate and media world, the printed word is invested with far greater prestige and authority than speech.

10. See David Graeber, *The Utopia of Rules*.

C & D

1. The purpose of capitalism is for those who do not contribute anything meaningful to an undertaking—owners and managers of capital—to profit from / appropriate the surplus of those who do—workers. It is, therefore, *impossible* for workers to be *ever* paid a fair wage by owners, as a 'fair' distribution of profit would mean that nothing were left over for owners to cream off (i.e. to steal) in the form of their unfair salaries, bonuses, share-dividends and wotnot. See Richard Wolff, *Democracy at Work*.

2. The modern idea of childhood was created to protect the young from an *adulterated* working world (see Philippe Aries, *Centuries of Childhood*).
    The current disappearance of childhood (childish games, language, dress, etc.) is, understandably, lamented by many (e.g. Neil Postman in *The Disappearance of Childhood*) who fail to understand that the problem is not that children are becoming like adults; but that adults are failing to become like children.

3. Young children, before they are corrupted, are miraculously sensitive, perceptive, spontaneous, wild, playful,

creative and competent to do many of the things that adults do. It is for this reason that they are not allowed to participate in unsociety in any meaningful way, nor to be consulted about anything of value. They are so dangerous that, like the dying and the dead, one must be a PROFESSIONAL to consort with them.

4. See Lewis Mumford, *Technics and Civilisation*.

5. See Naomi Klein, *This Changes Everything*, Katherine Richardson et al, *Climate Change*, Oreskes and Conway, *Merchants of Doubt*, Roy Scranton, *Learning to Die in the Anthropocene*, Eric Holthaus, *The Point of No Return...* or pretty much anything written about climate change, biodiversity, deforestation, pollution or water-depletion in *Nature*, by NASA, the UN, the IPCC or by any of the *oil-and-gas-industry-independent* climate-scientists of the world. But keep reading; each report is more horrifying than the last.

6. As Umberto Eco pointed out.

7. Includes the removal of status symbols (hierarchical titles, large offices, etc.) that might lead to dissent, class-conscious antagonisms or the 'why the fuck bother?' that hierarchies usually generate amongst the lower levels (see Robert Ozaki, *Human Capitalism*) as well as a pervasive BIOMORALITY (coined by Alenka Zupančič in *The Odd One In*) that stigmatises ill-health, conscience and any lack of eye-shining, enlightened, enthusiasm for WORK.

8. From Ivan Illich, *Energy and Equity*.

9. See William Davies, *The Happiness Industry*.

10. All of these, of course, are, to varying degrees impossible within the system. It could be said that the history of the world is a millennial war on your conscience.

11. Science (and ABSTRACT PHILOSOPHY) focuses exclusively on [the ownership, memories, qualia and whatnot of] describable hard-consciousness, either ignoring timeless, indescribable soft-consciousness altogether or conflating it with hard-consciousness, and then concluding that consciousness is 'really' an illusion created by the material brain. Well-known rational thinkers who make this silly, but *profitable*, post-modern mistake include Pinker, Jaynes and Dennett. As their critics point out, we know almost nothing about the matter that mind is supposed to have come from and have not the tiniest inkling of the causal arrow that links mind and body. The so-called 'illusion' of consciousness is because we can possess no *rational* knowledge that can possibly lead us to postulate the existence of conscious experience. Only EXPERIENCE can obliterate such fruitless, abstract, debate.

12. Tor Nørretranders, in *The User Illusion*, quoting studies by Manfred Zimmermann, Karl Küpfmüller, George Miller, Helmuth Frank and others.

13. Indeed, in only being able to deal with familiarity, fact and concentrated clarity (e.g. staring through the miniscule point of focus of the human eye), it will not offer its reasons, theories and opinions as possibilities but as clear, unquestionable, unambiguous certainties.

14. There is evidence that hard and soft consciousness are *associated* with left and right brain architecture. Damage to the left brain leads to impairments of time-awareness, language, abstract cognition and so on, while damage to the right brain leads to impairments of empathy, creativity, humour, ability to understand metaphor (or PARADOX) and contextual perception.
    See Ian Mcgilchrist, *The Master and his Emissary*.

15. soft-consciousness + self = consciousness / self-awareness.
    hard-consciousness + ego = un- / self-consciousness

16. There is no better way to see the fundamental sameness of scientism, religion, corporatism, mystishism or any other egoic subcult than when they are threatened by unconditional love, old, dark forests, silly behaviour, freedom from work and the simple, paradoxical truth.

17. e.g. pupils, patients (or 'service-users'), punters, customers, readers, viewers, voters, clients and 'the public'.

18. Ivan Illich points out that people who feel modern experience needs that correlate to commodities rather than to everyday human (VERNACULAR) activities. The need to play mario kart, get a better degree or buy a new kitchen has superseded the need to eat sardines on the street, carve a door knob, master sleight of hand or sit in silence.

19. *The average man does not linger long over the mere perception, does not fix his eye on an object for long, but, in everything that presents itself to him, quickly looks merely for the concept under which it is to be brought, just as the lazy man looks for a chair, which then no longer interests him. Therefore he is very soon finished with everything, with works of art, with beautiful natural objects, and with that contemplation of life in all its scenes which is really of significance everywhere. He does not linger; he seeks only his way in life, or at most all that might at any time become his way. Thus he makes topographical notes in the widest sense, but on the consideration of life itself as such he wastes no time. On the other hand, the man of genius, whose power of knowledge is, through its excess, withdrawn for a part of his time from the service of his will, dwells on the consideration of life itself, strives to grasp the Idea of each thing, not its relations to other things. In doing this, he frequently neglects a consideration of his own path in life, and therefore often pursues this with insufficient skill.*
Arthur Schopenhauer.

20. Artistic expressions and artistic movements are routinely co-opted, and thereby degraded; their monikas becoming

synonymous for sentimentality or decadence and their vigour vitiated by reproduction. Classic examples include gothic, baroque and romantic (all words for vibrant artistic movements which came to be used pejoratively). Modern examples include the music of blues, jazz, reggae and funk (which degraded into guitar and saxophone wanks and the moronic fuckbeats of ragga and rap) and the beat, hippy and punk movements (which began as bright out-breaks of revolutionary energy and artistic truth, before ossifying into hollow, anaemic or fashionable postering). Very often artists become famous and co-opt their *own* younger selves (see SHUFF OUT).

21. Note the tendency of corporations to become people (to be legally defined as deathless human beings) and for people to become corporations ('flexibly' precarious micro-start-ups expected to MARKET their entire beings).

22. Craft is obviously essential for activities that involve matter. We know when a cowboy has tiled our bathroom or a careless cook has served us a pap. It's also not too much of a stretch for most people to appreciate how important craft is for great music (through learning harmony and the mystery-tradition of chord progressions, etc.) or great writing (through a scholarly understanding of language, profound familiarity with myth and story-craft, learning to hear tales told by spiders, etc.) or dance (through years of tendon-stretching discipline, broadening and deepening musical taste, living in a forest, etc.), or magic.

But modern artists have found a get-out-of-apprentice-ship-free card which they can wave around at 'philistines' who suggest that they have a duty to learn composition, physiognomy, fractality or how to draw a hand. There are two reasons for this. Firstly artists are no longer expected to serve society (that degraded task has been hand-me-downed to illustrators and cartoonists), and secondly, they, like everyone else, are not only not expected, but actively prevented from serving the genius of life.

Instead, the artist is expected to exclusively focus on his or her own world—the more trivial and 'personal', the better. The result is widespread scorn amongst modern artists for REALISM and TRADITION (see TASTE), ponderously realist or political works by illustrators and a prevalence of utter mediocrity amongst what should be the most powerful revolutionary force in the world.

23. Debt is not just used by the custodians of the SYSTEM to imprison the functional classes in peonage, or to funnel, through USURY, their land, labour and creative power up the pyramid of evil; it is also a means of absorbing the effects of predatory elite activities, and of passing them off into the fabled futureland of infinite PROGRESS.

24. There are some people in the world who unconsciously *enjoy* being in debt (or in a mess) as it gives them purpose or an excuse to be harried and bound.

25. As Noam Chomsky points out. Democracy is a means of taking all of the thoughts, perceptions, instincts and suggestions of the individual on how her society should be run, how her workplace should be organised, how she should produce the necessities of life, what should be done about the various problems she and others are facing and distilling them all down to an x placed on a piece of paper every five years. This is called PARTICIPATION.

26. See Barry Long, *Seeing Through Death*.

27. See Ivan Illich, *Medical Nemesis* and Bruce Levine, *Why Anti-Authoritarians are Diagnosed as Mentally Ill*.

28. Which might actually be true.

29. Including hierarchical groups, which, provided they do not have *any* independent power, are as useful as specialism. See notes to UTP.

E & F

1.   Also applies to societies.

2.   What is ordinarily called 'egotism', or arrogance, is really just a subset of ego, which comprises a far deeper, subtler and more pervasive selfishness (which can masquerade as humility and niceness) than mere poncing around.

3.   The words 'feeling' and 'emotion' are, obviously, inter-changeable in normal speech (they are synonyms). Each word has a different meaning here (they are antonyms) not to lay down what these two words Really Mean, but to highlight a distinction that normal (especially educated) speech masks. See SYNONYM for other fundamentally different phenomena, experiences and realities which can best be understood and expressed by making new antonyms (or opposites) out of old synonyms.

4.   The perceptions and thoughts created by emotion are limited, coarse (catastrophically destructive of nuance) and prone to grotesque error. It has been repeatedly demonstrated that emotion restricts flexibility of thinking and increases the likelihood of the AVAILABILITY ERROR (see SECOND IMPRESSION), the NORMALCY BIAS (a refusal to accept or plan for disasters that have never happened, such as COLLAPSE, or your own DEATH), the SEMMELWEIS REFLEX (instinctive refusal to accept any kind of evidence or experience that might disturb your opinion), CONFIR-MATION BIAS (the tendency to only look for what you want or are already expecting to find), the FOCUSING EFFECT (ruling out an entire SOCIETY, world-view or human being because of one or two things you don't like), NAÏVE REAL-ISM (the laughable BELIEF that you see reality as it really is) and all the 'cognitive biases' of GROUPTHINK and GROUP-FEEL (see also VILICISE, VILIPAND, VILICUSE, FALLACY and PANJECTIVE). The consequence of emotional thinking is self-pity or contention.

5. Coined by Arlie Hochschild, in *The Managed Heart*, and thoroughly investigated by Ivor Southwood in *Non-Stop Inertia*.

6. Empathy is routinely confused for CARING. Women are regularly determined to be more empathic than men and adults more empathic than children. This is true, but what is overlooked is that men and women, and adults and children, tend to care about *different* things. Women, for example, tend to care more for real things (children, animals, clothes, bedrooms, bodies) and men tend to care more for unreal things (chord patterns, maps, archetypical plots, circuit diagrams, risky futures), and this has nothing to do with empathy, quality or morality; it is possible (indeed very common) to *selfishly care*.

    It is also possible to get exhausted caring; the so called 'compassion fatigue' of people who spend a great deal of time around pain and suffering, while empathy, being a natural state, never runs out (see Matthieu Ricard, *Altruism*, although Ricard calls empathy caring and compassion empathy).

    Empathy is not a value or an interest, but an experience of unself—childlike immersion in what I am not—of the quality-of-suchness in the morning light, of the hum and hue and tone of a friend's gesture, of the deep, inviting vibration of *this* cup (and not *that* one), of the ineffable character that makes one performance electric and another flat, or of what it is to be a cow; all equally available to men, women and children. There could be no great works of art without this me-less experience, no miraculous communion between parents and infants, no heart-rending offers of help from toddlers, and no self-detonating mutual-merge during love-making (you, me and the centre of the universe), but for selves to become soft enough to feel what they are not, they either have to be raised in a room of liquid vibe or, more often than not, pummelled by the horrors of life, death, loss, madness and profound sorrow, into literal tenderness.

This pummelling helps explain why the poorer classes, who are routinely subject to self-softening pressures (physical work, reliance on others, uncertainty, discomfort, etc.), along with the disabled, tend to be more empathic than the middle class and elites. See Michael Kraus et al, *Social Class, Contextualism, and Empathic Accuracy* Gary Sherman et al., *Perceiving Others' Feelings*, and Paul Piffa et al., *Higher Social Class Predicts Increased Unethical Behavior*.

7. In 1968 Garrett Hardin created the fiction of the 'tragedy of the commons'; that self-interest will drive a community to exhaust its commons in short order. Although Hardin's paper was one of the most quoted and cited in history, it was based on no more substantial evidence than the author's assumption that man is fundamentally a rational wealth-maximising consumer.

    Hardin's demented thesis was exposed in *Governing the Commons* by Elinor Ostrom. See also Ian Angus, *Debunking the 'Tragedy of the Commons'*.

8. See Ivan Illich, *Silence is a Commons*.

9. Expressing non-standard feelings is akin to planting potatoes in a nearby field. Ordinary people are deterred from it in conversation by the reactions of 'polite society' to spontaneity and honesty (which are so unusual in ordinary life that their appearance is usually received with an astonishment that borders on panic) and they are deterred from it in artistic expression by institutional OFFENCE (which tends to find originality distasteful), by systemic strangulation of unself (preventing ordinary people from leading an inspiring life) and by the inordinate expense of artistic apprenticeship, which leads to middle and upper-class usurpation of the artistic commons and the hollowing out of artistic life. Nobody notices the abomination of PRIVILEGED actors attempting to express genuine feelings, because those feelings are functionally illegal in daily (commercial and professional) life.

10. As Wittgenstein, Huxley, Kafka and others have noted.

11. In fact the idea that something other than blind luck or blind 'survival' influences genetic mutation—so-called 'Epigenetic LAMARCKISM'—is making a [re]appearance in biology; although only crude consequences of lifestyle or environment have been shown to be heritable. True as this is, the role of UNSELF, or CONTEXT will always be excluded by scientific study of heritability because science—SCIENTISM, rather—is based on HARD-CONSCIOUS egoic mentation, which filters reality into thinkable, relative, context-independent concepts and so can only understand the meaning of beauty, truth, love, life and other Q-WORDS in terms of comprehensible utility. For all evolutionists (Darwinian or Lamarckian) the majesties of art are means of ensnaring large-hipped wives, intelligence a means of manipulating the environment, mystic truth a way of binding groups together, love a way of binding partners together, life a self-replicating and largely self-informed mechanism and complex behaviour reducible to a few simple-minded [eu]genetic causes. The evidence they use to illustrate these interpretations is sound, but, to anyone who can perceive the world softly and selflessly, the meaning is ridiculous—for reasons that can *never* be articulated to the satisfaction of scientists (from Darwin to Dawkins) who *want* selfish violence to be the foundation of nature (BIOLOGICAL PANCULPISM; or, as Steve Hall put it, the ideology that life is selfish, spread by the selfish, to stop them feeling guilty about being selfish).

12. Coined by Douglas Adams and John Lloyd.

13. See Michel Foucault, *Discipline and Punish*.

14. Of course there is a land where factories are citadels of living death; where workers execute plans they have no role in formulating, as part of a work process that reduces workers to a pair of hands constructing a product they

have little or no relation to, and for which they see, at best, but a distant and indirect benefit; a land where factories are unremittingly ugly, where every second of the worker's time is policed, where only mutilated half-men can possibly flourish and where skilled work amounts to nothing more noble than baby-sitting machines; an endless INTERZONE of excruciating misery from which all the products of the whole world are produced.

15.   Most of this description is uncontroversial (See *The Cambridge Encyclopedia of Hunters and Gatherers* for copious evidence on the sexual and social egalitarianism of those groups that most resemble early humans; pre-conquest hunter-gatherers). Even right-wing anthropologists and historians (e.g. Jared Diamond, Yuval Noah Harari) concede that hunter-gatherers had fewer illnesses (see Arnold DeVries, *Primitive Man and his Food*, and Gurven et al., *Longevity Among Hunter-Gatherers*) and were far more egalitarian (see Christopher Boehm, *Egalitarian Behavior and Reverse Dominance Hierarchy*) than the farming communities which supplanted them. It is also fairly uncontroversial that if they did not work less than later groups (see Marshall Sahlins, *The Original Affluent Society* and Ted Kaczynski's important corrective, *The Truth about Primitive Life*), this work was far more rewarding and enjoyable and far less alienating than agricultural [and, of course, industrial] work.

More controversial is the claim that pre-agrarian people did not go to war. There is vast evidence that early people were peaceful, but there is also scattered evidence of warfare and violent mass-deaths. This evidence was recently popularised, and warped, by Lawrence Keeley (in *War Before Civilisation*), but the source of many of his claims, Keith Otterbein (not exactly a hippy) disputes the interpretations that Keeley makes of cherry-picked evidence, most of which is open to multiple interpretations and is 'scattered at the end of the Neolithic period' (i.e. when warfare began; around 10,000 years ago, at the time of the fall). The incompetent work of Napoleon Chagnon is also routinely used to support such claims (e.g. in the fanatical, power-loving fantasies of Stephen Pinker). See *Pinker's List* by R. Brian Ferguson (and *Reality Denial* by Ed Herman) for a thorough correction to the disgraceful distortions of Pinker, *The Ancient Origins of Warfare and Violence* by I.J.N. Thorpe for an antidote to Keeley and *Fuck Jared Diamond* by David Correia for a decent overview of Diamond's colonial-whitewashing.

This leads to the question; how can we know for sure that early humans were peaceful, much less that they were 'at ease with life, fearless before death and were able to commune, or improvise, with miraculous presence and sensitivity'? The answer comes partly from the anecdotal evidence of perceptive anthropologists who have lived with remote hunter-gatherer societies (R.B. Lee, Stanley Diamond, W.J. Perry, Elman Service, E. Douglas Turnball, Daniel Everett, etc.). These accounts, although instructive, are also, as is widely recognised, problematic. Even the lightest brush with civilisation (i.e. the conditions through which anthropologists are able to reach such people in the first place) radically changes the character and the quality of life of hunter-gatherers who have, further, often already been pushed to marginal habitats by violent, distrustful and 'civilised' agriculturalists.

Although it is reasonable to extrapolate from the historical deterioration (sickness, violence, etc.) of hunter-gatherer societies, and to assume, or at least accept the probability, that the further back one moves from uncivilisation (via the non-egalitarian sedentary horticulturists that are routinely included in reviews of hunter-gatherers, skewing the data towards bellicosity) the less sickness, inequality and violence in and among humans one is likely to find; the only *indisputable* proof that early people were unfallen cannot come through such external scientific evidence.

What, after all, is under discussion when we ask ourselves what early people were like, is what people *can* be like, which means the nature of consciousness; which, ultimately, means the nature of *my* consciousness. If a scientist seeks to explore the conscious experience that children, animals or primal people have of reality, without, first of all, exploring his own consciousness, he is ignoring the *only* evidence of conscious experience he can possibly have *direct* access to. Studying consciousness (and the Q-word experiences it animates; love, joy, art, etc.) OBJECTIVELY leads to findings that (no matter how meticulous the research or exhaustive the study) must ultimately be objective also; which is to say secondary, misleading, debatable and unconscious.

Investigating consciousness *directly* gives most scientists the willies—and they would certainly scoff at the idea that any 'proof' could be obtained in this way—because it means to experience one's own consciousness of life, without the attenuating and impoverishing influence of professionally-managed dependencies (i.e. grants), without a distorted, INDIRECT (market or media-mediated) relationship with one's fellows, without demeaning, alienating work, without being dominated by THOUGHT and EMOTION and without focusing exclusively on facts, evidence, ideas and objects. Ultimately it is only through soft-conscious unselfish awareness that one can understand one's own essential humanity and, by extension, humanity as revealed in pre-history: but scientists are as afraid of this as any other professional, priest or addict.

In fact self-knowledge is the foundation upon which all academic, political, social, religious, philosophical and scientific debate rests, regardless of how well or poorly informed the disputants. Discuss human nature for long enough with a psychologist, or the limits of science with a scientist, or the nature of God with a monotheist and you will eventually find your disagreements do not rest on objective evidence—or even on 'faith'—but on how your family, your culture and your own experiences have shaped your perception, on how powerful your ego is and on how narrow your consciousness is. Those resistant to exploring their own banishment from paradise are those most resistant to accepting its correlation in pre-history (see PUC). That's not to say that evidence is irrelevant—it *must* be honoured—just that, finally, if we agree about the nature of pre-conquest humans (indeed about NATURE herself) it is not because we have both studied every one of the countless hunter-gathererers that existed up to the modern age; which is close to impossible, nor because we have any significant objective evidence on the nature of hunter-gatherers, or of their innumerable cultures, more than ten thousand years ago; because we never will. If we agree about what it really means to be human, or what we have in common, it is because we are FRIENDS, that's all.

16. Culture and nature also became separated at this time (see Philippe Descola, *Beyond Nature and Culture*), as did WORK (painful 'slog', 'toil', 'labour', etc.) and PLAY (relief from work). The most catastrophic effect, however, was that LOVE-MAKING became separated from (and subsumed by) SEX, which, along with an accompanying craving for sex-attention and purchasing-power, took the place of the careless connected ease of primal togetherness (see Barry Long, *Making Love*).

17. The problems of the agricultural revolution were preceded by a decadent phase of hunter-gatherer shamanism which relied on the charisma of individuals and ever more elaborate rituals and ordeals (similar to the self-indulgent mystishical 'shamanism' practiced today). See Terence McKenna, *Food of the Gods*.

18. *There is a world in which children almost always feel 'wanted' and where 'there is no cultural preference for babies of either sex' (Howell 1988). Infants are suckled on demand by their mothers and by other women in her absence. They are indulged and cosseted by their fathers, grandparents, and siblings. Children wean themselves over a long period and are given nutritious foods (Robson and Kaplan 2003). They are subject to little or no restraint or coercion... (Henry 1941/1964).*

They are rarely or never physically punished or even scolded (Hernandez 1941). They are not expected to make a significant contribution to the household economy and are free to play until the mid to late teens (Howell 2010). Their experience of adolescence is relatively stress free (Hewlett and Hewlett 2013). This paradise exists among a globally dispersed group of isolated societies—all of which depend heavily on foraging for their subsistence. They are also characterized by relatively egalitarian and close social relations, including relative parity between men and women (Hewlett et al. 1998).

David Lancy, *The Anthropology of Childhood.*

19. Man did exploit nature before the fall. The Americas and Australia were covered in so-called 'megafauna' (enormous sloths, colossal walking owls, sleepy winged kangaroo) before unfallen man arrived there, which vanished upon his arrival. Although early people had a reverent relationship with the game they hunted, it seems they were unable to foresee the effects of strolling out of their huts, whenever they pleased, and tonking huge, passive, friendly, festivals of meat for a week's good eating. This lack of foresight (or possibly, restraint) is of an entirely different character to the rapacity of early uncivilisations.

20. Removing RESPONSIBILITY, through replacing actions with things, is also the means by which professionals generate the illusion that they supply health, education, food and so on. By replacing 'I learn' with 'education', 'I walk' with 'transportation', or 'I play' with 'Playstation', personal activities are replaced with packaged commodities, and the responsibility of man to feed, entertain, protect, inform and move himself magically disappears.

See Ivan Illich, *Disabling Professions.*

21. The academic demand for an argument is a demand that one enter the world of abstract philosophy; an idealised, structured, linear, spacetime arena of chronically literal thought. It is APT to do this when discussing facts and

evidence—the mechanical form of the universe, the data of academic life or even, perhaps, who last saw the keys to the garage. But it is inapt to approach the meaning of Q-words in this way; the meaning of beauty, or truth, or love, of what is going on in the world or even, perhaps, what a garage really is; which have nothing to do with evidence. Such questions can only be answered through the direct experience of paradox, myth, non-literal art and through learning to SEE in new, radically direct ways.

A similar ABREACTED objection is that an account that takes responsibility for what is beautiful and ugly, or selfless and selfish, or real and unreal, is 'black and white' or 'overly simplistic'. 'Simplistic', in this case, nearly always means 'a simplicity I am paid not to accept'.

22. So, to avoid criticism, one can rationally swing between two perfectly reasonable responses—the black-and-white of false antonyms, or the shades-of-grey of false synonyms—without attending to what is actually happening or being said. See SYNONYM and notes to EMOTION.

23. The difference between fallacies and blocks is that fallacies are ego-defence against *explicit* intellectual threats and blocks defend ego against *implicit* threats. Blocks are usually, therefore, deeper than fallacies, which tend to be restricted to conversation, rather than action.

24. See Douglas Adams and John Lloyd, *The Meaning of Liff*.

25. The fiend feeds on emotion. If it can't get positive emotion (excitement, getting, winning), it will feed on the opposame emotions of hatred, complaining, craving, anxiety and depression. See *Making Love* by Barry Long (who first used fiend in this way and first cleared up the difference here between feeling and emotion).

26. Fractality is a paradoxical blend of order and chaos. This can no more be duplicated by the non-paradoxical mind

than a tree can be represented by an exact copy, but must, first of all, be expressed from one's own paradoxical consciousness; that within which *is* the 'shape of the universe', which creates tools, poems and buildings that are inevitably as beautiful (i.e. as fractically formed) as they are useful (i.e. as capable of interacting efficiently with fractal reality).

With 3D printing, for example, computers can create, without the restraints of having to manufacture individual parts, literally the most useful (lightest, strongest, most efficient and so on) machine components possible; which, of course, end up being fractal structures; but, as Gaudí discovered, along with our greatest inventors, engineers and artists, this capacity is not one that requires vast processing power and magical printing facilities; natural fractal consciousness, or adoration of nature, is enough.

27. Systematic failure to recognise this elementary fact has led to thousands of years of fruitless debate over 'nature vs nurture'. Knowledge, language, morality, gender, etc. are neither entirely innate, nor are they entirely acquired from culture after birth—standpoints which have both been exposed as ultimately ridiculous. Rather the self has a beautiful, intelligent, living, paradoxical and flexible fractal nature, which is shaped and filled by the various vibes, feelings, ideas and skills of culture.

The reason natural culture is not RECOGNISED is that UNCIVILISATION (non-fractal anti-culture) blunts it. The wide tree of consciousness is narrowed, sickened and its sensitivity stifled by intensely specialised WORK, poor nutrition, restricted movement, vibeless domestication and a pathological over-emphasis on *fruit*.

28. Capitalism, as André Gorz points out in *Critique of Economic Reason*, has absolutely no use for freedom which must be converted into the consumption of holidays, fun, techno-frills, handbags and that grey, bloodless little dribble of human initiative called the HOBBY.

1. The myth is common to most of the world's religions; but the oldest and truest of those stories—far older than the female-hating Hebrew Eden—do not depict the garden in SPACETIME, but as ever-present, a secret garden in the city.

2. For influence of class, modernity and, indirectly, the influence of conditioned gender on homosexuality see (e.g.) Julien Barthes et al., *Male Homosexual Preference: Where, When, Why?* and Nigel Barber, *Ecological and Psychosocial Correlates of Male Homosexuality.* The point here is that there is no good reason to rule out the influence of 'society' on sexuality.

3. See Marshall Sahlins, *Stone Age Economics and the Original Affluent Society.*

4. The difference here between masculine and feminine and their application to men and women is, of course, necessarily schematic. In reality selves are composed of many components, layers and predispositions, each of which can be masculine or feminine, or even coloured quite neutrally. The point here is to outline some basic qualitative differences, the nature of their complementarity and how they are degraded in the WORLD.

5. See Irwin Silverman et al., *The Hunter-Gatherer Theory of Sex Differences in Spatial Abilities* and M. Dyble, et al., *Sex Equality Can Explain The Unique Social Structure of Hunter-Gatherer Bands.*

6. The only kinds of work rewarded by the post-industrial economy are those that men are, by dint of their greater capacity for shutting down their sensory and apperceptive awareness, better able to do. The eight hours a day of extreme specialisation and abstraction, the rigid time pressure and the suppression of generosity, spontaneity

and sensitivity of the industrial revolution were felt much more disturbingly by women, who were either relegated to an unpaid SHADOW ECONOMY of cleaning, cooking, raising children and so on, or forced to compete in a non-gendered environment in which they were at a disadvantage:

Women complained that men suddenly ordered them around at work, a totally new experience for them. No matter how much the gender-defined work of women might seem subordinated to that of men, the notion that men could direct women in the work itself had so far been unimaginable. Women resented the loss of domain. Women also complained that, while men had time after working at the rhythm of the plow to relax at the inn, they had to hurry back and forth between the hoe and the kitchen. Envy of a new kind, envy for the other gender's schedule and rhythm, thus appeared, a [feminishist] envy destined to remain as a central characteristic of modern life, an envy fully 'justified' under the assumptions of unisex work but unthinkable under the shield of gender.
Ivan Illich, *Gender* [my parenthesis]. See also WORK.

7. *Sex can be discussed in the unambiguous language of science. Gender bespeaks a complementarity that is enigmatic and asymmetrical. Only metaphor can reach for it… Gender-specific speech is not a variety of 'the' language, but one of its two fundamental, constitutive complements. The moment you treat it as a variety, you have already introduced both a genderless, or 'unisex', norm and, with it, the idea of deviance.*
Ivan Illich, *Gender*.

8. It was the Romantics, at the beginning of the nineteenth century, who first conceived of genius not as that which a great man channels, but as the man himself, just as they conceived of the imagination not as a means of expressing the soul, but as the soul itself.

The Romantic movement was a necessary correction to the rational insanity of the preceding 'enlightenment' — one of the darkest ages in human history — and it produced works of art and craft the likes of which we are unlikely to see again for a long time; but the intense egotism of the romantic conceptions of will, feeling, genius, imagination and the like helped create a much deeper sickness, one that the [modernist] arts have been unsuccessfully trying to heal themselves of for 200 years.

9. Being lucky, like creating a place for genius, is a skill. Unlucky people are much more tense and therefore miss opportunities, they also do not listen to intuition and are easily defeated—all skills, like will, which can be learnt. See David Shenk, *The Genius in All of Us*.

10. As Picasso pointed out, if la geniusette arrives and finds you're not in the workshop, she'll probably go home.

11. Keith Johnstone in *Impro* points out that our idea of art being 'self-expression' is culturally very unusual; that artists used to be seen as mediums or servants of something else. Teenagers asked to do something 'creative' are exposed by the insane modern idea that they are or are not 'talented', rather than that they transmit quality from elsewhere through talents, or crafts, which can be honed.

12. This is because genius comes from the void of the present-moment UNSELF. It is only when [a form-fixated] society has acclimatised to the formal expressions of the moment that it is prepared to accept expressions of its earlier timeless eruptions (which it calls '*before* their time'). Genius-hosts always contend with such societies.

13. See Orlov, *The Five Stages of Collapse* and Mauss, *The Gift*.

14. *At the moment whatever struck you was god. If it was a pool of water, the very watery pool might strike you: then that was god; or the blue gleam might suddenly occupy your consciousness: then that was god... or thirst might overcome you at the sight of water: then the thirst itself was god; or you drank, and the*

*delicious and indescribable slaking of thirst was the god; or
you felt the sudden chill of the water as you touched it; and
then another god came into being, 'the cold'; and this was not
a quality, it was an existing entity…*
  D.H.Lawrence, *Apocalypse.*

15. See *The Upanishads;* Barry Long, *The Way In* (for the 'do
     you believe in x' observation); *The Teachings of Ramana
     Maharshi; The Bhagavad Gita;* Aldous Huxley, *The Per-
     ennial Philosophy;* Joseph Campbell, *The Masks of God;*
     Thomas à Kempis, *On the Imitation of Christ; The Sermons
     of Meister Eckhart;* and, if you can discard the nonsense
     of the early Church, the *five* gospels.

16. See Stuart Sutherland, *Irrationality.*

17. See Douglas Adams and John Lloyd *The Meaning of Liff.*

18. Where the job of doctors is to *prevent* the patient from
     understand the true SYSTEMIC cause of her ailments
     ('you're working too hard' is probably the best you can
     hope for), the job of journalists, politicians, academics
     and other opinion-shapers is to actively *blame* the patient
     for her ill-health; or, more subtly, to suggest that it is her
     lack of proactive self-belief, inability to meditate or woeful
     ignorance of the guidance of celebrity chefs that is the
     cause of her depression, acne, obesity or alcoholism—
     with being born on the bottom rung of the ladder of life
     being far off in the 'angry' land of la-la or 'woo'. See Carl
     Cederström and Andre Spicer, *The Wellness Syndrome.*

19. The founding myth of the standard WORLD-STORY is that
     everything is getting better (a.k.a. PROGRESS). The 'free'
     and 'open' POST-MODERN (late-capitalist) world, the myth
     has it, is better than the 'closed' and 'inflexible' MODERN
     (classic capitalist) world, and the modern world, is better
     than the medieval world or the ancient world, all of which
     were superior to the pre-historic world. The myth is upheld

by focusing on the [very real] horrors of earlier cultures and ignoring their liberties (see BIASTIFY). The medieval world, for example, is presented by progressives as nothing but a time of indentured slavery, grinding poverty, early death and constant misery. The enormous amount of free time medieval peasants enjoyed, their free access to nature and to common land, their non-alienating work, the stupendous expertise of their crafts and so on, are routinely ignored, as are the deleterious effects of the techniques and ideas that the pre-industrial modern 'renaissance' brought with it at the close of the medieval period; such as sense-dimming literacy, clock-regulated behaviour, greater distrust of the senses, greater self-conscious awareness of the body, greater restrictions on spontaneity (through the invention of 'manners'), the creation of childhood, new perceptions of the externality of the natural world, USURY and ENCLOSURE, greater class separation, consciousness-fragmenting SPECIALISATION (of work and of the senses) and new negative conceptions of death and of madness; all of which led to an impoverishment of ordinary people's experience of reality. There is no question that the pre-modern world was saturated with grotesque violence and corruption, but before the modern dominance of technique in society, work was not as important as leisure, comfort was not as important as quality and tool perfection was not as important as using tools well; all priorities which the modern world has a vested interest in effacing. See Lewis Mumford, *Technics and Civilisation*, Ivan Illich, *In the Mirror of the Past*, Marshall McLuhan, *The Gutenburg Galaxy*, George Woodcock, *The Tyranny of the Clock*, William Morris, *Useful Work v. Useless Toil*, Philippe Ariès, *Centuries of Childhood*, Chris Wickham, *The Inheritance of Rome* and William Chester Jordan, *Europe in the High Middle Ages*.

The BIASTIFIED myth of progress is also present in standard media comparisons of the *Brave New World* of late-capitalism with the dreary *Airstrip One* of Fordism, but perhaps its starkest expression is in common (especially journalistic) depictions of pre-agrarian hunter-gatherer societies which are caricatured as sick and violent struggles for existence in a hostile universe (see notes to FALL).

None of this is to suggest that we must [even if we could] recreate pre-historic, medieval or hunter-gatherer society, or that they were all pain-free paradises; rather to dispel the reactionary fiction that, over the past 10,000 years, 'society' has progressed in anything but a technical sense—least of all 'morally'—when, at best, the modern ego has replaced the horrors of its own *directly* violent pre-modernity with the horrors of *indirect* violence, institutionalisation and virtual confinement. With such ideological filtering out of the way it is possible to re-introduce the liberties and pleasures we have lost, while retaining our tools, if need be, within their UTPs.

I & J

1. See Ben Crewe, *The Prisoner Society*.

2. Of these presence comes first. Great impro cannot be described because you *'had to be there'*. You had to be there because, to create great impro, *you have to be here*.

3. Not that animals are unconscious—not a bit of it—nor that there isn't ecstatic majesty in the marvellous animal drama of status-play and complementary genders—but that status *confinement*, being unconscious, runs blindly off the animal feed-fight-fuck code.

4. There is a notable lack of unstatus in improv theatre, which manifests as a lack of superb tragedy. The social PAIN of status is as important to the dramatic self as physical pain is to the body, but the intense (comic-flecked) seriousness that tragedy demands is impossible without death, love and other statusless states of self annihilation. These do appear in improvised theatre, but they are swamped by theatricality, levity and spectacle.

5. From the perspective of high status, unstatus seems low (because it has no desire) and from the perspective of low status, unstatus seems high (because it has no fear).
   Note also status isn't necessarily connected with class.

6. A surprisingly good chat-up line.

7. This does not mean submitting or giving your guts up; if the heart sinks with a feeling of coercion or confinement, then, after a world-shaking *'no!'* offer a finer *'yes!'*
   Note also that *'yes and...'* is a *state*, not an utterance. It is possible to BLOCK with an OPTIMISTIC, subservient or slap-happy series of yesses (see notes to UNVERSATION).

8. For improvised theatre, see White *&* Salinksy *The Improv Handbook*. Naturally though impro, theatrical or otherwise, cannot be learnt by reading about it, much less by summoning that enormous red-herring 'talent'; you must *repeatedly* leap up onto the stage (i.e., as White *&* Salinksy point out, take *lots of turns*).

9. Just as there is no drama without status, so there is no interest, in drama or in life, without change; but just as unstatus must be behind status, so the changeless (*timeless*) UNSELF must be behind SELF, or self becomes SELF-INFORMED, and therefore ADDICTED or HOLLOW: see SELF.

10. One reason why supermarkets and malls are unpleasant.

11. Note that the ongoing trend is for these separate institutional organs to blend into one INTERZONAL panopticorp, which it is impossible to be completely done with.

12. *So the interview, regardless of the job, becomes a kind of talent show audition hinging on generic questions about change, teamwork etc. (the equivalents of the standard repertoire of x-factor ballads), while the interviewee must project an all-purpose positivity by extemporising around this script*

without revealing its artificiality. The candidate must project the right image and hit the right notes, and must put his 'heart and soul' into every performance, even for the most dreary role. Preparation for the interview therefore ceases to be about the actual content of the job and instead becomes a theatrical rehearsal, concerned primarily with costume, demeanour, eye contact, stage presence, learning one's lines.

Ivor Southwood, *Non Stop Inertia*.

13.   Coined by William S. Burroughs.

K & L

1.   Coined by Ivor Southwood.

2.   Coined by Philip K. Dick.

3.   Laws apply to all situations and all people, and so they can only ever be APT by accident. Which is why you can't trust a LAW-ABIDER—one who deforms himself to fit laws.

4.   See Daniel Everett, *Don't Sleep, There Are Snakes* for a superb account of the kind of things that the remote preciv Pirahãs find worthy of laughter; everything.

M & N

1.   From Ambrose Bierce, *The Devil's Dictionary*.

2.   Alice Schlegel points out, in *Male Dominance and Female Autonomy*, that when property or dowries do not exchange hands with marriage, that virginity is of little interest.

3.   a.k.a. Eric Berne's game of WOODEN LEG, an excuse-creation process (*'well I'd love to go ballooning with you but you see I have this wooden leg'*) which, in extremis, leads to 'the plea of insanity', or *'of course I murdered her; what do you expect of someone as screwed-up as I am?'*

4.   The more common version of minging is outlined in David Reynolds' *Constructive Living* (based on the Morita therapy), in which he details the widespread blaming of emotions for irresponsible behaviour; *'I didn't kiss her because I felt shy / I shot him because I felt angry'*, etc. Not so long ago this kind of thing was seen as immature or selfish, but now such negative emotions are medicalised, in order to incorporate the sufferer into the narco-diagnostic system in a vast game of SANIFECTION.

5.   It is of course untrue that every cultural creation described as modernist is an expression of the schizoid mind. The unfathomable, timeless primal void and delightful comic shocks of self-awareness can find expression in the strangeness that modernism (and even post-modernism) allows; although the rare appearance of genuinely mystic insight in modernist art and literature is despite the modernist trend described here, not because of it.

6.   See Michael Rowbotham, *The Grip of Death*, Mark Boyle, *The Moneyless Manifesto*, Charles Eisenstein, *Sacred Economics* and Dmitry Orlov, *Five Stages of Collapse*.

7.   *…a man was found gathering sticks on the sabbath day… The LORD said to Moses, 'The man must be put to death; he must be stoned by the whole community outside the camp'. So the whole community took him outside the camp, where he was stoned to death, as the LORD had commanded Moses.*
       Numbers 15: 32

     They put every one to the sword [in Jericho], men and women, young and old, as well as the cattle, the sheep, and the donkeys.
       Joshua 6:21

     Every person must submit to the authorities in power… those who resist [authority] have themselves to thank for the punishment they will receive.
       Romans 13: 1/2

Therefore, when ye meet the Unbelievers (in battle), [cut off their heads]; At length, when ye have thoroughly subdued them, firmly [tie up the captives]...
   Quran 47:4

...those [women] on whose part [you] fear disloyalty and ill-conduct, admonish them, refuse to share their beds and beat them (lightly)...
   Quran 4:34

And so on and so forth... Believers go to absurd lengths to explain away these kind of things, to dismiss criticism of the coercive violence, outrageous misogyny (the Jewish Testament of Reuben is a feminist classic), groupthink tribalism (far more important to believers than doctrine), hostility to NATURE and to CHILDREN, superstition, ludicrous inconsistencies and occasional genocide that riddle the Torah, the Bible and the Koran as cherry-picked or context-free or incorrectly translated. It is much more difficult for monotheists to intelligently respond to criticisms of monotheism itself; that a causal god, separate from his creation, necessarily leads to violence, despair, sin, intense literate selfhood and violent hatred of unself, but such arguments are rarely offered. The usual critics of monotheist cults are members of scientific cults, who are also bound by the same causality as religion, and committed thereby to superficial critiques of it.

Note, however, that Christianity, Judaism and Islam have been the dominant cultural narrative of a vast group of people for thousands of years; as such, the tradition is not—nor possibly could be—bereft of sensuality, originality and inspiration, although wherever enjoyment of the senses, pantheism, paradox, unself or adoration of genuine mystery have surfaced, it has usually been crushed by religious authorities of the past, as it is today by secular authorities. Such 'heretical' movements included the teachings of Jesus of Nazareth, Sufism and the medieval mysticism of Meister Eckhart and Jacob Boehme.

8.   Iain McGilchrist, in *The Master and his Emissary* and Robert N. Bellah in *Religion in Human Evolution*, offer persuasive evidence that music precedes language in children and preceded language in human culture. Not that you need evidence to confirm the obvious, that the earliest societies were illiterate, onomatopoeic operas of yibbling, younding tweef and rhythmic chittering zinch.

9.   *The thoughts that are expressed to me by music I love are not too indefinite to be put into words, but on the contrary too definite.*
     Felix Mendelssohn.

10. See E. Richard Sorenson, *Preconquest Consciousness* (and *The Edge of the Forest*).

11. c.f. MILITARY: rich people paying thick people to kill poor people, MEDICINE: rich people paying educated people to get poor people back to work and POLICE: rich people paying 'moral' people to prevent poor people from disrupting the market.

12. The most dangerous and vulnerable news medium is that on the leftmost border of the spectrum. It is left-liberal newspapers (and their STAGVERSIVE, elite-educated, corp employees) that police the outer limits of acceptable thought. No writer, comedian or journalist can be employed by the left-wing mainstream media if he intelligently addresses the institutional limitations of his host media, the limits of standard ego-thought or the reality of propaganda in a 'democratic' society. Writers of tabloids and right-wing media, with no integrity to sell, just peddle official OPINIONS. Left-liberal 'mainstream' journalists are also selling their integrity (which the host uses to pull people into their market-wasteland). This is why stagversive writers react with far more outrage and violence to intelligent, honest criticism than truly reactionary ones, who just tend to stare it out / smirk it off.

13. NEWS SPEAK here just describes terms commonly used in modern, Western NEWS PROPAGANDA. It is not the same as the far more pervasive and disabling NEWSPEAK of George Orwell, which was an early attempt to describe a reduced, technical language, handed down from on high, with no system-threatening connection with subversive ordinary reality. The newspeak we use today is, as Ivan Illich and Barry Sanders point out in *ABC: The Alphabetization of the Popular Mind*, a 'uniquack' or 'expertese' of Q-WORDS and technical jargon, (based on earlier standardisation of 'correct language') handed down from professional academic discourse, invested with the quasi-religious authority of Scientific Truth, but with no power to express life as it is actually lived by those who actually live it. Ordinary speech is now peppered with terms, like *energy, disorder,* and *conscious,* which you have to be a qualified expert, or professionally coded computer, to use 'correctly'.

14. If something is in the news, it is serving the agenda of the system by being there, so if the news covers it, it *must* be fundamentally irrelevant (e.g. strikes, elections, the crimes of enemies, fears about civil rights and privacy, distant moral outrages, the crimes of politicians or institutions, or the ill-health and stress of work, instead of the criminal and sadistic market-system itself).

15. When the US invaded South Vietnam, it was presented as 'defence against internal aggression'—the 'aggression' of South Vietnamese peasants against the 'defensive' US air force, army and well-supplied US-run mercenaries. In the same way Soviet Russia 'defended' Afghanistan and Hitler 'defended' Poland.

16. Note also that the conditions for the creation of official terrorists—e.g. the bombing of Cambodia that led to the Khmer Rouge, the annihilation of Iraq that led to Isis, the funding and training of Al Qaida and so on—are never mentioned on the news.

17. The 'Peace Process' is usually understood to refer to efforts to seek peace in the Isreal–Palestine conflict. Such efforts, as Noam Chomsky points out, might include numerous UN security council resolutions to provide a two-state settlement. However these efforts are not officially included in the official definition of 'peace process' because the US does not seek peace and rejects all offers to reach it. 'Peace process' in the news refers to the US–Isreali elites doing what they want to do; which is to convert Palestine into peaceful ruins.

18. Also Communist, Marxist and, for supporters of Ed Herman's thesis that the word 'genocide' is frequently manipulated to serve western interests, 'Genocide Denier'. Examples include, Noam Chomsky, John Pilger, Harold Pinter, MediaLens and Julian Assange. If the threat pushes beyond politics into ego, the insults switch to mystic, hippy, cult-leader, navel-gazer, pseud, pretentious and so on, for example, Oscar Wilde, Eckhart Tolle, Russell Brand, etc. See MediaLens for a more detailed analysis.
    (PRETENTIOUS = calling attention to self / AUTHENTIC = calling attention to REALITY; for those insufficiently acquainted with reality the distinction = calling attention to a self like mine / calling attention to a self unlike mine).

19. Examples include STAGVERSIVE journalists (George Monbiot, Christopher Hitchens, etc.), Western leaders (Winston Churchill, Barack Obama, etc.), successful businessmen (Henry Ford, Steve Jobs, etc.), TED/TEDX lecturers and any nice, harmless people who cheer people up without upsetting the apple-cart too much (The Dalai Lama, Pope Francis, Stephen Fry, etc.). Dead people frequently make it on to the officially approved [unspoken] list of worthies, but only if they tend to criticise official enemies (George Orwell, Walt Whitman, etc.), support power (Shakespeare, Hegel, etc.), promote market-friendly views (Freud, Darwin, etc.), or have had any uncomfortable revolutionary intent expunged (Jesus, William Morris, etc.).

O & P

1. You are walking along the top of a cliff with a friend and they fall into an unreachable cove and break their leg. The tide is coming in and in two hours they will drown. It takes an hour to get to the nearest town and will take an hour for help to return. The path back is narrow.

   In this situation there is one right thing you can do, and only one thing, for the whole two hours; and there are literally an infinite number of wrong things you can do.

   Most situations are like this.

2. Note also 'now', which needs a 'right' in front of it to mean what it used to mean. Also 'sick' and 'insane', which have come to mean 'cool', and the word 'cool' itself, which means cold, technically able, independent, fashionable and so on—all of which have their place of course; but why do we not admiringly breathe 'warm' at displays of genius, when great warmth, sweetness or serenity are always at the heart of the coolest actors and musicians?

   Finally, note how *vulgus, plebeian, villein, idiot, peasant, common, barbarian* and other words for people below or beyond the polite, literate, MAINSTREAM, were used as insults, or have ended being up so.

3. Coined and used by Byron Katie.

4. A subset of psychological panculpism is the belief, based on a limited sample of corrupted moderns, that women are erratic creatures addicted to subservience and security (or perhaps crystalline structures that shatter upon 'sexist' compliments); and not utterly mysterious avatars of the void, and that men are simplistic walking-talking penises and not mythic heroes engaged in a long and challenging mission of unself-discovery.

5. The same as a computer chip, which flashes between discrete either-or 0/1 switches.

6. Note also the enormously popular slur 'narcissist', which can mean either a vain, manipulative egomaniac or someone who rejects egoic GROUPTHINK. As with any other psycho-smear-word, ego is completely incapable of telling the difference between the two. Both (egomaniacs *and* ego-resisters) will seem arrogant and 'above-it-all' to ego.

7. See *Oblique Strategies* by Brian Eno.

8. *The biggest load you are carrying in your life is your personality; the strain of pretence. Keeping it up weighs you down and sucks the life out of you. You blame so many things for the feeling of heavyness and lack of life. You blame your work, your relationships, your diet, your problems. And yet it is your personality that has cut you off from your natural joy and vibrance. The personality makes you worried and emotional. It's the cause of your moods and self-doubt, your depressions and times of misery. It confuses your mind. It's fearful of the future and guilty or regretful of the past. It gets listless, bored or restless with the present. It is the unsuspected shadow that slides in between you and your partner. It's the cunning and knowing in the eyes. It lives off every kind of stimulus, good and bad, depression and excitement, and it is utterly terrified of being found out, discovered as the phony and spoiler it is. The personality is the face of dishonesty.*
    Barry Long, *Only Fear Dies.*

9. *Above all the genuine philosopher will generally seek lucidity and clarity and will always strive not to be like a turbid, raging, rain-swollen stream, but much more like a Swiss lake, which, in its peacefulness, combines great depth with a great clarity that reveals its great depth.*
    Schopenhauer, *The World as Will and Representation.*

10. To point to something beyond time and space is obviously not a matter of unparadoxically indicating a time or a place where truth can be found, but of expressing the QUALITY of timelessness; in word, gesture, house or sketch. This

is how children, animals and lunatics often make better philosophers than professors, who—as Heidegger pointed out—study their own concentrated, temporal selves and then assume that consciousness is a constrained temporal thing rather than the mysterious means by which that thing comes to awareness.

11. See *On Photography* by Susan Sontag.

12. The reason for this is that onions are the guru, or prophet, of vegetables; they see all. The potato is the king of vegetables, the tomato is the queen of vegetables, and the onion is the guru, or prophet, of vegetables.

13. i.e. it is an *expression*, not a cause. Like the pretty brain-patterns that nueroscientismists (and corporate media) claim show us what creativity, or language, or love 'really is', physiognomic features do not cause character-personality, but express it. The difference is that the living tapestry of the vibe-beaming or vibe-hiding face in context is infinitely more expressive, apt and human than a colour-enhanced photograph of a brain in a laboratory.

14. Although it is not so easy to judge books with covers made by other people.

15. Which is why it is also taboo to intelligently discuss physiognomy. To criticise or refuse someone because they look like a sausage-wrapped android is considered at best irrelevant—when, often, nothing could be *more* relevant.

16. See P.D. Ouspensky, *Tertium Organum*.

17. *In fact religious affairs were at a very low ebb; all such matters sat very lightly upon the thoughtless inhabitants; and, in the celebration of many of their strange rites, they appeared merely to seek a sort of childish amusement.*
    Herman Melville, *Typee*.

18. See Peter Gray, *The Play Deficit*. Note also how play must be banished from EVOLUTIONIST accounts of nature and SCIENTISMIST accounts of the universe.

19. See David Graeber, *The Utopia of Rules* for the 'bureau-crats with swords' idea; and why the police do not get involved with crimes that do not involve paperwork.

20. Individual police men and women, are often, like any other professional, kind people trying to do a good job under very difficult circumstances. But try not paying your rent or filling in your tax-returns and watch those kind people kindly kick you out of your home.

21. See *Amusing Ourselves to Death* by Neil Postman for his now famous comparison of 'what Orwell feared' (book-burning, truth-concealing, information-depriving, fear-based authority) and 'what Huxley feared' (no desire to read books, stupefaction from oceans of information and distraction, and a leaderless desire-shaping system), then make up your own mind who was closest to the truth, and why we (in the UK) have an Orwell prize — regularly won, of course, by employees of the Ministry of Truth — but not a Huxley prize — because it wouldn't be cost-effective to send out fifty million gongs.

22. The official meaning of 'bureaucracy' is 'inefficient gov-ernment meddling in the market', but, as David Graeber points out, removing this 'meddling' so that 'government can run more like a business' just replaces government bureaucracy with corporate bureaucracy. This, Graeber points out, is how we should understand the corp-elite campaign for 'deregulation', which actually means 'chang-ing regulations so that I benefit', and 'decentralisation', which actually means 'placing the company HQ in Jersey'.

23. See Gary Wilson, *Your Brain on Porn*. The term PORN-STARE was coined by Ali Davis, in *True Porn Clerk Stories*

24. For the giants of twentieth-century intellectualism—Levi-Strauss, Lacan, Saussure, Barthes, Derrida, Foucault, Baudrillard, Lyotard and Žižek—there is no meaning outside literate LANGUAGE, except, perhaps, power. The outrageous poverty of their thought must be concealed by intellectual jugglery and stupefying verbosity or its schizoid hollowness would be open to mass-derision.

    On rare occasions an insight from a post-modern philosopher can be understood, and, rarer still, they offer a few crumbs of insight into the nature of experience. Usually it is critiques of postmodernism, offered (within its framework) by Mark Fisher or (without) by Noam Chomsky and Louis Sass, that are of the most use; although some postmodern techniques—such as reading pop-songs and films as if they were 'world-dreams'—are also of value, and something of an honourable exception should be made of Michel Foucault, who wrote some good critiques of the subtleties of modern power-techniques and Slavoj Žižek, a kind of friendly uncle meaninglessly blathering away to himself over the barbecue, who, every once in a while, says something half-decent.

25. *As soon as a man appears who brings something of the primitive along with him, so that he doesn't say, 'you must take the world as you find it', but rather 'let the world be what it likes, I take my stand on a primitiveness which I have no intention of changing to meet with the approval of the world', at that moment, as these words are heard, a metamorphosis takes place in the whole of nature. Just as in a fairy story, when the right word is pronounced, the castle that has being lying under a spell for a hundred years opens and everything comes to life, in the same way existence becomes all attention. The angels have something to do, and watch curiously to see what will come of it, because that is their business. On the other side dark, uncanny demons, who have been sitting round doing nothing and chewing their nails for a long time, jump up and stretch their limbs, because, they say, 'here is something for us...'*
    Søren Kierkegaard.

26. See Jeff Schimidt, *Disciplined Minds*.

27. See *House of Cards* by Robyn Dawes for an investigation into the fraudulent nostrum of psychotherapy and a summary of the evidence that mental health professionals debase the common sense of their patients, that the accuracy of their judgement does not increase with clinical experience (i.e. that it is not a craft, but a species of guesswork) that the attentions of so-called 'paraprofessionals' (ordinary people) are equally effective and that their methods are often not even scientifically sound.

28. *For more than a century, analysis of disease trends has shown that the environment is the primary determinant of the state of general health of any population. Medical geography, the history of diseases, medical anthropology, and the social history of attitudes towards illness have shown that food, water, and air, in correlation with the level of sociopolitical equality and the cultural mechanisms that make it possible to keep the population stable, play the decisive role in determining how healthy grown-ups feel and at what age adults tend to die…*

    Just as at the turn of the century all men were defined as pupils, born into original stupidity and standing in need of eight years of schooling before they could enter productive life, today they are stamped from birth as patients who need all kinds of treatment if they want to lead life the right way. Just as compulsory educational consumption came to be used as a device to obviate concern about work, so medical consumption became a device to alleviate unhealthy work, dirty cities, and nerve-racking transportation…

    Iatrogenesis will be controlled only if it is understood as but one aspect of the destructive dominance of industry over society, as but one instance of that paradoxical counterproductivity which is now surfacing in all major industrial sectors. Like time-consuming acceleration, stupefying education, self-destructive military defense, disorienting information, or unsettling housing projects, pathogenic medicine is the result of industrial overproduction that paralyzes autonomous action…

The destructive power of medical overexpansion does not, of course, mean that sanitation, inoculation, and vector control, well-distributed health education, healthy architecture, and safe machinery, general competence in first aid, equally distributed access to dental and primary medical care, as well as judiciously selected complex services, could not all fit into a truly modern culture that fostered self-care and autonomy.
Ivan Illich, *Medical Nemesis.*

29. Note also that the manager must be functionally inept or have no experiential knowledge of the industry he or she managers, as hands-on experience engenders profit-threatening practicality and sympathy; see Peter Fleming, *The Mythology of Work.*

30. *Progress is the central lie of our culture and there are illusions and fantasies of it everywhere: There's the schooling system, where we go from 'lower' to 'higher' grades—but this rising is not real, just a story they tell, and the change is just to make us fit better in the dominant system, as we trade experience for rigid stories, intuition for intellect, diversity for uniformity, independence for obedience, and spontaneity for predictability. Then there's the wage labor system, where we're supposed to go from 'lower' to 'higher' positions, but few of us do, and anyway 'higher' just means the dominant system has a tighter grip on our attention, our values, our souls. Then there's the history of technology, where the changes are declared 'better' when their effects are to increase our forceful transformative power over the world while also increasing our emotional distance, or to make us more dependent on specialists, or to surround humans more and more with things humans have created, a process that Jerry Mander has identified as psychic inbreeding. The deepest place yet in our inbreeding is the world of computer games, games which almost without exception are built on the myth of progress, training us to self-administer dopamine for visions of ever increasing power, and then letting us off with a 'win' instead of showing us how this kind of story really ends.*
Ran Prieur, *Seven Lies about Civilisation.*

31. See Jacques Ellul, *Propaganda*, Noam Chomsky and Edward Herman, *Manufacturing Consent*, Medialens (David Cromwell and David Edwards) *Guardians of Power* and *Newspeak in the 21st Century*.

32. Orwellian illusions are threatened by criticism, while verbal criticism of huxleyan illusions, far from being a threat, are encouraged; because criticism can be co-opted, sold and used as an ADVERT (see STAGVERSION). Huxleyan propaganda is not the master telling lies, but the slave building his own counterfeit world from facts.

33. The class divisions here are schematic. In fact there are, on the one hand, bright exceptions, created by an intrepid few, and, on the other, the monocultural grey-area-spread of a global class-structure; which gives working classes a dab of higher education, property, aspiration and TASTE; and divests all classes of those few MARKET-resistant characteristics they once had; the integrity of the lower-class artisan, for example, or the nobility of the higher-class outsider, have, like masculinity and femininity, no place in monotopia and are ousted by RICH chavs and POOR elites.

Q & R

1. Feminishism and queerishism usually go together, but they mask a contradiction between social and sexual identity. Feminishists, in order to justify their *social* (esp. professional) identities, are forced to claim that *gender* is socially constructed, because they don't want their identity (as doctors or CEOs) to be ascribed to their gender, but to their will. Queerishists, on the other hand, to justify their *sexual* identities, are forced to claim that *sexuality* is innate, because they don't want their homosexuality to be ascribed to their will, but to an innate predisposition.

2. Celebration of middle-class multiculturalism is a justification of working-class uprootedness.

3. See Matt Kennard, *The Racket*.

4. Rationality is based on ego. Mental. REASON (or, in its original sense, logic) is the same scientific process of thought, but based on soft-perception of the context.

5. *In the case of a creative mind… the intellect has withdrawn its watchers from the gates, and the ideas rush in pell-mell, and only then does it review and inspect the multitude. You worthy critics… are ashamed or afraid of the momentary and passing madness which is found in all real creators…*
   Friedrich Schiller.

6. And justifying it by pointing to its opposame; the cold, bored, taking-for-granted ghost-world of long-term compromise.
   Also ENCLENK 1 to pretend that he is interested in you for your mind and for your personality (see Jean-Paul Sartre, *Being and Nothingness*) 2 to convince yourself that 'love' is the reason you have waited for years for your man to change; and not your doormat fear of being alone.

7. The iniquities of the WORK SYSTEM, and particularly the horrors and frustrations of COLLAPSE, tend to seem like personal failings to those who [are encouraged to] insufficiently understand the deep reality of the world.

8. Along with architecture. Both can only arise from a SOCIETY of geniuses acting without constraints of time, profit, property or professional management (i.e. without egos, markets, priests or architects).

9. Where ego-addiction to small ritual tends to become OCD, ego-addiction to big-ritual tends to become RELIGION.

10. It is, of course, a standing disgrace to western 'civilisation' that we do not all regularly, actively, participate in a home-grown blend of Kecak and Beethoven's 9th.

1.   Coined by Brian Eno.

2.   Where clinical schizophrenia swings between grandiosity and paranoia and between total derealised detachment and absolute literalness (inability to understand any metaphor, vibe, or joke), the earlier schizoid state swings between feeling special and feeling worthless, between etiolated irony and sopping sentimentalism and between intense self-interest and a denial of authorship or self.

    Such FALSE ANTONYMS create a sense of false variety amongst full schizophrenics (i.e. those subsumed totally by ego) and early-stage schizoids (i.e. the staff).

3.   Hieronymus Bosch's sixteenth century vision of hell (the third triptych of *The Garden of Earthly Delights*) is a perfect representation of the only thing in existence which can rightly be called hell, the imaginative self-informed-ego, in which nothing relates to anything else. It is also an amazingly accurate portrayal of TEEVEE.

4.   The common cliché of schizophrenia, that it is synonymous with genius, with access to higher realities and with primal Dionysian psychological liberty, is partly because schizophrenia shares some attributes with mysticism, spirituality and union with the void (timelessness), but mainly because most accounts of schizophrenia originate from scientists with a vested interest in ignoring its similarities to the modern mind. See Louis A. Sass, *Madness and Modernity*.

5.   See Jeff Schmidt, *Disciplined Minds*.

6.   See Ivan Illich, *Deschooling Society*; also John Holt, *Teach Your Own* and *Instead of Education*, John Taylor Gatto, *Dumbing Us Down*, Krishnamurti, *On Education*, Paulo Freire, *Pedagogy of the Oppressed* and *Tolstoy on Education*.

7. See *The Anthropology of Childhood* by David F. Lancy for an extensive review of one of the most unequivocal findings in the ethnographic record; that children in PRIMAL societies acquire their culture not through teaching but through participation; and that refusal to coerce either children or adults is, in primal societies, universal.

   And note also that the word 'learning' which I have used negatively, in scare-quotes, is not the same as *learning*, which means acquiring skills and doing.

8. See Aldous Huxley, *Brave New World Revisited*.

9. See *The Teachings of Don Juan* by Carlos Casteneda.

10. 'Ancient Greeks', here and elsewhere, refers to the small group of maniacs that founded Western rational 'civilisation', not to Parmenides, Empedocles, the miraculous, illiterate, mythic poets or the mighty Stoics.

11. What was the Big Bang, how did it happen and what existed before it? Unknown. What is the nature of dark energy and dark matter, the dominant entities of the cosmos? Unknown. How did life arise? Unknown. How did consciousness arise and what is the nature of consciousness? Unknown. Why is the machine-metaphor of the universe better than the organism metaphor, and how could either be tested or refuted? Unknown. Is life further experienced after one's body dies? Unknown. How do genes specify the size and location of every organ and bone in the body and direct nascent cells to the correct location? Unknown. How do quantum physics and mathematics apply to biology? Unknown. How does consciousness effect quantum measurements? Unknown. How could the universe be so perfectly tuned to support consciousness? Unknown. What is time? Unknown. Are the laws of nature fixed or are they evolving? Unknown. What is the universe expanding into? Unknown. Why is there anything at all? Unknown.

One or two of these questions can perhaps, in principle, be answered by science. The majority, however, like so many of the bald statements in this book, refer to soft-consciousness of the context; which science can *never* understand, no matter how much factual evidence it can discover about its constituent elements, any more than a digital image can accurately represent analogue reality, no matter how many pixels it contains. This is why science deliberately (and necessarily) excludes the *infinitely* subtle CONTEXT (which it calls 'noise') from its *finite* object, fact and theory-creating activities—and why scientists, like the monotheistic priests that they usurped, are scared witless by the prospect of having to investigate the role of their own consciousness in the reality they [merely] OBJECTIVELY study.

See Rupert Sheldrake, *The Science Delusion* (which is a bit loopy, but contains lots of good points) and Curtis White, *The Science Delusion* (which contains a fairly thorough critique of the smarmy optimism of scientism, and of its inability to understand the artistic terms it bandies about, such as 'dazzled', 'elegant' and 'beautiful').

12. The only way to literally describe self [to your self] is as an understandable machine comprised of parts—just as the only way to literally, and practically, describe 'matter' is as discrete, solid bits—but this is not what self [or matter] *is*, which can *never*, ultimately, be understood; only EXPERIENCED. See UNSELF and PARADOX.

13. Note, however, that early people did not necessarily have an idea of the universe as a feminine entity or 'goddess'. I use the word 'conceive' here to make my point, not theirs. That said, see Joseph Campbell, *The Masks of God*, Peggy Reeves Sanday, *Female Power and Male Dominance: On the Origins of Sexual Inequality* and Marija Gimbutas, *The Living Goddesses* for an idea of the huge amount of evidence supporting feminine conceptions of reality amongst early, peaceful and egalitarian people.

14. Also the blood of menstruating women which, in fallen, agricultural tribes became a source of intense anxiety.

15. These negatively-exciting controlling techniques went side by side with a positively-exciting enjoyment of lying.

16. While horticulture was a useful technique for early man, agriculture was misery, adding the capacity for hoarding, class-stratification, specialism, brutally unpleasant work and disease onto the burden that ego was now pressing upon the world.

17. e.g. Marduk vs Tiamat in Babylon, Indra vs Vritra in Vedic India, Jahweh vs Satan in Judaism, Zeus vs Typhon in classical Greece. These ego-honouring male-worshipping myths all superseded earlier cosmologies in which the femi-snake had been a benevolent, mysterious creatrix.

    The mono-religion also erased the creative, amoral, paradoxical, boundary-crossing trickster god from original myth and replaced him with a blandly immoral devil.

18. This, of course, is just an outline. In principal true; but the exact factual process of ego's spread — an enormously complex process, integrating with innumerable contexts, covering thousands of years of obscure history, and possibly arising independently in different areas — is obviously impossible to know or to neatly summarise.

19. In most religious traditions there were and are strands of original non-egoic pre-superstitious APPERCEPTION and GENIUS that persisted. The non-dualist Hinduism of the Upanishads (later Advaita), the Bhagavata and early schools of Tantric Yoga, The Tao Te Ching, some mystic strands of Buddhism (esp. Zen), the teachings of Jesus (without their Paulist-Christian distortions) and [later] a few elements of Sufism all expressed timeless, original pre-egoic experience. Because of this they were usually labelled heresy and persecuted, often brutally.

20. Only a few hundred years previous to Socrates, Plato and Aristotle, so-called 'irrational' contemplative philosophers, such as Parmenides and Empedocles, had provided the answer—something like zen meditation—but by the time of the rationalists, this, along with the illiterate magic of Homer, was now literally inconceivable.

See Peter Kingsley, *Ancient Philosophy, Mystery and Magic* and *Reality*.

21. The emotional component of ego is the one most frequently ignored; it is possible to be friendly, generous, non-intellectual—even 'spiritual'—and yet emotionally egotistical. Similarly, it is possible to talk often of oneself, to vaunt one's own excellence, to be fascinated in oneself and to take (temporary / flamingly flamboyant) charge of a group, while being humble and selfless.

22. A self-informed machine is incapable of self-sacrifice (a.k.a. ALTRUISM) unless that sacrifice is either not fundamental (i.e. superficial, such as CHARITY), or, as self-informed EVOLUTIONISTS and ECONOMISTS repeatedly stress, for the benefit of similar selves (who share the same genes), those who might reciprocate at a later date or (as a virtuoso display of mating fitness) future partners.

23. Because SCIENCE focuses exclusively on the manifest, objective self, it finds that, fundamentally, there is no such thing; the self is an illusion and we are all 'really' a multiverse of shifting mes. This modern duck-*fact* is the opposame as the commonly-held pre-modern rabbit-*fact* that there is one fixed me for all eternity. The unselfish originating PARADOXICAL drabbit *reality* of I is, of course, far subtler, more intimate and living-vivid than either of these crude—but useful—either-or facts.

24. The schema used in this book, the division of self into matter, mind, viscera and energy (or into masculine and feminine) is not of course, like any other map, a perfectly

accurate representation of the terrain. There are plenty
of exceptions (or PLATIPI) and contradictions, but the
primary purpose of a map is not to perfectly represent
the landscape, but help you, or me, navigate through it.

25. Ego will necessarily over-inflate the benefits and joys of its
own addictions, while focusing laser-like on the dangers
and depravities of addictions it is not constitutionally
prone to. In fact ego will actually go looking for stunts in
others that negatively correlate to its swellings. This game
of BLEMISH is characterised by prying, morbid curiosity
and bitchy asides (*'She's got last year's hat!', 'He hasn't even
read Lacan', 'Snicker, can't hold his erection I've heard'*).
  Blemish comes from Eric Berne's *Games People Play*.
He finishes by pointing out that the game of blemish is
used to shoo away depression and avoid the intimacy
that might reveal one's own blemishes.

26. The self-directed self creates stereotypical personalities,
ever more 'themselves', as well as stereotypical GENDER;
either bloating male and female into slave–master sub–
dom psychosis or effacing gender difference completely.

27. See Erich Fromm, *To Have or To Be*, for a comprehensive
account of self's psychopathic *need* to possess (money,
objects, people, good ideas, physical beauty, etc).

28. See Steve Taylor, *The Fall*, which is a bit mystishist, but
contains a fair overview of cross-cultural studies that
correlate low female status with social-stratification, private property with warfare and repressive child-rearing
with social and sexual violence. See also James DeMeo,
Saharasia, also a bit loopy, but which contains some good
evidence and interesting observations on this theme.

29. See Mark Fisher, *Capitalist Realism* and Peter L. Berger
et al., *The Homeless Mind*. Note also that as well as being
uniquely addictive to self, the world also obliterates the

capacity for unself to be conscious [and thereby master] of the feeble voice of *'can't stop'* or *'must have'* from which addiction gains power. It is impossible to ignore a voice in your head that you have no way of telling is you or not.

30. Full-blown schizophrenia was rare in hunter-gatherers and non-Western societies. See *Louis A. Sass, Andrew Halliday, George Deveraux* and *Meyer Fortes*.

31. The healthy self, like the [traditions of a] healthy society, is soft and temporarily absent, never permanently. The garden, like the cell, needs permeable and discerning— which is to say *living*—walls (or hedges).

32. See *Meditation: A Foundation Course* by Barry Long (and the recordings, *How to Stop Thinking, Start Meditating Now* and *Who Am I?*).

33. Your own particular practice depends less on any one of the tips mentioned here as on facing your own particular selfmare. You might find it easy, for example, to walk through a corpse-strewn battlefield or meditate for twelve hours a day, but play clunkily with children, have secret sexual shames, talk down to your mother, be uncomfortable around plumbers or weird about money.

    See the works of George Gurdjieff, Barry Long, Jiddu Krisnamurti, Shunryu Suzuki, Eckhart Tolle and the Bonzo Dog Doo-Dah Band.

34. Agitated, unpresent anger, not deep, passionate IRE.

35. True sexuality, like its synonym, DEATH, is unimaginable, ungovernable and, in its joy, undependent; and so must be controlled by the SYSTEM. This *begins* with suppression of the natural sexuality of children, which makes them obedient or anxious and suppresses rebellious forces; as Wilhelm Reich pointed out (before he went out of his tree), the brainwashing family is a kind of mini-state

which forces the child to submit, enabling the child to later fit into the wider system. It *ends* with sex—like its opposame, sentimentality—being absolutely everywhere. You can't use love, or true sexuality, to sell shampoo.

36. *Woman has learned to make love through man who does not know how to make love. Hence the dreadful mess that love is in. Since time began she has been manipulated and encouraged to feel that the finest expression of her love is to please man sexually. The truth is the other way around. The finest expression of love is to have man delight her sexually. This he can only do when he can forget his preoccupation with orgasm and be sufficiently selfless or present in love...*
By teaching her to please him and satisfy him down through the ages, man has taught woman to desire him, to project herself sexually, to make herself attractive to him. He addicted her to an emotional and physical craving for his sexual attention. And he did this by neglecting to love her.
Barry Long, *Making Love.*

37. As noted by Normal Mailer.

38. When the ear of self hears the void of silence it's voice says (in nourished awe or primal ego-fear) *'I am not that!'* If ego rules, silence is abolished wherever it goes.

39. Coined by Glenn Albrecht.

40. Reality has a spacetime aspect paradoxically blended with timeless, spaceless eternity, likewise the present has a solid (SCIENTIFIC) past-future matrix blended, through unself, with the eternal present. Schizophrenia and modernism, by obliterating unself and the context, get stuck in a frozen now of objects (each thing hovering in its suchness) without process and with no context upon which consensus can reliably agree. This leads to the uncanny pseudo-paradoxical schizoid KINERTIAL experience of feeling that all is shifting yet nothing is alive.

41. From Samuel Johnson's *Dictionary of the English Language*.

42. Scientism, being purely egoic (rigidly focused on what I can know best, of what can be known), necessarily tends to hyper-specialism, just as hyper-specialism tends to intense [groundless, and therefore insane] rationality.

43. *Always chained to a single little fragment of the whole, man himself develops into only a fragment; always in his ear the monotonous sound of the wheel that he turns, he never develops the harmony of his being; and instead of putting the stamp of humanity upon his nature [or, rather, allowing nature to stamp her genius onto his humanity] he becomes nothing more than the imprint of his business or science.*
    Letters upon the Aesthetic Education of Man by Friedrich Schiller [my parenthesis].

44. Human beings who cannot compose groovy love-songs, design fractal buildings, gut fish, bake biscuits, execute a slick swingout, back-flip, build a dry-stone wall, navigate by the stars, tell a false bolete from a penny bun, let out a dress, dig all day with psychotic intensity, chuck a frisbee, sweep a room as it should be done, make an exceptionally fine coffin in a day, deliver a baby, knock up a bivvy, impersonate autumn, weep like a pig or fashion a nice organised vagina out of blu-tac [or something like that] are—*in this respect*—no better than insects.
    Robert Heinlein said something similar to this, although he specialised of course, as I have, as a writer. Our point really is that specialism alone is for insects. See also *Teach Your Own* by John Holt, and his account of the unschooled Hiram Salisbury or Ivan Illich's account of his unschooled friend's language skills in *Shadow Work*.

45. Standardbeautypeople are usually more anxious, selfish and uptight than non-standard because they are more powerful and, over generations, they marry into power.

46. Obviously old people, like craft-masters, disabled people, foreign guests, parents and the homeless, must be *given* special consideration; unless—the point here—they *use* their 'speciality' to try to *take, wheedle* or *demand* it.

47. See Mark Fisher, *Capitalist Realism*.

48. Or, if you hold power, deflating genuinely revolutionary fervour with a temporary half-measure (or 'reform').

49. To say that men are physically stronger than women is a useful generalisation (a context-dependent, and therefore flexible summary of a state of affairs) that is not invalidated by Russian women shot-putters. To say that Russian women are either tarts or shot-putters, on the other hand, is a stereotype (an inflexible ego-directed descriptive pathway / conclusion).

    The difference between generalisation and stereotype is therefore the same as that between self and ego, or routine and rut, or butter and margarine.

50. *You can hold yourself back from the sufferings of the world… but perhaps precisely this holding back is the only suffering you might be able to avoid.*
    Franz Kafka.

51. *The whole cosmos was alive and in contact with the flesh of man, there was no room for the god idea… God and gods enter when man has fallen into a sense of separateness and loneliness.*
    D.H. Lawrence, *Apocalypse.*

52. Suttery—and its correlates; laughing at fat and ugly immoderates, or at people who have an imperfect grasp of grammar—is a cover for class-guilt, fear and disgust.

53. Those who control the world are terrified of great art; i.e. socially meaningful, boundary-crossing, insanely joyous, death-recognising, foolish, crafted and free GENIUS.

54. Although subversion is an integral part of SELF-MASTERY, the people of tomorrow will not thank you for your protests, petitions, polemics but for the extraordinary way you faced the enormous catastrophe to come. Nothing is more subversive than facing death full on.

55. Coined, I think, by David Icke, all of whose views are quite, quite, demented; but I like this term.

56. Likewise the 'perfect' entertainment industry makes it impossible to be idle for a nanosecond, the 'perfect' energy industry makes *everything* dependent on massive quanta of energy, and so on and so forth.

57. See Jacques Ellul, *The Technological Society*.

58. See Michel Foucault, *Discipline and Punish*.

59. These are a re-application of the filters of Chomsky and Herman's PROPAGANDA MODEL, which explains how institutionally-favourable views predominate in the media without any overt control. These filters are:

1ST FILTER	Business interests of owner companies
2ND FILTER	Reliance on selling audiences to advertisers
3RD FILTER	Sourcing information from [institutional-professional] power
4TH FILTER	Flak; pressure on journalists, and threats of legal action from corporate establishment
5TH FILTER	Ideological belief in LAW, WORK, 'markets', 'progress' and 'our side'

    Unsurprisingly the propaganda model, despite its unsurpassed ability to predict and explain systematic media bias, is never mentioned by [disciplined and subservient] corporate journalists, nor can it be.
    See Edward S. Herman and Noam Chomsky, *Manufacturing Consent* and David Edwards, *Free to be Human*.

60. *Employers have at their disposal a whole range of convenient terms — confidence, presentation, commitment, personality — upon which to hang any ideological conflict.*
    Ivor Southwood, *Non-Stop Inertia*.

61. See Paul Babiak, *Snakes in Suits*, *The Corporation*, Belinda Board et al., *Disordered Personalities at Work* and Simon Baron-Cohen, *Zero Degrees of Empathy*.
    Or just talk to a successful senior manager.

62. Along with, as Camille Paglia points out, the banal totalitarian literalism of 'yes means yes' and FUTILE attempts to police thought or control feeling by criminalising verbal or written deviations from [mono] 'gender-neutrality'.

63. Likewise, the lower class manual worker is likely to say, when confronted in the Tate Modern with a doll's head on a satsuma, that he 'doesn't get it'. He does not realise that this 'art' is not trying to express something real and that, in this situation, to talk about what is in front of your eyes, or to mention reality, is TABOO (or 'distasteful').
    These kind of experiences confirm, in the lower classes, either the pointlessness of art that is not functionally decorative or instructional, or it belittles them by confronting them with an implicit status-code that they have been unable or unwilling to grasp.
    See Pierre Bourdieu, *Distinction*.

64. See Norbert Elias, *The Civilising Process*.

65. The laws, institutions, manners and tastes of advanced modern society are BIASTIFIED by highlighting the nauseating immoderacy, snobbish intolerance and personal violence of pre-civilised people, which the modern ego assumes to be indicative of human nature (PSYCHOLOGICAL PANCULPISM), but these same laws also, inevitably, suppress spontaneity, sensuality, non-verbal intimacy and radical generosity, which are equally threatening to the

uncivilised ego, despite being the root of genuine, natural refinement, civility and modesty.

66. Specialisation, demanded by technique, separates man from man, makes him unable to understand his neighbour—except through technology and technique. Combined with hierarchical power, specialism also introduces massive amounts of unnecessary time between action and reaction, catastrophically limiting SPONTANEITY.

67. Jacques Ellul, in *The Technological Society*, explains that A) there are not different types of technique; you cannot apply it *badly*, just less B) technique is bourgeois; they force the world to adopt it, they run, worship and play in it, but technique has overtaken them too, and made them redundant C) the more techniques develop the more unobtrusive they become (until they are as invisible as reality in VR *and can only be perceived by the unemployed*) and D) all techniques are related to all others and to the anti-context; isolate one and it becomes reasonable.

68. Includes half-hearted 'coolness' and living in a universe of 'yes, but...' in order to protect oneself from exposure.

69. Temenos was first used, in this sense, by Camille Paglia and the no-I parable is Steven Norquist's.

70. Coined by Russell Brand.

71. See P.D. Ouspensky, *Tertium Organum*, Roger Jones, *Physics as Metaphor* and Carl Sagan, *Cosmos*.

U & V

1. See Thomas Szass, *The Myth of Mental Illness*.

2. Or getting tremendously excited about getting something, then tremendously disappointed that it wasn't what you

thought it would be like, and then *so* excited about getting someone, and then *so* upset that he died or left you or turned out to be a bastard (and so on; repeat until death).

3. Coined by Barry Long.

4. Art and science are divided from each other, CRAFT is removed from ART, TRUTH is banned from PHILOSOPHY, MYTH is separated from HISTORY and RESPONSIBILITY and meaning are excluded from SCIENCE. All unconsciously.

5. This term, introduced by Kant (a.k.a. NOUMENON), can refer either to what the separate individual things are that my mind turns into ideas of furry cats and red spheres and so on, or to the entire context.

   In the first, largely quantitative, sense it is often impossible to know if we experience the cat or the sphere in quite the same way—thank God. Although we can, and should, be confident that we can build a correct objective representation of a thing, our selves are constituted and positioned differently and so refract experience differently to us. This enables us to build a multi-faceted society, song or four-storey spherical cat-totem.

   In the second—more important—qualitative sense, it is not just possible for us both to experience reality (because I am it), and to be certain that we are experiencing the same reality; it is essential. Without this unselfish sharing of what is, we will always be ultimately alien to each other, and suspicion, and law, and lawyers, will reign.

6. Manifests in a child's life as various as-yet-unknown situations—or TRANSITIONS (see BRAINWASH). Where the unbrainwashed child overcomes crises by being in feeling contact with the fundamental fearlessness of unself, able to confidently approach the genuinely new (food, person, country, activity, etc.), the [sabotaged] brainwashed child, is, through vibe-conditioning, implicitly taught to fear crises and frantically avoids them; through ADDICTION.

7. See Galen Strawson, *Realistic Monism.*

8. Just as it is impossible to define unself, so there can be no definable description of the relationship between unself and self; i.e. it is neither inside nor outside 'me'

9. Note the unversational tactic of agreeing with, approving of and *apparently* building on another's comment while *actually* ploughing along in one's own furrow as if it had never happened. This is the shifty FALSE YES-AND... See White & Salinksy's *Improv Handbook.*

10. Cringe = shame-pain + empathy

11. a.k.a. Crime Prevention Through Environmental Design.

12. a.k.a. THE GRUEN TRANSFER, an unconscious anxious-addictive response to 'disorientation cues' in the environment, such as confusingly spatious layouts, unmusic, unart, lack of fractality, and the classic emotion-provoking urban-planning opposames; relentless sensory-overload alternating with monotonous sensory deprivation.

13. Only the origin of the unnatural, ego, could create a substance, money, that does not decay or die and that, through usury, proliferates endlessly. Ego also had to create institutions that do not decay or die to carry out this impossible feat, as well as reconfigure the entire universe as a debtor-creditor contract to justify it and put in place a vast bureaucratic apparatus of constant WAR to POLICE it. See David Graeber, *Debt: The First 5000 Years.*
    Attempting to deal with all this by *first of all* circumventing money, destroying capitalism, rewriting myths or ending war is the quintessence of FUTILITY. Casting the merchants from the temple is not *first of all* a literal event.

14. Resistance to what? If it could be named, it wouldn't be resisted.

15. Which includes specialisation as a parent; without the need for nuclear families free-range children are not a burden on parents', particularly mothers', time.

16. Joy can change you, but it is not expressed literally and it needs a *wide* open—or broken—heart to make its way in.

17. One unable to orient himself away from a life without moodies is unlikely to feel a great urge to so orient himself towards a world really worth living in.

18. See Ivan Illich, *Energy and Equity*. Note that systems that exceed UTP limits are also impossible to scale back into smaller, human units. Intensively farmed land cannot just be handed over to hunter-gatherers any more than an oil tanker can realistically be used to transport a bag of prawns. They first need to be broken down.

19. Magic mushrooms and LSD are not *really* addictive; in fact they can be used to cure addiction, depression and work, which is why they are banned in every country on earth.

20. Small-scale 'horizontal', 'local' or 'direct' organisation, free of all power-constraints, is the indispensable basis of human SOCIETY, and an antidote to structural domination; but it is also inherently limited—in large-scale activism for example (see Srnicek & Williams, *Inventing the Future*). It *is* possible to create indirect, SPECIALISED, OMNARCHICAL, non-dominating, societies or movements coordinated or voiced by *powerless* leaders; but CAPTAIN UNSELF *must* be at the helm, with LIEUTENANT REASON at the charts, or oppressive TOTALITARIA, DEMOCRACY, DEMAGOGUERY or ANARCHY will result (see SUBVERSION).

21. And the insane [inapt] modern ideas that the written word is more trustworthy than speech, that Q-WORDS have meanings independent of context or that the truth is a kind of book that the reading self must learn.

22. *However fine the mosaic may be, the edges of the stones [pixels] always remain, so that no continuous transition from one tint to another is possible. In the same way, concepts, with their rigidity and sharp delineation, however finely they may be split by closer definition, are always incapable of reaching the fine modifications of perception...*

    Arthur Schopenhauer [my parenthesis].

W, X, Y & Z

1. See Douglas Fry et al., *War, Peace, and Human Nature*, Noam Chomsky, *Year 501*, David Cromwell, *Why Are We the Good Guys?* Mark Curtis, *Unpeople* and *Web of Deceit*, John Hobson, *Imperialism*, John Pilger, *Hidden Agendas*, Gabriel Kolko, *Century of War*, John Newsinger, *The Blood Never Dried*, Howard Zinn, *A People's History of the United States*, John Perkins *Confessions of an Economic Hit-Man* and Matt Kennard, *The Racket*.

2. See *1984* by George Orwell (the 'Goldstein Book') for a good analysis of the market-enhancing purpose of war. As Orwell suggests, elites are never as worried about the threat of foreign enemies as they are the threat of their own populations living in peace.

    Note also the related millennial objective of restructuring society so that it mimics an army barracks.

3. And—where revolutionary fury should be—body-anxiety, COMFORT ZONE BIOMORALITY and guilt. See Carl Cederström and Andre Spicer, *The Wellness Syndrome*

4. Why points towards causality, or to timespace explanations; useful, like science, but, as Edmund Husserl and Maurice Merleau-Ponty pointed out, unable to see into the life of things, or feel out the solution to the central problems of life; which reside in the purely perceived [pre-scientific] actuality, experience or bodily whatness of what is happening.

A child must continually ask *'yes but why?'* to satisfy his understanding—but eventually, if he starts getting off on whying, the parent has to reply *'just because'*.

5. See Frederick Taylor, *The Principles of Scientific Management*. Taylor was the first modern capitalist to understand the importance of placing THE SYSTEM before all human concerns, and of the pre-eminent role of the manager in dealing with the enormous pessimism that hierarchies create in the workforce, in recapturing power from skilled or self-sufficent workers and in feeding this power into a vast machine designed to further bloat and armour the owner class. TAYLORISM was enthusiastically taken up by evolutionists, scientismists, marxists, communists, Nazis and capitalists who then, as now, form more or less the same cadre of professionals employed to repair, upgrade, armour, extol or camouflage the machine.

6. Note the vast and ever-increasing quantity of unpaid SHADOW WORK that modern men and women are required to provide to the economy that was previously supported by society, playfully free of market concerns or unnecessary—child-raising, commuting, housework (as genuine feminists note, but TABOO for feminishists), self-service, self-sales, self-bureaucracy, self-promotion, and now even socialising and *job-seeking!*—all of which contribute to sickening, will-sapping 24/7 SERFDOM, and require techniques of EXSUPERATION and SUBVERSION to overcome. (See Brett and Kate McKay, *Shadow Work and the Rise of Middle-Class Serfdom* and Ivan Illich, *Shadow Work*)

7. See Peter Fleming, *The Mythology of Work*, David Frayne, *The Refusal of Work*, J. Douglas, *The Pixar Theory of Labor*, Bob Black, *The Abolition of Work* and Jonathan Crary, *24/7*

8. Said, and lived, by William Morris.

9. See Barry Long, *From Here to Reality*.

———— SELECT KALEIDOGRAPHY ————

If you have enjoyed *The Apocalypedia*, you might also like to pack some of the following audio, literary, audio-visual and graphic source-delights onto the ark. I have left out some of the books already mentioned in the notes, as well as most relevant technical (history, philosophy, popular science, etc.) works and anthologies.

A   Aavikko. *Holiday Inn* (from *History of Muysic*).

A   Afrosound. *El Eco y El Carretero* (from *The Afrosound of Colombia Vol. 1*).

L   Akutagawa, Ryunosuke. *Rashōmon* (*and Seventeen Other Stories: trans.* Rubin, Jay).

A   Allegri. *Miserere* (King's College, 1963).

A   Amen Corner, The. (*If Paradise is*) *Half as Nice*.

V   Anderson, Paul Thomas. *Magnolia*.

V   Andersson, Roy. *Songs from the Second Floor*.

-    ———— *You the Living*.

G   Anonymous. *Lascaux Cave Paintings*.

-    ———— *Chauvet Cave Paintings*.

-    ———— *Hedgehog Stealing Apples*.

-    ———— *The Book of Kells*.

A   Armstrong, Louis. *Louis Armstrong Plays W. C. Handy*.

V   Arndt, Micheal. *Little Miss Sunshine*.

V   Attenborough, David. *The Life Series* (all of them)

L   Austen, Jane. *Pride and Prejudice*.

V   Axel, Gabriel. *Babette's Feast*.

A   Bach, J.S. *Brandenburg Concertos* (Britten, 1968).

-    ———— *Violin Concertos* (Perlman & Stern, 1983).

-    ———— *Mass in B minor* (Richter, 1961).

-    ———— *Cello Suites* (Gendron, 1994).

A   Banhart, Devendra. *The Body Breaks*.

G   Bauer, John. *Swedish Fairy Tales*.

A   Beatles, The. *The Beatles* (a.k.a. *The White Album*).

-    ———— *Revolver*.

-    ———— *Rubber Soul*.

-    ———— *Because* (from *Abbey Road*).

A   Beethoven, Ludvig van. *Piano Sonatas* (Brendel, 1975).
–   —— *Late String Quartets* (Végh, 1974; Italiano, 1968).
–   —— *Symphony No.7* (Kleiber, 1975).
–   —— *Symphony No.9* (Szell, 1961).
–   —— *Violin Concerto in D* (Perlman, 1981).
A   Beiderbecke, Bix. *The Okeh And Brunswick Recordings.*
A   Beirut. *Gulag Orkestar.*
A   Belle & Sebastian. *Dog on Wheels.*
–   —— *Tigermilk.*
L   Berger, John. *About Looking.*
L   Berne, Eric. *The Games People Play.*
A   Bezos, Kostas. *Ta Aspra Poulia Sta Vouna.*
L   Bickel, Lennard. *Mawson's Will.*
V   Bird, Brad. *The Iron Giant.*
A   Bishop Allen. *Butterfly Nets* (from *The Broken String*).
L   Blake, William. *Songs of Innocence and of Experience.*
–   —— *Auguries of Innocence.*
V   Bleasdale, Alan. *Boys From the Blackstuff.*
V   Blier, Bertrand. *Going Places.*
L   Blyth, Jonathan. *The Law of the Playground.*
V   Bogdanovich, Peter. *Paper Moon.*
A   Bon Iver. *For Emma, Forever Ago.*
G   Bosch, Hieronymus. *The Garden of Earthly Delights.*
A   Bowie, David. *Hunky Dory.*
–   —— *Low.*
–   —— *The Rise and Fall of Ziggy Stardust and the Spiders from Mars.*
A   Bowlly, Al. *Love is the Sweetest Thing & Heart and Soul.*
A   Brassens, Georges. *La Mauvaise Réputation.*
–   —— *Les Amoureux des Bancs Publics.*
A   Brel, Jacques. *La Chanson de Jacky* (from *Ces Gens-Là*).
–   —— *Amsterdam* (from *Enregistrement Public à l'Olympia*).
L   Brontë, Emily. *Wuthering Heights.*
L   Bryant, Edwin F. (*ed.*) *Bhagavata Purana.10.*
A   Bryars, Gavin. *The Sinking of the Titanic.*
G   Bruegel the elder, Pieter. *The Triumph of Death.*
L   Bukowski, Charles. *Ham on Rye.*
A   Byrne, David. *Glass Operator.*

A   Byron Lee *&* The Dragonaires. *Live and Let Die.*

L   Campbell, Joseph. *The Masks of God* (vol 1–3).

-    ——— *The Hero with a Thousand Faces.*

L   Camus, Albert. *The Fall.*

A   Can. *Ege Bamyasi.*

-    ——— *Saw Delight.*

G   Caravaggio, Michelangelo Merisi da. *Saint Matthew and the Angel.*

L   Carter, Asa Earl. *The Education of Little Tree.*

L   Cassirer, Ernst. *Language and Myth.*

A   Cat Stevens. *Harold and Maude.*

L   Chomsky, Noam. *Year 501.*

-    ——— *Understanding Power.*

-    ——— *On Anarchism.*

L   Chomsky, N. *&* Herman, E. *Manufacturing Consent.*

A   Chopin, Frédéric. *Nocturnes* (Moravec, 1966).

A   ——— *Preludes* (Argerich, 1977).

L   Chuang Tzu. *The Book of Chuang Tzu.*

A   Cletin, Benis. *Jungle Magic.*

A   Cliff, Jimmy. *You Can Get it If You Really Want.*

A   Comelade, Pascal. *Musique Pour Films, Vol. 2.*

-    ——— *Ragazzin' the Blues.*

L   Conrad, Joseph. *Heart of Darkness.*

A   Crew Cuts, The. Sh-Boom (from *Earth Angel*).

A   Crumb, Robert (*ed.*). *That's What I Call Sweet Music.*

G   ——— *Sketchbooks.*

A   Cumbia en Moog. *Cumbia de Sal* (from *The Afrosound Of Colombia Vol. 1*).

A   Dekker, Desmond. *Intensified.*

-    ——— *Music Like Dirt.*

A   Delgados, The. *Pull the Wires from the Wall* (from *Peloton*).

V   Demme, Jonathan *&* Byrne, David. *Stop Making Sense.*

A   Devo. *Gut Feeling / Slap Your Mammy* (from *Q: Are We Not Men? A: We Are Devo!*).

V   Dhawan, Sabrina. *Monsoon Wedding.*

L   Dick, Philip K. *Do Androids Dream of Electric Sheep?*

-    ——— *Valis.*

-    ——— *The Three Stigmata of Palmer Eldritch.*

L   Dickens, Charles. *David Copperfield.*

\-   —— *Bleak House* (also the Andrew Davies adaptation).

A   Divine Comedy, The. *Casanova.*

L   Dodds, E.R. *Greeks and the Irrational.*

V   Donnersmarck, Florian Henckel von. *The Lives of Others.*

L   Dostoyevski, Fyodor. *The Karamazov Brothers* (*trans.* Avsey, Ignat).

G   Dürer, Albrecht. *Study of a Man Aged.*

\-   —— *The Four Horsemen of the Apocalypse.*

A   Dury, Ian. *Do it Yourself.*

V   Eastwood, Clint. *Unforgiven.*

A   Edwards, Cliff (a.k.a. Ukulele Ike). *Night Owl.*

\-   —— *I'll See You in My Dreams* (from *I'm a Bear in a Lady's Boudoir*).

A   Electric Light Orchestra. *Mr. Blue Sky* (from *Out of the Blue*).

L   Eliade, Mircea. *Tales of the Sacred and the Supernatural.*

V   Elliot, Adam. *Mary & Max.*

A   Elliott, Matt. *Drinking Songs.*

\-   —— *Only Myocardial Infarction Can Break Your Heart.*

\-   —— *The Broken Man.*

A   Eno, Brian. *Another Green World.*

\-   —— *Ambient 1: Music for Airports.*

A   Eno, Brian & Cale, John. *Wrong Way Up.*

L   Erickson, Milton. *My Voice Will Go With You.*

L   Eschenbach, Wolfram von. *Parzival.*

G   Escher, M.C. *Puddle.*

A   Faust. *It's a Bit of a Pain* (from *Faust IV*).

V   Fellini, Federico. *Nights of Cabiria.*

A   Fifth Dimension, The. *Let the Sunshine In* (from *Hair*).

L   Fisher, Mark. *Capitalist Realism.*

A   Flight of the Conchords. *Pencils in the Wind.*

A   Foreigner. *I want to Know What Love Is.*

V   Forman, Miloš. *One Flew Over the Cuckoo's Nest.*

\-   —— *Man on the Moon* (*esp.* The Funeral Scene).

L   Foucault, Michel. *Discipline and Punish.*

L   Frayne, David. *The Refusal of Work.*

V   Fricke, Ron. *Koyaanisqatsi.*

L Friere, Paulo. *Pedagogy of the Oppressed.*
L Frisch, Karl von. *Animal Architecture.*
L Fromm, Erich. *The Sane Society.*
- ——— *To Have or To Be?*
- ——— *The Art of Being.*
A Funkadelic. *Can You Get to That* (from *Maggot Brain*).
A Gainsbourg, Serge. *La chanson de Prévert* (from *L'Étonnant Serge Gainsbourg*).
V Gilliam, Terry. *Brazil.*
A Glass, Philip. *Glassworks.*
- ——— *Violin Concerto No. 1.*
G Gogh, Vincent Van. *The Starry Night.*
- ——— *Peasant Woman, Stooping with a Spade…*
L Graeber, David. *Debt: The First 5000 years.*
L Grandin, Temple. *Animals in Translation.*
A Green, Adam. *Losing on a Tuesday* (from *Gemstones*).
- ——— *You Get So Lucky* (from *Sixes & Sevens*).
L Harman, Chris. *A People's History of the World.*
V Hartley, Hal. *Trust.*
G Hayami, Gyoshū. *Persimmon.*
A Heptones. The. *Sea of Love.*
V Hertzfeldt, Don. *World of Tomorrow.*
- ——— *Rejected.*
V Herzog, Werner. *Cave of Forgotten Dreams.*
V Higgins, Colin. *Harold and Maude.*
L Hölldobler, Bert & Wilson, Edward O. *Journey to the Ants.*
A Holst, Gustav. *The Planets* (Loughram, 1976).
L Homer. *The Odyssey* (*trans.* Richmond Lattimore)
L Hughes, Ted. *The Hawk in the Rain.*
L Huxley, Aldous. *Brave New World.*
- ——— *Brave New World, Revisited.*
- ——— *The Perennial Philosophy.*
V Hykade, Andreas. *Love and Theft.*
- ——— *Ring of Fire.*
L Illich, Ivan. *Celebration of Awareness.*
- ——— *Medical Nemesis.*
- ——— *Deschooling Society.*
- ——— *The Right to Useful Unemployment.*

V   ——— *Tools for Conviviality*.

V   ——— *Disabling Professions*.

V   Itami, Juzo. *Tampopo*.

V   Jackson 5. *I Want You Back* (from the 1971 *Goin Back To Indiana* teevee special).

A   Jam, The. *Going Underground* (from *Snap!*).

L   James, Oliver. *The Selfish Capitalist*.

L   Jay, Ricky. *Learned Pigs and Fireproof Women*.

L   Jerome K. Jerome. *Idle Thoughts of an Idle Fellow*.

V   Jodorowsky, Alejandro. *The Holy Mountain*.

A   Johnston, Daniel. *True Love Will Find You in the End*.

–   ——— *Walking the Cow* (from *Hi, How Are You?*).

L   Johnstone, Keith. *Impro*.

–   ——— *Impro for Storytellers*.

A   Kaizers Orchestra. *Min Kvite Russer* (from *Evig Pint*).

L   Kempis, Thomas à. *The Imitation of Christ*.

L   Kerouac, Jack. *Dharma Bums*.

L   Kingsley, Peter. *Reality*.

–   ——— *Ancient Philosophy, Mystery, and Magic*.

A   Kinks, The. *Waterloo Sunset*.

–   ——— *Strangers*.

–   ——— *Apeman*.

G   Klimt, Gustav. *Danae*.

–   ——— *Beethoven Frieze*.

V   Knight, Steven. *Dirty Pretty Things*.

A   Kosmischer Läufer. *The Secret Cosmic Music of the East German Olympic Programme*.

A   Kraftwerk. *Autobahn*.

–   ——— *The Man-Machine*.

–   ——— *Radio-Activity*.

L   Krishnamurti, Jiddu. *The Impossible Question*.

–   ——— *Freedom from the Known*.

–   ——— *The Krishnamurti Reader* (ed. Lutyens, Mary).

L   Kropotkin, Petr Alekseevich. *Mutual Aid*.

V   Kubrick, Stanley. *The Shining*.

–   ——— *2001: A Space Odyssey*.

V   Kurosawa, Akira. *Red Beard*.

–   ——— *To Live*.

L   Lawrence, D.H. *The Rainbow.*

-    —— *Women in Love.*

-    —— *Sketches From Etruscan Places.*

L   Lee, Laurie. *Cider With Rosie.*

-    —— *As I Walked Out One Midsummer Morning.*

V   Leigh, Mike. *Nuts in May.*

-    —— *Grown Ups.*

-    —— *Naked.*

-    —— *Topsy Turvy.*

-    —— *Vera Drake.*

L   Levi, Primo. *If This is a Man* (*trans.* Stuart Woolf).

L   Long, Barry. *From Here to Reality.*

-    —— *Only Fear Dies.*

-    —— *Making Love.*

-    —— *Meditation: A Foundation Course.*

-    —— *Wisdom, and Where to Find it.*

V   Lynch, David. *The Elephant Man.*

-    —— *Rabbits.*

V   Lynch, David & Frost, Mark. *Twin Peaks* (*ep. 1-6 of first series, last four of second*).

A   Magnetic Fields, The. *Get Lost.*

-    —— *69 Love Songs.*

L   Maharshi, Sri Ramana. *Be as You Are.* (*ed.* David Goodman).

A   Mahler, Gustav. *4th movement, Adagietto* (from *Symphony No. 5.* Barbirolli, 1970).

L   Mamet, David. *A Whore's Profession.*

A   Mangeshkar, Lata. *Haunting Melodies.*

G   Martin, John. *The Destruction of Sodom and Gomorrah.*

L   Mascaro, Juan (*trans.*). *The Upanishads.*

L   Matsuo, Bashō. *On Love and Barley* (*trans.* Stryk, Lucien).

L   McGilchrist, Ian. *The Master and his Emissary.*

V   McGoohan, Patrick. *The Prisoner* (*ep. 1-6 and last two*).

L   McKirahan, Richard D. (*ed.*). *Philosophy Before Socrates.*

A   Melodians, The. *Rivers of Babylon.*

L   Melville, Herman. *Moby Dick.*

-    —— *Cock-A-Doodle-Doo!*

A   Mendelssohn, F. *Songs Without Words* (Barenboim, 1974).

A   Microphones, The. *the Glow pt.2.*

\-   ———— / Mount Eerie. *Mount Eerie.*

L   Miller, Henry. *The Colossus of Marousi.*

\-   ———— *Tropic of Cancer.*

\-   ———— *The Rosy Crucifixion Trilogy.*

L   Milne, A.A. & Shephard, E.H. *Winnie the Pooh.*

L   Miyazaki, Hayao. *Princess Mononoke.*

\-   ———— *My Neighbour Totoro.*

L   Mizuki, Shigeru. *Kitaro.*

V   Morris, Chris. *The Day Today.*

A   ———— *Radio 1 Show.*

L   Morris, William. *News from Nowhere.*

\-   ———— *Signs of Change.*

G   ———— *The Kelmscott Chaucer.*

\-   ———— *The Woodpecker Tapestry.*

A   Mott the Hoople. *All the Young Dudes.*

A   Mozart, Wolfgang Amadeus. *Piano Concertos No. 20 — 27* (Brendel & Marriner, 1973).

\-   ———— *Requiem* (Karajan, 1975).

\-   ———— *Symphony No. 40* (Böhm, 1961).

G   Munch, Edvard. *The Sun.*

\-   ———— *Starry Night.*

\-   ———— *Madonna.*

A   Muppets, The. *The Muppet Show Album.*

\-   ———— *Rainbow Connection.*

A   Nash, Johnny. *Hold Me Tight.*

\-   ———— *I Can See Clearly Now.*

L   Natsume, Sōseki. *I am a Cat.*

A   Neu! *Seeland* (from *Neu! '75*).

A   Newley, Anthony. *Oompa Loompa*

V   Newton, Teddy. *Day and Night.*

L   Nietzsche, Friedrich. *The Gay Science.*

\-   ———— *Beyond Good and Evil.*

A   Nyman, Micheal. *Nyman / Greenaway Revisited.*

V   O'Brien, Richard. *The Rocky Horror Picture Show.*

A   Onyeabor, William. *Fantastic Man.*

A   Orb, The. *The Orb's Adventures Beyond The Ultraworld.*

\-   ———— *U.F. Orb.*

A   Orbison, Roy. *In Dreams.*

L   Orwell, George. *Down and Out in Paris and London.*

\-   ———— *1984.*

L   Ouspensky, P.D. *Tertium Organum.*

L   Ovid. *Metamorphosis.*

V   Ozu, Yasujirō. *Tokyo Story.*

V   Park, Nick. *Creature Comforts (first series).*

V   Park, Nick, Burton, Mark & Starzak, Richard. *Shaun the Sheep (first and second series, and the film).*

V   Parker, Alan. *Bugsy Malone.*

L   Patterson, William Patrick. *Struggle of the Magicians.*

A   Perry, Lee. *Super Ape.*

\-   ———— *Return of the Super Ape.*

\-   ———— *Kentucky Skank* (from *Son of Thunder*).

G   Picasso, Pablo. *Young Cock.*

\-   ———— *Le Singe Assis.*

A   Pink Floyd. *St. Tropez* (from *Meddle*).

A   Pixies, The. *Doolittle.*

\-   ———— *Surfer Rosa.*

\-   ———— *Santo.*

V   Pollak, Kay. *As it is in Heaven.*

A   Postal Service, The. *Such Great Heights.*

V   Potter, Dennis. *Pennies From Heaven.*

\-   ———— *The Singing Detective.*

L   ———— *Seeing the Blossom.*

L   Proust, Marcel. *In Search of Lost Time (trans. Terence Kilmartin & Scott Moncrieff).*

V   Python, Monty. *Quest for the Holy Grail.*

\-   ———— *Life of Brian.*

\-   ———— *Series (I & II).*

A   Quantum Jump. *Lone Ranger.*

A   Queen. *Good Old Fashioned Lover Boy.*

\-   ———— *Don't Stop Me Now* (from *Jazz*).

A   Rachmaninoff, Sergei. *All-Night Vigil* (Sveshnikov, 1965).

\-   ———— *Piano Concertos Nos. 2 & 3* (Ashkenazy, 1970).

G   Rackham, Arthur. *Illustrations for Wagner's Ring.*

\-   ———— *Illustrations for The Sleeping Beauty.*

V   Ramis, Harold. *Groundhog Day.*

A   Raphael. *Digan lo que Digan.*

A   Real Tuesday Weld, The. *Live at the End of the World.*

L   Reich, Wilhelm. *Function of the Orgasm.*

-    ———— *The Mass Psychology of Fascism.*

V   Reiner, Rob. *This is Spinal Tap.*

A   Reinhardt, Django. *Swing de Paris.*

V   Reitherman, Wolfgang. *The Jungle Book.*

G   Rethel, Alfred. *Der Tod Als Erwurger.*

V   Robinson, Bruce. *Withnail and I.*

V   Rogen, Seth & Goldberg, Evan. *Superbad.*

V   Rogozhkin, Aleksandr. *Kukushka.*

G   Rothko, Mark. *Untitled (Black on Grey).*

L   Sacks, Oliver. *The Man Who Mistook his Wife for a Hat.*

A   Sakamoto, Kyū. *Sukiyaki.*

L   Salinksy, Tom & White, Deborah. *The Improv Handbook.*

L   Sass, Louis. *Madness and Modernism.*

A   Sayer, Leo. *You Make Me Feel Like Dancing.*

G   Schiele, Egon. *Portrait of Gerti Shiele.*

-    ———— *The Embrace.*

L   Schopenhauer, Arthur. *The World as Will and Representation Vol. 1 & 2 (trans.* E.F.J.Payne).

A   Schubert, Franz. *Impromptus* (Brendel, 1988).

-    ———— *String Quintet* (Melos, 1978; Berg, 1985).

A   Screaming Tea Party. *Cracked Up Dietrich.*

L   Shakespeare, William. *King Lear.*

-    ———— *Hamlet.*

-    ———— *Macbeth.*

-    ———— *The Tempest.*

L   Sharaf, Myron. *Fury on Earth.*

A   Shatner, William. *You'll Have Time* (from *Has Been*).

L   Shelley, Mary. *Frankenstein.*

L   Shurtleff, Micheal. *Audition.*

V   Siegel, Don. *Invasion of the Body Snatchers (1956).*

A   Simon and Garfunkel. *Bridge over Troubled Water.*

-    ———— *Homeward Bound* (Live, 1988).

A   Simone, Nina. *Who Knows Where the Time Goes?*

A   Smiths, The. *Strangeways, Here We Come.*

-    ———— *The World Won't Listen.*

L   Southwood, Ivan. *Non-stop Inertia.*
A   Spacemen 3. *The Perfect Prescription.*
-    ——— *Dreamweapon.*
A   Squeeze. *Take Me I'm Yours* (from *Squeeze*).
A   Stanshall, Vivian. *Yelp, Bellow, Rasp Et Cetera.*
L   Steinbeck, John. *East of Eden.*
-    ——— *Grapes of Wrath.*
V   Stenner, C, Wittlinger, H & Uibel, A. *Das Rad.*
A   Stranglers, The. *Hanging Around.*
-    ——— *Golden Brown.*
-    ——— *Waltzinblack.*
L   Szasz, Thomas. *The Myth of Mental Illness.*
V   Takahata, Isao. *The Tale of Princess Kaguya.*
-    ——— *Pom Poko.*
A   Talking Heads. *Fear of Music.*
-    ——— *Remain in Light.*
-    ——— *The Name of This Band is…*
G   Tan, Shaun. *Eric.*
A   Teleman. *Breakfast.*
L   Tezuka, Osamu. *Buddha.*
-    ——— *Phoenix.*
A   They Might Be Giants. *Hearing Aid* (from *Flood*).
-    ——— *Kiss Me, Son of God* (from *Lincoln*).
L   Thoreau, Henry David. *Walden and on the Duty of Civil Disobedience.*
A   Tiersen, Yann. *Le Fabuleux Destin d'Amélie Poulain.*
A   Tokumaru, Shugo. *Exit.*
L   Tolstoy, Leo. *War & Peace* (*trans.* Maude).
-    ——— *The Death of Ivan Ilyich* (*trans.* Maude).
-    ——— *Master and Man* (*trans.* Maude).
A   Tommy James & the Shondells. *I'm Alive.*
A   Tracey, Arthur. *Pennies From Heaven.*
A   T.Rex. *Cat Black* (from *Unicorn*).
-    ——— *Planet Queen* (from *Electric Warrior*).
A   Troubadours Du Roi Baudouin, Les. *Sanctus.*
G   Turner, J.M.W. *Steamboat in a Snowstorm.*
-    ——— *Study of the Sea and Sky, Isle of Wight.*
L   Twain, Mark. *Adventures of Huckleberry Finn.*

L   Tzu, Lao. *Tao te Ching* (*trans.* Ellen Chen).

G   Ungerer, Tomi. *The Underground Sketchbook.*

\-   —— *Far Out isn't Far Enough.*

G   Utagawa, Hiroshige. *Sudden Shower over Shin-Ōhashi bridge and Atake.*

G   Utagawa, Kuniyoshi. *Takiyasha the Witch and the Skeleton Spectre.*

A   Vangelis. *Blade Runner.*

A   Various Artists. *Kroncong vol. 1.*

G   Velázquez, Diego Rodriguez de Silva y. *Christ on the Cross.*

A   Velvet Underground, The. *The Velvet Underground & Nico.*

\-   —— *The Velvet Underground.*

\-   —— *Loaded.*

V   Vinci, Leonardo da. *The Battle of Anghiari.*

G   Vinterberg, Thomas. *Festen.*

A   Vivaldi, Antonio. *Magnificat / Gloria* (Muti, 1999).

A   Wailers, The. *The Best of the Early Years* (w/ Lee Perry).

V   Waititi, Taika. *Eagle vs Shark.*

V   Waititi, T & Clement, J. *What We Do in the Shadows.*

A   Waits, Tom. *Swordfishtrombones.*

\-   —— *Cold Cold Ground* (from *Frank's Wild Years*).

\-   —— *All the World is Green* (from *Blood Money*).

A   Ward, M. *Requiem* (from *Post-War*).

G   Waterhouse, John William. *The Lady of Shalott.*

A   Wayne, Jeff. *The Eve of the War* (from *The War of the Worlds*).

V   Weir, Peter. *The Truman Show.*

V   Wenders, Wim. *Wings of Desire.*

L   Wilde, Oscar. *The Soul of Man Under Socialism.*

A   Wiley, Geechie. *Last Kind Word Blues.*

L   Wilson, Colin. *The Outsider.*

V   Wit, Michaël Dudok de. *The Monk and the Fish.*

L   Wittgenstein, Ludwig. *Philosophical Investigations.*

L   Wolff, Richard. *Capitalism Hits the Fan.*

A   Yamasuki. *Yamasuki.*

A   Yoshikawa, Jacky & his Blue Comets. *Blue Chateau.*

A   Zé, Tom. *Todos os Olhos.*

V   Zeffirelli, Franco. *Jesus of Nazareth* (parts 3 & 4).

V   Zwigoff, Terry. *Crumb.*

INDEX

Play 'connect the dots' by linking up the following ideas in your brain and colouring in the surprising shape they make.

A & B

C & D

E & F

G & H

I & J

K & L

M & N

O & P

Q & R

S & T

U & V

W, X, Y & Z

This book was designed by Darren Allen.

The text face is Plantin, set in 10-point type on a 12-point line. Plantin is named after Christophe Plantin, a Renaissance humanist and book printer. It was first cut in 1913 by Fritz Stelzer, based on a '*Gros Cicero*' face cut in the 16th century by the designer Robert Granjon.

The paper in this book is of archival quality. It is made from clusters of Kentish Kolomnasberry, Hotnitsan Tagus and the sweet flesh of the wild Kurashiki Coo; lovingly soaked, pounded, stretched, softened with pumice and hand-bound in pterodactyl-vellum by the free people of Evolia.